peak district : bouldering

peak district : bouldering

Copyright© 2004 **Vertebrate Graphics Ltd**

Published by **Vertebrate Graphics Ltd**

ISBN 0-9548131-1-1

Cover photo: *Ray Wood*
All other photos as credited.

Vertebrate Graphics

Design, typesetting and illustrations by **Vertebrate Graphics** and **Rupert Davies**.

www.v-graphics.co.uk

◀ Jon Fullwood on The Alliance: *Mike Birkby*

Contents

Acknowledgments

Every effort has been made to achieve accuracy of information in this guidebook. The authors, publishers and copyright owners can take no responsibility for: loss or injury (including fatal) to persons; loss or damage to property or equipment; trespass, irresponsible behaviour or any other mishap that may be suffered as a result of following descriptions or advice offered in this guidebook. The inclusion of a bouldering area or approach to a bouldering area does not guarantee a right to climb there or a Right of Way to reach it - if conflict with landowners arises, we advise that you act politely and leave by the shortest route available. If the matter needs to be taken further, please take it up with the Peak Park or other relevant authority.

For up to date information on access please visit **www.thebmc.co.uk**

This guide builds on the excellent work in Allen Williams' two previous guidebooks to the Peak, Jason Myers' Peak Plus bouldering guide and the BMC Roaches guide. A big thank you to them for showing the way.

Very many people have been involved in bringing this guide to print. Without their help, you would still have a meaningful life; you might still have fingertips and you wouldn't be £20 worse off. Checkers, authors, photographers - a big thank you to you all.

Special thanks to Andy Harris for compiling and writing the Stoney section – a place that needed the input of someone who truly appreciates it!

Also special thanks to Mark Hundleby, John Coefield, Adam Long and Jon Fulwood for a mega effort in checking the script.

Thanks to everybody at **Vertebrate Graphics** particularly Paul Mellor for his outstanding design work on this guide.

And thanks, of course, to all the photographers, proofers, climbers and other helping hands that have brought this project to fruition:

Mick Adams, Zaff Ali, Lee Anderson, Mike Annersley at **www.ukbouldering.com**, Robin Barker, Percy Bishton, Dave Buchanan, John Coefield, Matthew Coutts, Nik Crawshaw, Sarah Davies, Chris Doyle, Jon Fulwood, Niall Grimes, Andy Harris, Richard Heap, Matt Heason, Andy Higginson, John Houlihan, Simon Hudson, Mark Hundleby, Paul Ingham, Alan James, Carl Kelsall, Neil Kershaw, Stuart Littlefair, Adam Long, Graham Lynch, Alex Messenger, Jerry Moffatt, Ben Moon, Jason Myers, Pete O'Donovan, Simon Panton, Dave Parry, Gareth Parry, Richie Patterson, Chris Plant, Mark Pretty, Simon Richardson, Steve Roberts at Scarpa, Rob Smith, Kim Thompson, Andi Turner, Martin Veale, Ian Vickers, Sam Whittaker, John Welford, Allen Williams, Ray Wood and Paul Worsdale.

Thanks also to the BMC and their access workers for looking over the script.

Foreword

I first saw these rocks after a bus ride up from Nottingham, away from school and home. I had just read The Hard Years and my first pair of EBs had come by post the day before.

Ten years later, I have hitched out to the Roaches to escape college life in Stoke, and am back in the same place. The winter sun is on my back, and my breath mists over the hard ground. All the colours seem to jump out, extra red, green and blue. The light sparkles, and there isn't much noise. A tractor chugging around, a cow groaning, and a pony tearing at the frosted grass. I can smell wood smoke from the farm. This is all I've ever wanted from climbing. I am compelled to try the arete again, even though last week it felt impossible. Everyone else has gone to Dovedale. I rub my boots on a Tetleys beer mat, slap the shoulder of impeccable grit, and everything goes quiet, the smells evaporate, and the colours disappear. The rock texture becomes hyper real, and I can see every molecule of grit on the flake. I don't even notice the drop. All my senses taper to a sharp point. Everything feels right, my palm works the sloper, new 'Fires' stick, and I reach the easier wall. It's over. I am joined at the hip, merged with my surroundings and complete. A bird starts to sing, the sky is extra blue, and the sun seems a little bit closer.

Fifteen years on and I am underneath the same boulder. Everything and nothing has changed. The pad I last used in Bishop covers the grass. My 5.10's feel tight. There is still sand from Fontainebleau in my chalkbag. I clean the arete with my rifle brush I found at Targasonne and powder up with my extra dry chalk.

Bouldering has gone all global. The magazines showcase the latest bouldering venues, just a Ryan Air flight away. There is a perfect venue for any time of the year. It is now a shared experience. We cross reference moves from different continents, and compare one test piece with another. It is now officially a culture and we are targets. But the Peak is like a beating heart for climbers, deep and subtle and once you get it, you will never leave.

At the boulder with friends, touching the same holds as I did years before, this problem is like an old friend and this rock will ground me. It feels easier but harder than it used to. This is still all I want from climbing.

Al Williams, *author of the first guide to bouldering in the Peak.*

Introduction

The Peak District is one of the most developed climbing areas in the world. There are few, if any, other places that offer the same breadth and volume of easily accessible climbing in so many different styles in such a small geographical area.

Since Al Williams produced the last guide, Peak bouldering has come of age. All of the old desperates have been repeated, and the intense development of the last few years has opened up many new problems and areas. But despite all of the changes, one thing remains the same: pulling over the top of the perfect grit boulder problem, with your friends spotting you below, at the end of a crisp autumn day, the sinking sun turning the sky orange and the rock glowing amber, is the best feeling in the world.

Rupert Davies, *November 2004*

What's in and what's not

This guide contains virtually every problem above 7a in the Peak, almost every good problem from 6a – 6c+, and the best of the problems that are easier than that. Every major grit crag is covered, pretty much every minor crag is covered, and what is not covered in detail we point you at with instructions to go forth and explore. The three major limestone crags are covered in detail.

That's a lot of problems, but obviously some stuff has had to go, otherwise this would be volume one out of one hundred. Here's what's not in:

The moorland grit of Kinder, Bleaklow and Derwent is one major omission. There are several reasons for this. Firstly, the bouldering in these areas is only loosely documented and these areas represent some of the few remaining places in the Peak where one can still explore and discover new problems. The second reason is that much of the rock in these places is softer and thus more easily damaged than elsewhere. Guidebooks lead to increased traffic on all boulders and the wish to preserve these wilderness areas is a major motivation for leaving them out of this book.

Another omission is the majority of the small grit routes. Gritstone crags are rarely higher than 15m and there are many routes that are much smaller than this. What was once a dangerous solo can now, with mats and spotters, be a relatively safe proposition as a highball boulder problem. There are hundreds of grit routes that fit this bill and a line has had to be drawn.

This book therefore includes only those routes that are customarily attempted as highball boulder problems, along with all the highballs that were first done as such. For definitive information on the Peak's many superb routes, see the relevant BMC guide.

The next major category of problems that are not included is eliminates. Ideally you should be able to approach any problem and climb it in any way you see fit without wondering if you are doing something that is not allowed. However, eliminates are very much part of the history of Peak bouldering and some crags (such as Stoney Middleton) have almost nothing but eliminates, so the best ones are still included - along with those problems that have historically been climbed with the odd rule.

Almost every boulder in the Peak has probably been climbed at some stage, and in many different ways. This book intends to guide you up the best lines and the most interesting problems but it is not definitive. It is not necessary to illustrate every last problem but that doesn't mean that you can't climb it! There are some areas where the opportunities for exploration and invention are self-revealing – this guide will point you at these problems but does not list each one.

And lastly, some problems are quite frankly terrible. Dirty, brittle, too small, lacking in line or just plain pointless, the reasons why they are bad are many. Although this distinction is somewhat subjective only 'worthwhile' problems are included.

Safety statement

Climbing, bouldering and spotting are activities that carry a risk of personal injury or death. Participants in these activities need to be aware of, and accept, that these risks are present and they should be responsible for their own actions and involvement. Nobody involved in the writing and production of this guide accepts any responsibility for any errors it contains, nor are they liable for any injuries or damages that may arise as a result of its use.

For all emergencies and mountain rescue call 999

Not To Be Taken Away: *Pete O'Donovan* ▲

Looking after the rocks

Rocks are often very big, and compared to us they are very hard. Because of this many people are of the impression that they don't wear out very fast. By and large this is true, but it's not as true as we'd like. All climbing will cause some wear on the rocks, but to preserve the problems for others to enjoy we must minimise it. This means that if you really must clean the holds on a problem use a nylon bristled brush, and never use a wire brush, not even of the brass bristle kind. However tough you think the rocks are, problems have been irreversibly damaged by wire brushing. Often, simply whacking the holds with a clean dry cloth will remove excess chalk and may also cool the holds by that vital half degree. If you must use chalk tick marks (aka donkey lines), clean them off afterwards. Clean your feet so that the dirt on your shoes does not act like a scouring agent – this also damages the rock. Never use resin (rosin) or pof.

Similarly, if we exercise respect for the rest of our outdoor playground we will keep it nicer for longer. Take litter home, be nice to people you meet, keep dogs under control, don't damage vegetation, park with respect for others.

Finally, do not chip holds. If you can't do a problem, train till you can. Or go and climb an easier one – that's what they're for.

Countryside code

- Be safe - plan ahead and follow any signs.
- Leave gates and property as you find them.
- Protect plants and animals, and take your litter home.
- Keep dogs under close control.
- Consider other people.

Access

The inclusion of a crag in this guide is not a guarantee of a right of access to climb on it, but thanks to the CroW Act that has started to come into force in September 2004, many rights of access are now being authorised by statute. Restrictions may still apply in some areas due to nesting birds or other reasons so please read and respect any notices that may alter access at crags and if in doubt, check with the BMC. We, as boulderers, share our beloved crags with many other interested parties and it is through mutual consideration that everyone's interests can be maintained. Please keep to footpaths and do not climb dry-stone walls, close any gates that you open and keep dogs on leads if there is the chance of them worrying sheep or disturbing wildlife.

For up to date access info see **www.thebmc.co.uk**

By joining the BMC you will help provide continuing access to our crags.

Names disclaimer

Every effort has been made to track down the correct first ascentionist for each problem and to find out the original names. However, with many people climbing problems independently, there are often competing claims. Whilst many previous inaccuracies have been corrected, many more will probably surface, so apologies if you think that you have been robbed of your claim to a problem. If it helps, remember that they're just bits of rock.

A bit about grades

This book is full of grades. Previous bouldering guides to the Peak used an adapted system of grading that culminated in the B grading system used in the last guide. This was met with a mixed response and it has been dropped in favour of a more widely used system for this guide.

The two choices of grading systems available were the Fontainebleau system and the V system. The Fontainebleau system was developed to grade the rounded, technical and conditions dependant sandstone problems near Paris. Meanwhile, on the other side of the world the V system was developed by John 'Vermin' Sherman to grade the wildly overhanging, positive and powerful problems at Hueco Tanks in Texas. There is nothing to choose between grading systems in their raw state – all are just series of numbers – so the choice was be made on other grounds.

The Fontainebleau system of grading has been chosen for the following reasons:

Many of the Peak activists use the Font system as their default system to grade new problems and so this has been retained. Similarly most Peak climbers have climbed extensively in Fontainebleau and can accurately apply the grades to problems back in Blighty, but very few have climbed in America and have a feeling for the V system that is as good as their feeling for the Font system. It would be possible to convert all the grades to V grades using a conversion chart, but this would be derivative and would potentially make the grades less accurate. Other arguments for the Fontainebleau system are that the style of climbing on gritstone is similar to that on the sandstone blocks of Fontainebleau and that the rest of Europe has adopted it as their standard.

If you don't understand it, climb as many problems as you can, and you will soon get a feel for it. This brings us onto the other issue. Ideally we should climb for the love of the activity, and the grades should merely help us to decide what to try. But, alas, we are human and with grades we can compare ourselves to others, and thus their importance becomes magnified. We have made every effort to make the grades as correct as possible by getting the consensus opinions of as many climbers as possible, but individual differences in body shapes and sizes means there is no true grade for any problem. This is especially so on grit where problems often boil down to one or two moves and conditions are so vital.

So enjoy your bouldering and don't worry when you get spanked by an 'easy' problem shortly after cruising a 'hard' one.

If a problem's difficulty is very dependant on body shape or morphology (normally height) this is noted in the text as 'morpho'.

One thing to note is that there is no separate grade for traverses. An 'up' 7b+ is exactly the same difficulty as an 'along' 7b+.

Sam Whittaker on Low Rider: *Jon Fullwood* ▲

How to use the Fontainebleau grading system...

...especially for beginners.

If you've been to 'Bleau then all you need to know is that this book uses exactly the same system of grading as is used there, except that we've binned the idea of a separate grading system for traverses. In this book a Font 7a is a 7a no matter whether you go up or along.

If you've only used the V system then all you need to know is that it's the same idea, it's just called something different. See the grade conversion table below.

If you've no experience of either then listen up.

Firstly, don't panic, it's dead simple really. Starting at 1a the Font grading system goes 1a, 1b, 1c, 2a, 2b etc, all the way up to 8c+. The easiest problem in this book is about grade 3 as 1a would be ridiculously easy, about as hard as getting out of bed (ok, bad example, getting out of bed can be pretty tricky).

The grade is one of absolute difficulty, reflecting how hard it is to get from the bottom to the top for an average person of average height, with an average job, living in an average 3 bed semi in an average town such as Swindon. On average this person's name will be Andy, or John.

So, longer problems of a given grade will have easier moves, but you will get more tired, and shorter ones will have to have harder moves to make up for the fact that there are less of them.

But what will I be able to climb, I hear you shout (but only very, very quietly, as you're a long way away)?

Well the quickest way to find out is to try and climb some of them. Below is a list of good places to start your bouldering career. However, if you want to know now, sitting, as you are, in your chair at home then read on.

Let's presume that you can climb V-Diff on gritstone - well that's about Font 3+. Severes are anywhere from 3+ – 5, HVS is generally about 4 – 5+ but, thanks to the randomness of the British grading system some HVSs could be anything up to 7a (try Sulky Little Boys at the Slipstones!). E1 is anything from 4+ to 6a on average and so on.

Having said that, bouldering is generally close to the ground and is an environment in which you can really push yourself, so if you do climb V-Diff and are now thinking that this sport is not for you, then don't despair. You will probably surprise yourself and be able to climb 4s and 5s - and with a bit of practice you will whizz through the grades.

V:	V16	V15	V14	V13	V12	V11	V10	V9	V8	V7	V6	V5	V4	V3	V2	V1	V0+	V0	V0-
Font:	8c+	8c	8b+	8b	8a+	8a	7c+	7c	7b+	7b	7a+	7a	6c+	6c	6b+	6b	6a+	6a	5+	5	4+	4	3+	3

Where to start bouldering

Without doubt the best beginners venue in the Peak is the boulders below Burbage South. Pleasant and low, in a lovely setting, with many, many easy problems, it really is a great place to start a bouldering career.

Next, the top boulders at Cratcliffe are good. Again they are low, easy angled with great landings and there are some superb problems, but it's not as extensive as Burbage South. While you are there, check out Robin Hood's Stride.

A trip to the Roaches is in order next, especially if there has been a spell of good weather. More low, user friendly boulders below the Lower Tier will test your smearing and slab climbing skills on rough rock with impeccable friction.

After these areas it may be time to branch out a little. Try Stanage Plantation, Owler Tor, Newstones, Wimberry and Tody's Playground at Froggatt.

As we live in the Peak, we are perhaps not the best people to offer advice about accommodation, cafes and the like for visiting climbers. However, listed below are a few pointers that we hope will make eating, drinking and sleeping as pleasant as possible:

Cafes and pubs

Eastern and Limestone Crags

Outside Café, *Main Street Hathersage*

Outside Café, *Calver Crossroads*

Grindleford Station Café, *just off the B6521*

Lovers Leap Bistro, *Stoney Middleton*

Woodbine Café, *Hope*

Fox House Inn *on the A625*

The Grouse Inn, *on the A625*

The Norfolk Arms, *Ringinglow*

The Moon, *Stoney Middleton*

Three Stags Heads, *Wardlow Mires, A623*

The Monsal Head, *nr Ashford in the Water on the B6465*

Southern Crags

The Café, *Elton*

The Druid Inn, *Birchover*

The Rambler's Retreat, *Dimmings Dale*

Western Crags

The Roaches Tearoom

The Travellers Rest, *A53 Leek to Buxton Rd*

The Rock, *Upper Hulme*

The King William, *Greenfield*

The Lazy Trout, *Meerbrook, nr Tittesworth Reservoir*

Campsites and accommodation

We can recommend the following:

North Lees, *Hathersage*, 01433 650 838

Hardhurst Farm, *nr Hope*, 01433 620 001

Sladen Cottage Self Catering, *Hathersage*, 01433 650 104

Also try the local Tourist Information Centres for full details of accommodation, or try one of the trusty Youth Hostels dotted around the Peak, **www.yha.org.uk**

Climbing shops in the Peak

Outside, *Hathersage and at Calver Crossroads*, 01433 651 936

Nevisport, *Hathersage*, 01433 659 666

Hitch and Hike, *Bamford (at the garden centre)*, 01433 651 013

Jo Royles, *Buxton*, 01298 258 24

Climbing walls

There are many climbing walls within easy driving of the Peak. Leeds, Manchester, Nottingham, Sheffield and Birmingham all have excellent plastic pulling potential. The best source of info is The BMC climbing wall directory. The closest walls for when it turns wet are:

The Edge, *John Street Sheffield* 0114 275 8899

The Foundry, *Mowbray Street Sheffield* 0114 275 4802

The Rope Race, *Hibbert Lane, Marple* 0161 426 0226

The Matrix, *University of Sheffield, Goodwin Athletics Centre, Northumberland Road, Sheffield*

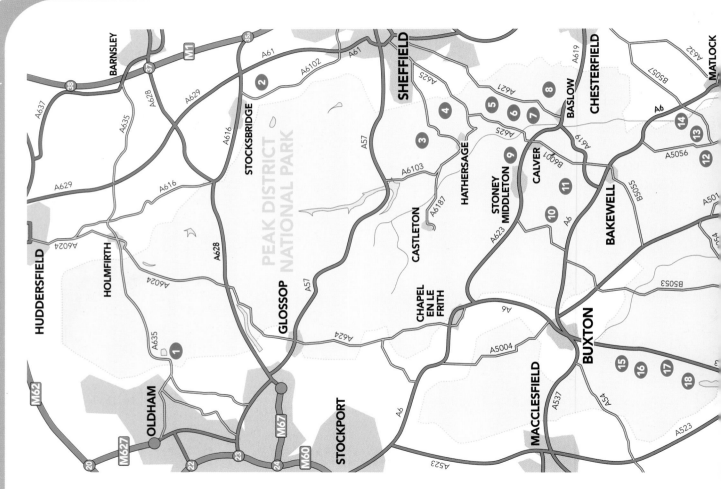

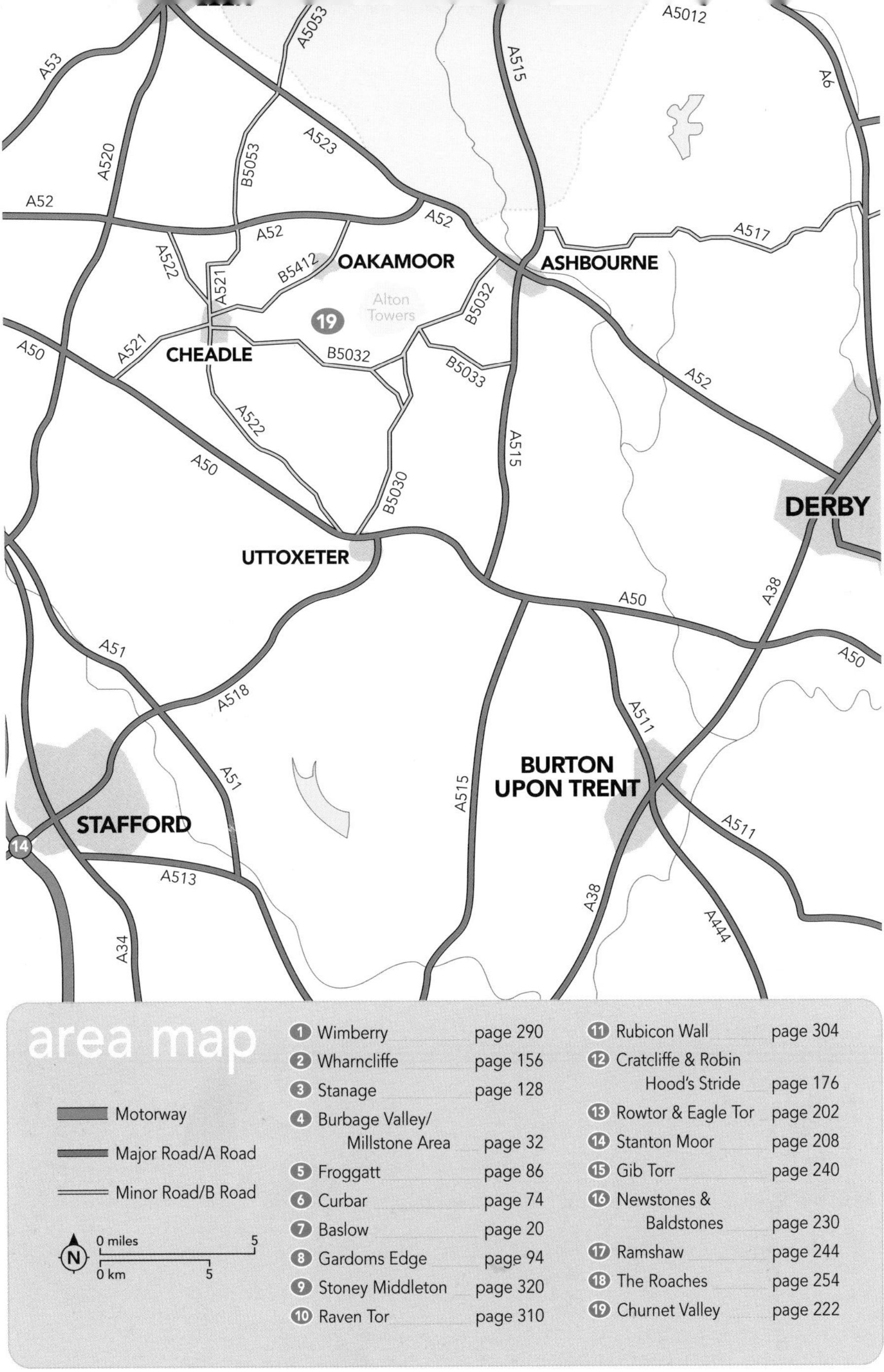
DERBY
ASHBOURNE
OAKAMOOR
Alton Towers
19
CHEADLE
UTTOXETER
BURTON UPON TRENT
STAFFORD
14
A53
A5053
A5012
A515
A6
A523
A520
A52
B5053
A517
A522
A521
B5412
B5032
B5033
A50
A515
B5030
A38
A51
A518
A511
A513
A34
A444

area map

Motorway

Major Road/A Road

Minor Road/B Road

N

0 miles 5

0 km 5

eastern crags

Baslow
Bell Hagg
Burbage Valley
Curbar
Froggatt Edge
Gardoms
Millstone Area
Rivelin
Stanage
Wharncliffe
White Edge
Yarncliffe

John Houlihan ▲

baslow

Though these half dozen or so boulders are a little too spread out to be deemed a circuit, a visit is still essential. The Eagle Stone is one of the best single boulders on grit, with a spread of technical and powerful problems that all take strong lines. The Walnut Whip block offers great traversing from the straightforward but pumpy to the devious, intricate and technical. Finally, Flatworld is a modern classic testpiece. Grades from 4 – 7c, but the better problems are from 6b upwards.

Simon Richardson ▲

Access and Approach

Park at the car park at the top of Curbar Gap (pay and display, I'm afraid) and walk back down the road until a track on the left leads through a gate and onto the moor. Take the right-hand path to get to the Square Stone and the left-hand path to get to the Eagle Stone. For access to the other blocks see the descriptions under their individual headings.

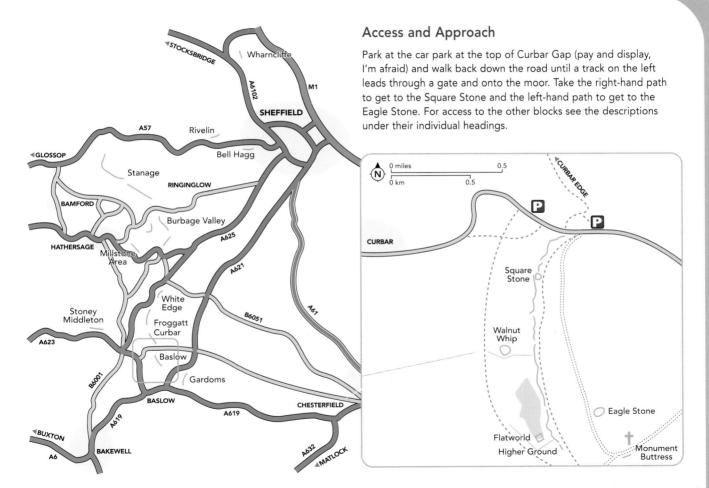

Square Stone

This is the obvious perched block on top of the main edge, visible from the track. It is approximately 250m from the gate.

1. *3*
The left-hand line is trivial but, in the interests of warming up, worthwhile.

2. *6a*
A sit-down start on the small edge below the lip. Pull through on good edges and flat holds to a flake and the top. Worthwhile.

3. *5+*
Direct from the back to a good flake under the lip, then direct to the top.

4. *3*
The arête on either side is a bit pointless, with difficulty depending on how high up you reach to start.

4
The front face has a contrived sit-down start, but it's a one-pull wonder otherwise.

6b+
Traverse the wall from the left, using the line of edges at mid-height, finishing up the arête. Quite tricksome.

The Walnut

Visible under the main edge, just north of the wall, this is a huge, isolated boulder with two classic Peak gritstone traverses. Approach either from the low-level path, or by dropping down under the Square Stone and picking your way along the network of sheep tracks to the block.

1. **The Walnut** 6c
   Traverse the undercut wall on the south-facing side of the boulder. Start as far left as you can, and finish as far right as you can for the full stamina workout. Excellent. *(Allen Williams)*

2. **Whip Me Whip Me** 7a+
   From the depths of the low cave (underneath final moves of traverse)... to daylight. *(Mark Pretty)*

3. **Walnut Whip** 7b+
   On the shady north-facing side of the boulder is a line of crimps and slopers. Traverse these from right to left at mid-height. A satisfying challenge. *(Allen Williams)*

   A harder eliminate traverse has also been added:

   The Choker 7c+
   Traverse from right to left starting as per Walnut Whip, drop down low via a sharp edge to a slopey ledge, gain the pinch on Little Richard, and push on at the same level around the arête and up the slabby wall. *(Percy Bishton)*

4. **Little Richard** 7a
   Sit-down start on a good flake on the underside of the steepest part of the block. Crimp more or less straight up to the good jugs. Excellent.

   Again, as is the norm, a few eliminates exist.

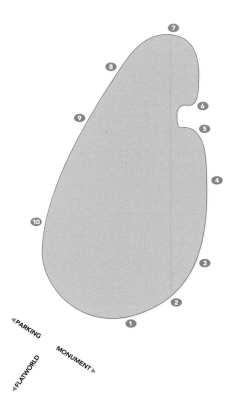

7

8

9

6

5

4

10

3

2

1

◄PARKING

MONUMENT ▲

◄FLATWORLD

Simon Richardson on *The Beagle Has Landed: Stu Littlefair* ▲

Eagle Stone

The large tor of rock on the left of the track is unmissable.
An ascent is proof of one's virility, and rumour has it that
the maids of Baslow will throw themselves at you.
Which would be nice.

1. **Men Only** *3*
   The descent route, which is worth bearing in mind as you struggle
   to climb it. The chipped holds are in, but don't tell the maidens.

2. **A Fist Full of Beagles** *7a+*
   From holds in the break, span out around the roof and campus
   to a mantel finish. The puddle which often forms underneath
   adds to the interest. *(Jason Myers)*

3. **Beagles About** *5*
   Up to and over the drainage tube.

4. **For a Few Beagles More** *7b*
   An excellent highballish problem. From the small corner go up
   then head left on breaks to the top. *(Jason Myers)*

5. **The Good, the Bad, and the Beagle** *7a*
   Another classic struggle, up the green streak. Finding enough
   holds to top-out with is the crux. *(Jason Myers)*

6. **A Beagle Too Far** *6b*
   Up the classy groove, use technique or claim a higher grade.

7. Two problems have been climbed, virtually on top of each other,
   taking the challenge of the big nose.

   The Bright Concept *7b+*
   The left-hand of the two, reaching from a small undercut/pocket.
   (David Kettle)

   Dreaming the Eagle *7b*
   The right-hand side of the nose using the break as a left-hand
   undercut to initiate another big reach. *(John Welford)*

8. **The Beagle Has Landed** *7a+*
   Nasty crimps don't detract from the quality of this problem.
   Climb the blank wall – preferably when it's cold. *(Jason Myers)*

9. **Where Beagles Dare** *7a+*
   Use a small pocket with your right hand to double dyno for the
   top. Using it with the left and reaching right to an edge is far
   easier, and the usual means of success. *(Jason Myers)*

10. **Like a Beagle over Troubled Water** *6b+*
    Up the wall and rounded breaks to the summit.

    Then, if you must, traverse the whole block.

Flatworld

This excellent block is situated by the fence, on the southern edge of the woods directly under the edge, across the moor from the Eagle Stone. Approach from the top of the crag.

1. **Flatworld** *7c*
   A stunning arête, powerful and tenuous. *(Allen Williams)*

   Flatworld Left-Hand *7c*
   As it suggests, locking out to the pocket on the west facing wall.
   (Adam Long)

3. **Hurry on Sundown** *7a+*
   Sit-down start and slap up the arête right of Flatworld.
   A grade easier from standing. *(John Welford)*

4. **Lichen Slab** *5+*
   Climb the centre of the green, lichenous slab, this being the east-facing side of the Flatworld block (note this slab when clean is climbable almost anywhere).

5. **Elmer Fudd** *7a*
   The centre of the slab is a frustrating smearing testpiece.

6. **Fat World** *6a*
   The excellent micro arête on the west-facing narrow block. *(Mark Pretty)*

20m right of Flatworld, on what is essentially the last buttress of the main edge, with oak trees at its base, is...

1. **Higher Ground**   *7c*
   Climb the centre of the high wall, with a hard move to finish. The key to success seems to be a span from an undercut.   *(John Welford)*

   The left arête is none too good, at 6b+.

Monument Buttress

At the end of the track is the Wellington Monument, looking out over the valley and Gardoms Edge. This small wall is located directly under the bench.

1. **Fact Hunt**   *7b+*
   Said slowly. The obvious rib from sitting is the easiest way up this central line.
   (Percy Bishton)

2. **That Which Does Not Kill Me Makes Me Stronger**   *7c*
   A squeezed-in line just right of Fact Hunt using some bad crimps. It's not a great problem but it's dirty hard.
   (Neil Travers)

3. **Dirty Bitch**   *7a*
   Sit start in the same place as for Fact Hunt, but move right using undercuts in the vague overlap to rock onto the slab.
   (Lucy Atkinson)

Baslow is a low, broken crag with a number of worthwhile problems scattered throughout its length. The following are described in the BMC guide and are worthwhile highballs: Hot Ziggerty, 6c+ (low start is Tony Gubba's Made of Rubba, 7a) and Poppers start, 7a+ to break. Bring pads and spotters for all of the above.

bell hagg

Bell Hagg is suburban climbing at its best. Located in a well-to-do neighbourhood of Sheffield, it doesn't suffer from much of the graffiti or any of the used needles and cider-soaked tramps that you may have encountered at less up-market city venues. Instead we have delightful, shady hillside bouldering with good views and the occasional admiring dog-walker.

The climbing is characterised by positive holds and - Bell Hagg being a 'real' crag - the problems can get quite high. Some of the rock is a little dubious, but suspect holds are easily identified (i.e. they rattle). Because Bell Hagg is situated within walking distance of probably the highest concentration of climbers in the world, every hold has its own set of eliminates and in light of this fact we have only described a selection of the problems.

That said, there is still one independent (and very hard) project waiting to go.

Good conditions are common. The crag is north-facing, so summer evenings can be tolerable even on the hottest days. The main climbing tends to stay dry and clean, but the top-outs can get green. You don't need to top-out everything, just make sure you spot the escape traverses before committing yourself and getting too high.

◀ Lurcher Direct

Access and Approach

Park at the end of Moorbank Road and follow the dirt track, then path, taking the steps up on the left. Follow the path for approximately 200m. The first climbing is on Burglar Buttress, the large flat-topped buttress adjacent to the path. Access is via the path that drops down just past the buttress top.

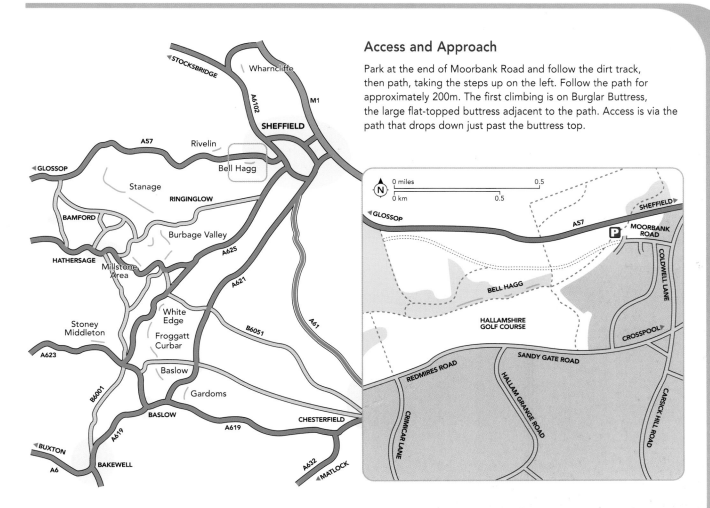

Burglar Buttress

A reassuringly steep buttress that stays dry in the rain. Littered with good holds, Burglar's offers massive potential for imaginative eliminates and - if you're very strict - some of these will be very hard indeed. Fun and games can be had with steep dynos, feet-first ascents, improbable heel-toe jams, etc, etc, etc.

A good low traverse exists at a powerful 6b, while the higher rail of jugs is quite easy. By the time you have done the traverse footless you should be warmed up.

Len's Buttress

1. *3*
   Slanting cracks.

2. *6a*
   Crimps to the break, using underclings to start.

3. **Len's Areet** *5*
   A classic.

4. **Alleluia** *3*
   More good holds.

Nunn's Eliminate Buttress

Fun is to be had on the stepped roof past the green wall a little further right.

1. *3*
   The left-hand line, useful as a descent if you traverse off the other problems rather than topping out.

2. *4*
   Two edges and a stiff pull gets the jug.

3. **Nunn's Eliminate** *5*
   Sidepull action.

4. *5*
   Right of the sidepulls.

5. *4*
   Spike to a leftwards exit.

6. *5+*
   Traverse right, variations exist.

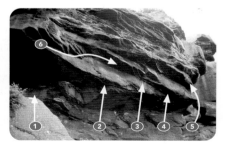

Lurcher Buttress

A compact, solid series of walls and overlaps, with several fine problems.

1. **Rodger's Arête** 5
   A high arête on good holds.

2. **Banner's Ridge** 5
   Right of arête is slightly less intimidating, but still excellent.

3. **The Brig** 5
   Crimpy wall left of the groove.

4. **Brown's Unmentionable** 5
   The scary groove.

5. **Lurcher Direct** *6a*
   A classic up the blunt rib. A brutal project sit-down start exists.

6. *Easy*
   Slabby wall.

7. *4*
   Sit start - the arête on its left or right.

8. *6c*
   Scratch up the undercut slab.

9. *5*
   Slim groove thingy.

10. *6c*
    Sit start - follow the crimps.

150m from Lurcher on a barrel shaped boulder just down from the edge is:

The Barrel Slap Problem *6c*
From ledge and undercut to layaway. Amazing. The problem on the left is 6b.

After crossing a small, often dry, stream, there is a short vertical wall with an obvious pocket. This is Sputum, 5+ and to its right on the next block is Hyde's Mantelshelf, 5+.

The last worthwhile problem is 80m further along up a short, slabby buttress.

Master's Revenge *6b+*

burbage valley

Better than Cuvier! Many, many classy problems of all grades are spread with abandon
throughout the valley. Shady or sunny, windy or sheltered; take your pick of crags.
There are some isolated classics, some compact buttresses of fun, a boulder field and,
if you are lucky, an ice cream van.

Access and Approach

The Burbage Valley climbing area is surrounded by car parks and well served by buses.
This broad valley, which the majority of the bouldering overlooks, is conveniently accessed
on foot via a rough track - the Green Drive. For access to Burbage Bridge, North & West,
park at Burbage Bridge. For Burbage South limited parking is possible in a little turn off just

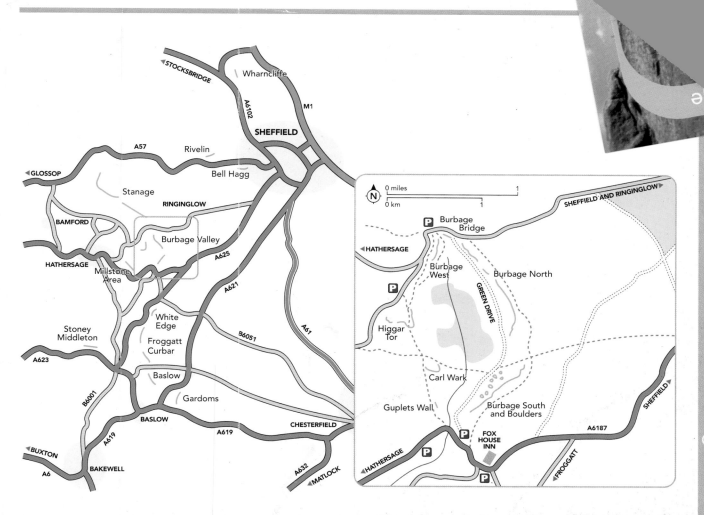

STOCKSBRIDGE

Wharncliffe

A6102

M1

SHEFFIELD

A57 Rivelin

GLOSSOP

Bell Hagg

Stanage

RINGINGLOW

BAMFORD

Burbage Valley

A625

HATHERSAGE

Millstone Area

A621

White Edge

Stoney Middleton

Froggatt Curbar

B6051

A61

A623

Baslow

B6001

Gardoms

BASLOW

A619

A619 CHESTERFIELD

BUXTON

A6

BAKEWELL

A632

MATLOCK

0 miles — 1
0 km — 1

N

P Burbage Bridge

SHEFFIELD AND RINGINGLOW

HATHERSAGE

Burbage West

Burbage North

P

GREEN DRIVE

Higgar Tor

Carl Wark

Burbage South and Boulders

Guplets Wall

P

FOX HOUSE INN

SHEFFIELD

A6187

HATHERSAGE

P

P

FROGGATT

Burbage Bridge

If you are a time-starved boulderer looking for an espresso-style hit, you've come to the right place. With an approach time of just under a minute, this splendid - and mostly pretty steep - little clutch of problems can be enjoyed with an absolute minimum of wasted time.

Approach

Hop over the stile from the car park at Burbage Bridge - the enticingly leaning twin cracks of Mermaid are clearly visible and nearly within arm's reach.

Conditions

Occupying a sheltered hollow, these rocks evade the wind nicely but can be sweaty in summer. The classic problem of Mermaid often seeps in winter when conditions are at their best.

There is at least one hard eliminate still to do here, lurking somewhere amongst these great little walls and buttresses...

Problem 4: *Alex Messenger* ▲

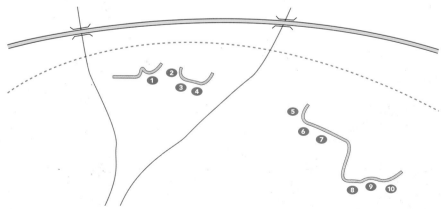

1. *6a+*
   Funky, undercutty shenanigans up the rib.

2. **Rocket Man** *7b+*
   Dyno from low slot to the top.
   (Rob Smith)

3. **Mermaid** *7a*
   The twin cracks from sitting. Often wet.

4. *6c*
   Arête from sitting, hands in slot. You can
   use the pinch on the arête at this grade,
   but not the holds on the right of the
   arête - which is annoying but a better
   problem. Avoiding the arête completely
   is better still, harder, but completely
   eliminate rather than just a bit eliminate.

5. *5+*
   Arête taken on the left-hand side.

6. *6b+*
   Wall from low start, no arête. Hard.

7. *4*
   Easy little arête.

8. **Wobble Block** *6b*
   Direct through the roofs.

9. *4+*

10. *4+*

Rupert Davies ▲

Burbage North

A very popular crag with all calibre of human being. The climbing is superb, from Font 3a to 8a.

Approach

Park at Burbage Bridge. The Green Drive path leads down under the edge from where all the problems can be accessed.

Conditions

The whole valley is more sheltered than Stanage. Burbage North is often a good cold weather venue, and Remergence buttress also stays dry in the rain.

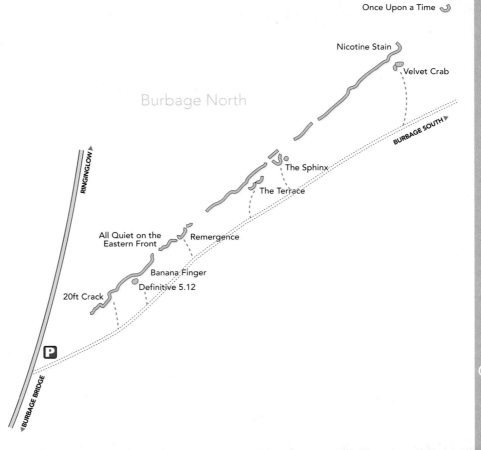

Once Upon a Time

Nicotine Stain

Velvet Crab

Burbage North

BURBAGE SOUTH

The Sphinx

The Terrace

RINGINGLOW

All Quiet on the Eastern Front

Remergence

Banana Finger

Definitive 5.12

20ft Crack

P

BURBAGE BRIDGE

20 Foot Crack Area

The first section you reach from the parking is the 20ft Crack Area, which provides some lovely warm-ups and a couple of classic teasers. There is loads to do here of which this is but a selection. All quite high, they are much more enjoyable as boulder problems if you are confident at these grades.

1. **The Chant** *4+*
   Solo the wall left of the crack.

2. **20 Foot Crack** *4*
   The lovely crack splitting the buttress.

3. **The Curse** *5*
   Classic tease.

4. **Lost in France** *6a*

Andy Harris on Cinzano Roof: *Rich Heap* ▲

Banana Finger Area

1. **Banana Reverse** *7a*
Traverse into Banana Finger Direct from the left.

2. **Banana Finger Direct** *6c*
The direct start to Banana Finger is superb.

3. *6c*
Pull on slopers just right of Banana Finger Direct.

4. **Banana Finger** *6a*
A classic traverse and up problem,
listed by English Heritage as a national monument. Follow edges
and slots left to a pull to the good hold in the upper break.
Knees are allowed. *(Ed Drummond)*

Definitive 5.12 *5.11c*
Just left of the Banana Finger buttress is a cave and roof crack
formed by the collision of two boulders. Ferret into the gap and
jam or undercling your way out. There is a harder left-hand finish.

Cinzano Roof *7b*
The roof formed by the boulder cluster above and left of Banana
Finger from an edge and pocket. Starting from the block right
and reaching out to the pocket is a more amenable 6c.
(Andy Harris /Rich Heap)

*Right of Banana Finger buttress, and just right of Wednesday
Climb is the classic big roof that is Life in a Radioactive Dustbin.
Highball 6c or E4, depending on the thickness of your mat.*

All Quiet Area

A small wall left of the Remergence buttress.

1. **All Quiet on the Eastern Front** *6a+*
   Traverse to the arête and up.

2. **All Quiet Direct** *7a+*
   Thin wall climbing to join the original at the end of the traverse.
   Harder if you go direct to the jug.

3. **All Sit-Down** *7b+*
   More thin wall climbing from the low jug.

4. **The Busker** *4+*
   Wall left of crack.

5. *4+*
   Wall right of crack.

Submergence: *Sarah Davies* ▲

Remergence Area

Although very popular and increasingly spoilt by the polish, this block is perhaps the best buttress in the valley, especially since the puddle was stolen. It's very sheltered which is great in the freezing wind, but bad nick can appear when the sun is out even when it's otherwise very cold.

1. **Arête Problem**   6b
   The left-hand nose/prow is rather good. Eliminates abound: eliminating the flat edge on the lip and using slopers left is 6c, and using just one sloper and powering through to the top in a campus stylee (well, you're allowed feet) is 7b+ at least.

2. **Submergence**   7c
   Start on a low jug under the roof, traverse the lip left and finish up the blunt prow (Arête Problem). This grade is for the original method matching on the polished sloper. Tallies can just go again from the sidepull - 7b+.   *(Jason Myers)*

3. **Blind Drunk**   8a
   Direct to break from the jug via a tiny dish. Unfortunately it's possible to slap from the lip to the same pocket missing out the hard move (at about 6c) if you have very long arms. *(John Welford)*

4. **Remergence**   6b
   Classic knee-on grovel, straight through the middle of the roof. Essential!

5. **Blind Date**   7b+
   This Peak rite of passage starts from the back of the roof, or more commonly with your right hand on the crimp on lip and left hand on the flake under the roof. Same grade either way.   *(Alan Rouse)*

6. **Blind Fig**   7c
   An eliminate on Blind Date (but better) matching the sloper and rocking left to a small hold on the lip of the next roof, pop up for crimps and rock-over.   *(Jason Myers)*

Several traverses exist for the bored, the best of which are:

Blind Ali   7b+
Left to right traverse of the lip of the lower roof (holds under roof are IN).
(Zaff Ali)

Break Traverse   7c+
From the start of the Arête Problem traverse the line of slots and edges below the roof rightwards (eliminate the holds above). Painful.

Tiny Slab

A tiny slab on a boulder 20m or so right of Remergence has some lovely delicate problems that all merge into one another. The slab immediately left of the right arête is 6b, and the problems get gradually easier as you move left. Seek and enjoy.

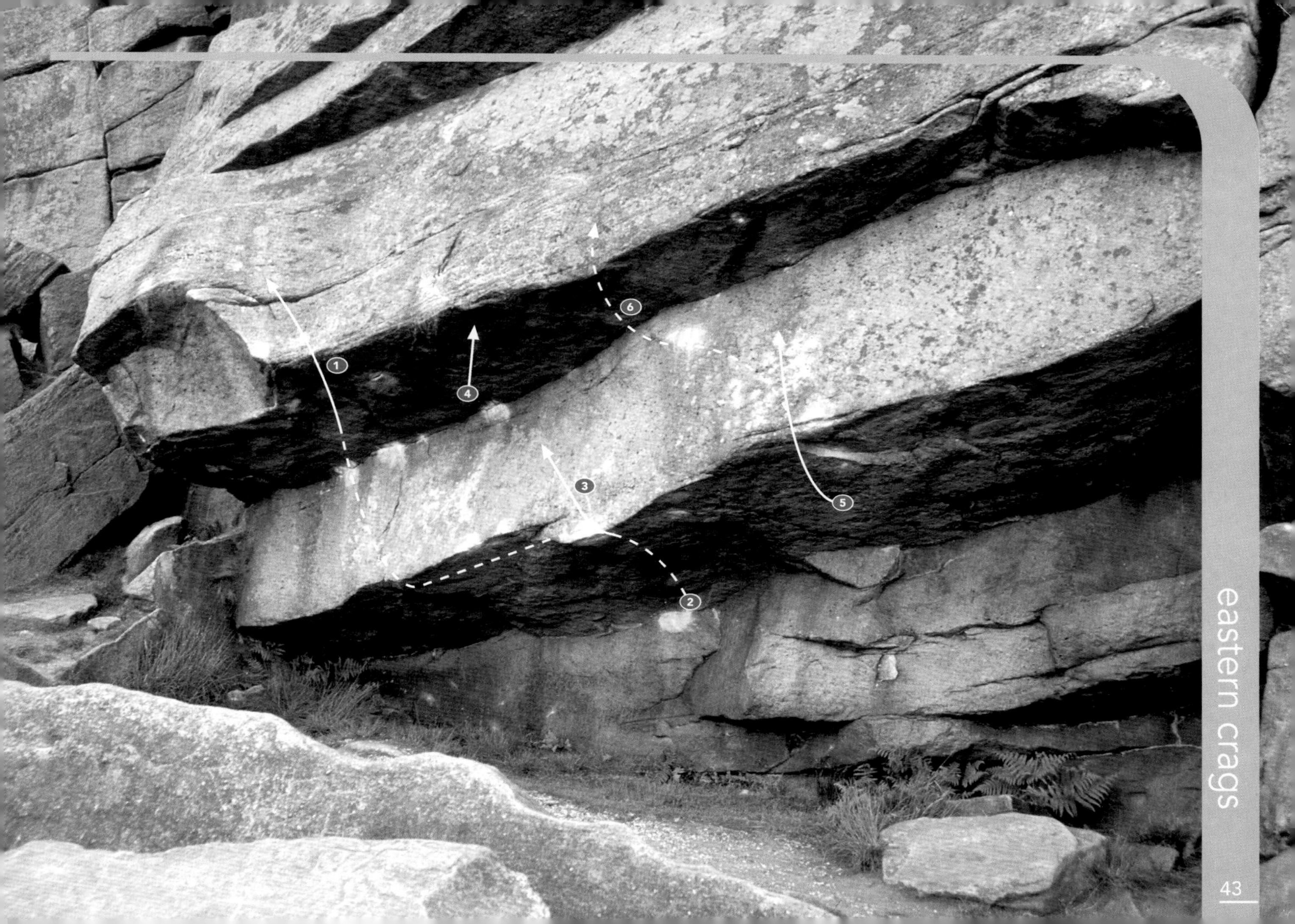
1
2
3
4
5
6

Ash Tree Wall Area

A couple of boulders masquerading as an area under the main crag.

1. **The Terrace** *7c+*
   The left-hand leaning block. A powerful yet technical arête from a sitting start, starting from the lowest undercling and arête. Totally brilliant climbing - lots of opinions on the grade. (Paul Houghoughi)

2. **Jason's Roof** *7b+ - 7c+*
   Out via keel from low start under the roof. Grade depends on wingspan. 6c+ from standing. *(Jason Myers)*

Ben Bransby on The Terrace: *Adam Long* ▲

3. *7a*
From a low start as per Jason's Roof move out to and up the hanging arête.

4. *7a*
Starts as above, but move out and climb the narrow wall to the right of the arête. Easier if you find the knee bar.

Both are still good, but easier, from hanging the lip.

Striker *7c+*
A very hard dyno. Essentially a direct start to Beach Tea One on the main edge. *(Ben Moon)*

La Terrace *8a*
A silly Fontainbleau style link up. Climb The Terrace to holds under the apex where the boulders meet, spin 180 degrees, climb down the facing wall and finish up problem 4. *(Rupert Davies)*

The Sphinx Area

100m further along the edge is the imposing prow of The Sphinx.

1. Giza *7c*
Straight up the wall from the start of The Sphinx. Harder than it looks with a sloping landing. *(Ian Fitzpatrick)*

2. The Sphinx *E5 6c/ 7a+*
The rising traverse line out to the big hanging nose is E5. But with a few mats it turns into…

…well, it's still E5 when you get up there. *(John Allen)*

3. Cleo's Edge *5+*
The superb looking obvious chalked arête just right.

4. Roof Goofe *6b*
The small roof and mantel from the back.

5. *6a+*
Jump to pocket.

6. *6b*
Two-finger pebble and sloper.

7. Safe Bet *6c*
Highball.

8. Yabbadabbadoo! *6c*
Jump to ledge.

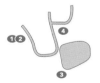

Green Drive

Nicotine Stain Area

Something worthwhile on the final part of the edge and a couple of classics on the big boulders down from the edge justifies the walk-in. Nicotine Stain is just beyond the trees right of the obvious prow of The Fin.

The Fin

1. **Nicotine Stain** *6b*
Before bouldering was invented in the Burbage Valley *(by John Welford in 1999 allegedly)* this was a perfectly good E1 which you flashed, 'cos that's what you do with grit E1s. Now you have to fall off it endlessly at 6b. It is the obvious faint crack on the main edge, with the worn landing. *(Alan Rouse)*

Down from the edge is a large cave formed by several large boulders.

2. **Velvet Crab** *7a+*
The big left arête of the cave beneath Nicotine Stain. The finish feels high and a bit gritty. Excellent. *(John Welford)*

3. **Zaff Skoczylas** *7c*
The shapely prow from a lying down start (big pocket on the left). 7b+ from sitting. *(Dawid Skoczylas/Zaff Ali/John Welford)*

If you found the above two problems easy, try the cracks in the roof. The left-hand one is slightly harder than the right-hand one, but it's unlikely you'll have the enthusiasm to do both.

Beyond The End Area

100m further south is an isolated block.

4. **Once Upon A Time** *7b+*
Climb the centre of the block.
(John Welford)

5. **Beyond The End** *3+*
Good right-hand arête of the small buttress, worth the walk. *(John Welford)*

Ben Moon on problem 1, Zeus Quarry: *John Houlihan* ▲

Burbage South

Spiritual home of Hard Grit, Burbage South offers varied bouldering that is always of impeccable quality. Best savoured with local knowledge, we have tried our best to guide you, but the visitor will need patience to get the best out of this circuit. Many problems are well spread out, and often well hidden, among the routes and jumbled blocks along the edge.

Approach

There is limited parking in a small lay-by on the road at the bottom of the valley from where the Green Drive can be followed to below the edge. Alternatively, park alongside the A625 between the B6450 turn off and the Fox House Inn, and approach across the moor. Or, if you enjoy a stroll, park at Burbage North and follow the Green Drive down the valley. The Fox House Inn is well served by buses from Sheffield.

Conditions

West-facing, the edge is shaded in the first half of the day and with a good breeze can hold good conditions well into summer. The quarries can be sheltered in a cold wind. The boulders get the sun all day – most pleasant.

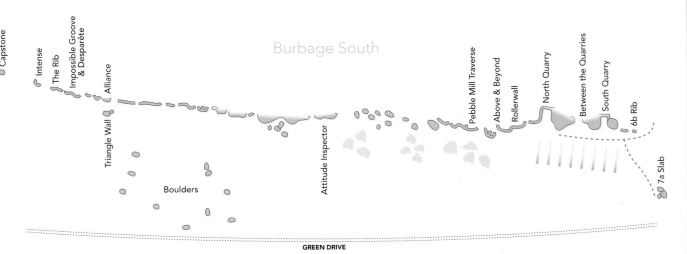

The Quarries and Edge

Perhaps the best bouldering on Burbage South is littered around the quarries and small quarried walls on the main edge, although it is far from a concentrated circuit. A good session here should leave you tired and satisfied (or just plain tired). See Burbage Overview for the location of the first two problems

7a
A good slab, but make sure you start from the floor at this grade - even a slight udge up reduces the difficulty a lot. Located on a small hillock in the first jumble of boulders that can be seen up and right from the Green Drive (above and right of a large, circular stone trough).

6b
The appealing rib was, unfortunately, born without a landing. Either balance your mats as best you can or do it old-skool style without. It's on the right of the path, just before the entrance to the south (Cioch) quarry.

South (Cioch) Quarry

Trellis *7a+*
Highball problem up the shield of rock opposite the vast Cioch block. Undercut, edge, edge, top. Watch that landing. *(Ben Moon)*

◀ Harry Pennells on Trellis: *Adam Long* Ben Bransby on Zorev: *Adam Long* ▲

Between the Quarries

Between the quarries is a pleasing plateau with a smattering of quality problems around it.

1. *5+*
   Classic concave wall.

2. *6a*
   Wall and breaks.

3. *5+*
   Lovely arête.

4. **Little Gem** *7b*
   The excellent seam in the small wall.
   Several methods at several grades. *(Andy Popp)*

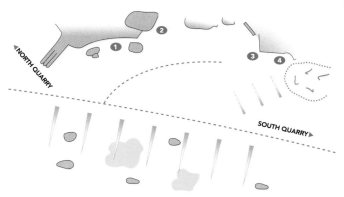

North (Zeus) Quarry

In the depths of the quarry is an inconspicuous block and on that block is…

1. *7a+*
   Sit start the arête on the obvious small block to a slopey finish. Intense.

   Ignore the slabby chipped block in the middle of the quarry floor. It's crap.

2. **Zorev** *7c*
   The arête on the edge of the quarry 50 feet left of Zeus. The broken patio landing hardly makes it any easier. *(Jerry Moffatt)*

   Zorev Sit Start *7c+*
   Desperete moves lead into the original problem. *(Mick Adams)*

3. *7b+*
   The isolated hanging prow facing back into the quarry from a squatting start with feet on the back wall. 6b from standing.

The Knock

Nosferatu

The Knack

Pit

◄ LEFT SECTION 100M

Trees

Trees

Burbage South Edge: Central Section

The quarries now give way to a mostly natural edge. It's a superb circuit with generally good landings, some shade and isolated problems appearing every twenty feet or so.

1. **Roller Wall** *7c*
   Highball slab, direct. Take yer stiffest boots and yer biggest pad. *(Ron Fawcett)*

2. **David Traverse** *7a*
   Climb (walk) along the shelf, drop round the corner and traverse the edges rightwards to reach flakes at the right-hand side of the wall. Finish at a finger jug.

3. **Above and Beyond the Kinaesthetic Barrier** *7a*
   High and scary – indeed not really a boulder problem at all. But as mat technology improves, it becomes ever more enticing. Climb out to the arête, then up and back left to finish. The direct start is harder. *(John Allen)*

4. **Dork Child** *5*
   The arête on its left-hand side.

5. **Pebble Mill Traverse** *7a+*
   Traverse from the undercut on the front face around the arête, and through the scoop to finish on the right arête. It's also possible to do it in reverse at the same grade. Rather good.

6. *6a+*
   The slabby rib is a great problem.

7. **7 Ball** *6c*
   Like an easy 8 Ball. Sit start right of the groove and move left and up the groove and rib. Brilliant.

8. *6a*
   Arête. The wall to the left is 4+.

9.10.11.
   An appealing slab that has a range of good, easy problems. The hardest problem climbs just right of the left arête without the arête or the groove (about 5+) and then they get easier as you move right.

12. *4*
    Easy arête.

13. *6c*
    The mantel just right of centre is much easier than...

14. **Jason's Mantel** *7a*
    Mantel onto the low slopey slab from a hanging start, just left of centre. *(Jason Myers)*

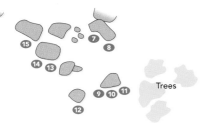

Pebble Mill

Trees

Trees

Trees

Trees

BETWEEN THE QUARRIES ▶

15. *6c*
Climb the wall left of the arête.

16. *5+*
Great arête, taken on the left.

17. *5+*
Edge, edge, top.

18. *6b+*
Tackle the front of the small block face-on from a sit start. Cute.

19. Electrical Storm   *7a+*
Sit start the lightning bolt rib in the pit and top-out up the sloping ramp.

20. Attitude Inspector   *7a*
Fantastic flying dyno up the arête. The tall will miss out on all the fun by doing it statically. *(Mark Wilford/Derek Bolger)*

21. *6c*
Crimpy flakes in wall just right of crack.

22. *6a*
Arête from jug.

23. *6c+*
Sit start on the pedestal, out to lip and rooocckk for the pocket.

24. Definitive *5.11*
Tunnel into the gap between the boulders and work your way back out along the crack.

25. *6b*
Rock onto the hanging slab.

26. *5+*
Pockets 'n' stuff.

27. *5+*
High arête.

28. *5*
Right arête on the left-hand side.

29. *5*
Left arête on the right-hand side.

30. *6b*
Wall via shelf.

31. *7b*
Traverse the block just right of The Knock from a jug on the arête to finish up slopes just right of centre.

eastern crags

53

 CAPSTONE 50M

Burbage South Edge: Left Section

Past Parthian Shot the edge starts to shrink, and comes into its own for the boulderer.

1. **Classic Arête Problem** *7a+*
   Start on front face, move up and left onto left-hand side of arête finish up this.

2. **The Alliance** *7a+*
   Great double arête. Highball. *(Pete Oxley)*

3. **Home Cooking Slab** *6c*
   Climb the slab side of the arête.

4. **Home Cooking** *7a*
   Just left, the double arêtes give more fridge-hugging climbing above a poor landing. Highball. *(Johnny Dawes)*

5. **Triangular Wall** *6c*
   The lovely, rippled triangular wall is a gem from a sit start.

6. **Desparête** *7b+*
   Another immaculate double arête feature formed by the right arête of the groove and the arête right again. *(Johnny Dawes)*

7. **The Impossible Groove** *impossible*
   The stunning groove on this wall is not known as The Impossible Groove for nothing, and has seen failure by the great and the good of international bouldering.

8. **The Rib** *7b+*
   Located in a small bay 50m further on is this small quarried rib. It looks a lot easier than it is, but it's also a lot better than it looks. Tenuous climbing with a final slap to a jug. *(John Welford)*

9. **Intense** *8a*
   A small overhung quarried wall. Jump to high right-hand sidepull and snatch to top. Stacking mats to reach the high holds is much easier and indeed the problem is somewhat incomplete without the obvious sit start from the slot. *(Jerry Moffatt)*

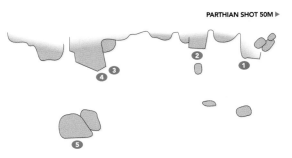

PARTHIAN SHOT 50M ▶

Capstone

After the last rays of bouldering disappear towards the northern horizon, and the edge merges into moor, one last capstone floats on heather and bedrock, halfway between the end of the edge, and a promising looking set of pinnacles 50m further on.

Two problems exist, rewarding for the man who has done everything.

The Whippet 6c+
Climb out from the break to the lip, and a stiff lock 'n' grovel to the top – no arête. (John Welford)

The Flat Cap 7a+
On the opposite, north-facing side, starting from the lowest part of the capstone. Traverse left and up from two crimps with a variety of heel hooks, shuffle moves and bunch-ups, to a top-out on the highest part of the block. (John Welford)

10. I'm Tense 7b
From low pocket on Intense, go up left via undercut and sidepull. (Mo Overfield)

11. 6b
Pocket to sloping break.

12. Fuji Heavy Industries 7b
Awkward sit start to right-hand side of arête. (John Welford)

13. Little Rascal 7a+
The starting groove of the route is tremendous. Escape right from the sloping ledge, or jump down. (Johnny Dawes)

At the far end, 20m further on is this worthwhile find.

Percy Bishton on I'm Tense: *Bishton Coll.* ▲

Burbage South Boulders

The Burbage South Boulders provide one of the friendliest circuits in the Peak. There are stacks of easy problems, all with perfect landings, and the occasional harder problem tucked in between them. The boulders are in a beautiful setting at the bottom of the Burbage Valley, sheltered from the worst of the winds.

Ellen Worthington on Problem 48: *Rupert Davies* ▲

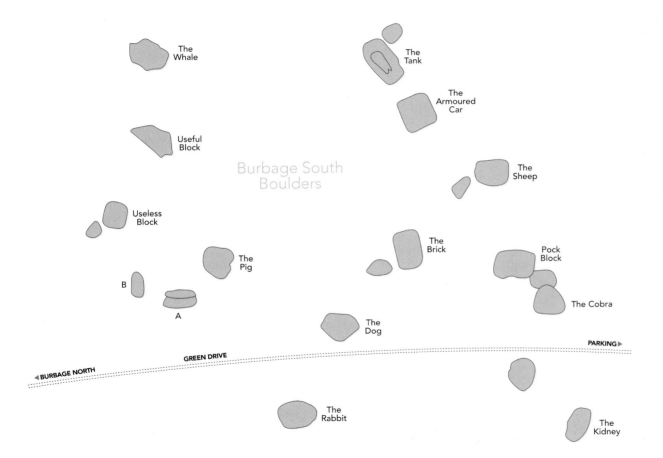

The Whale

The Tank

The Armoured Car

Useful Block

The Sheep

Burbage South Boulders

Useless Block

The Brick

Pock Block

The Pig

B

The Cobra

A

The Dog

PARKING ▶

GREEN DRIVE

◀ BURBAGE NORTH

The Rabbit

The Kidney

The Whale

1. 5
    Rising rightwards line along the arête/top of the block.

2. 5
    The wall past a pocket.

3. 5
    The wall past a break.

The Useful Block

4. 4+
    The small rib. The short crack just left is 4+.

5. 3+
    Crack.

6. 5
    The slab is one of the best problems on the boulders. An eliminate up the scoop to the left, without the crack is 5+.

7. 5+
    The sharp quarried arête is climbed on the right. Classic.

8. 6b
    The wall on crimpy edges.

The Useless Block

9. 5
    An inelegant mantel onto the top.

10. 4
    The blunt arête is easiest on its left.

11. 4
    Wall and pebbles.

12. 4
    The slab and arête on the other side of the gap between the boulders

A

13. 5+
    The arête on the next boulder along. Climbed on the left. 6a+ on the right.

B

14. 6a
    Left side of the arête.

15. 3+
    Scallops and rib.

The Pig

16. **Little Pig** 7c
    From a sitting start on thin pockets, slap up the rounded arête to finish via a mono. Lovely moves.
    (John Welford)

17. 4
    Pull into the scoop and occasional puddle from low.

18. 5+
    A good hidden slab and a good test of footwork.

The Brick

19. **Crash 'n' Gurn** 7a
    Pull on and dyno to the (often) puddle-filled scoop from a sitting start holding a large undercut and a mono.

20. 4
    The arête above the slot. From a sitting start this problem is a tricky classic.

21. 4
    The centre of the wall.

22. 4
    The arête.

23. 4+
    The slab just right of centre is very good.

24. 4+
    More slab climbing left again. Those without a bit of reach may find it harder.

25. 4
    The wall just right of the arête.

26. 5+
    The steep arête on the boulder just next to The Brick.

27. 3+
    Any which way up the rib and slab.

The Dog

28. *7a*
Sit start. Snatch up edges and dishes. The footblock is in at this grade.

29. *6a*
Jump to the edge and top-out.

30. *6a+*
Traverse the rising edge of the boulder from a sitting start.

31. *4*
The elephant's arse/bum feature.

The Rabbit

32. Bugs *5*
The short blunt arête, climbed on the right. An eliminate taking the arête straight on ('Bunny') is 6a.

33. *5*
The bulge to the left, via the edge.

34. *5*
A reachy arête.

The Tank

35. *4+*
Sit start the small steep block.

36. Tiger *6a*
Classic slap from sidepulls to incut.

37. *3+*
The big flake.

38. Panzer *6b+*
Traverse the top of the block from left to right, shedding skin as you go.

39. *6a+*
Jump to the hold and top it out.

40. Chieftain *5*
The delightful rib.

The Armoured Car

41. *4+*
The wall right of the arête.

42. *4*
The arête and flakes.

43. *4+*
The short wall just right of centre has one of the nicest pebble holds on grit.

44. *4*
The wall left again.

45. *5*
Traverse the face leftwards from the right arête.

The Sheep

46. *5*
Climb the arête on its left.

47. The Sheep *6c+*
The curving crack and slopey pocket. Superb.

> **The Sheep Assis** *7b*
> It's much harder from sitting.

48. Sickle Crack *6c*
The Sheep left-hand. Layback the crack on the left with help from slopers on the arête. 7a from sitting.

49. Talk to Me Martin *7b+*
A painful pull using the small edge. The rumoured problem to the left is just that, as is the sit start.

Ellen Worthington on Pock: *Rupert Davies* ▲

eastern crags

Pock Block

50. Puck *5+*
The blunt arête is climbed on shallow dishes. A tasty sitting start is 7a+.

51. Pock *5*
A classic wall climb up bullet hole 'pocks'. A good 6c from sitting.

52. Pick *3*
The blunt arête on big sandy scallops starting from the rock platform.

53. Pock Man *5+*
The precarious slab.

54. *7a*
Tricksome slab - work up the left side of the scoop.

55. *3+*
Mantel onto the slot.

The Cobra

56. The Cobra *4+*
A lovely easy traverse that climbs really nicely.

57. *5*
Mantel over the roof - watch your back on the boulder behind.

58. *3*
Around the other side of this block are some more 3s.

The Kidney

59. *3+*
The slab and hanging crack.

60. *4*
The right-hand crack.

61. *5*
A delicate traverse. Start on the extreme left and traverse rightwards, walking your feet along the bottom of the slab, to finish up the right-hand crack. The traverse can be continued rightwards, but quickly gets much trickier.

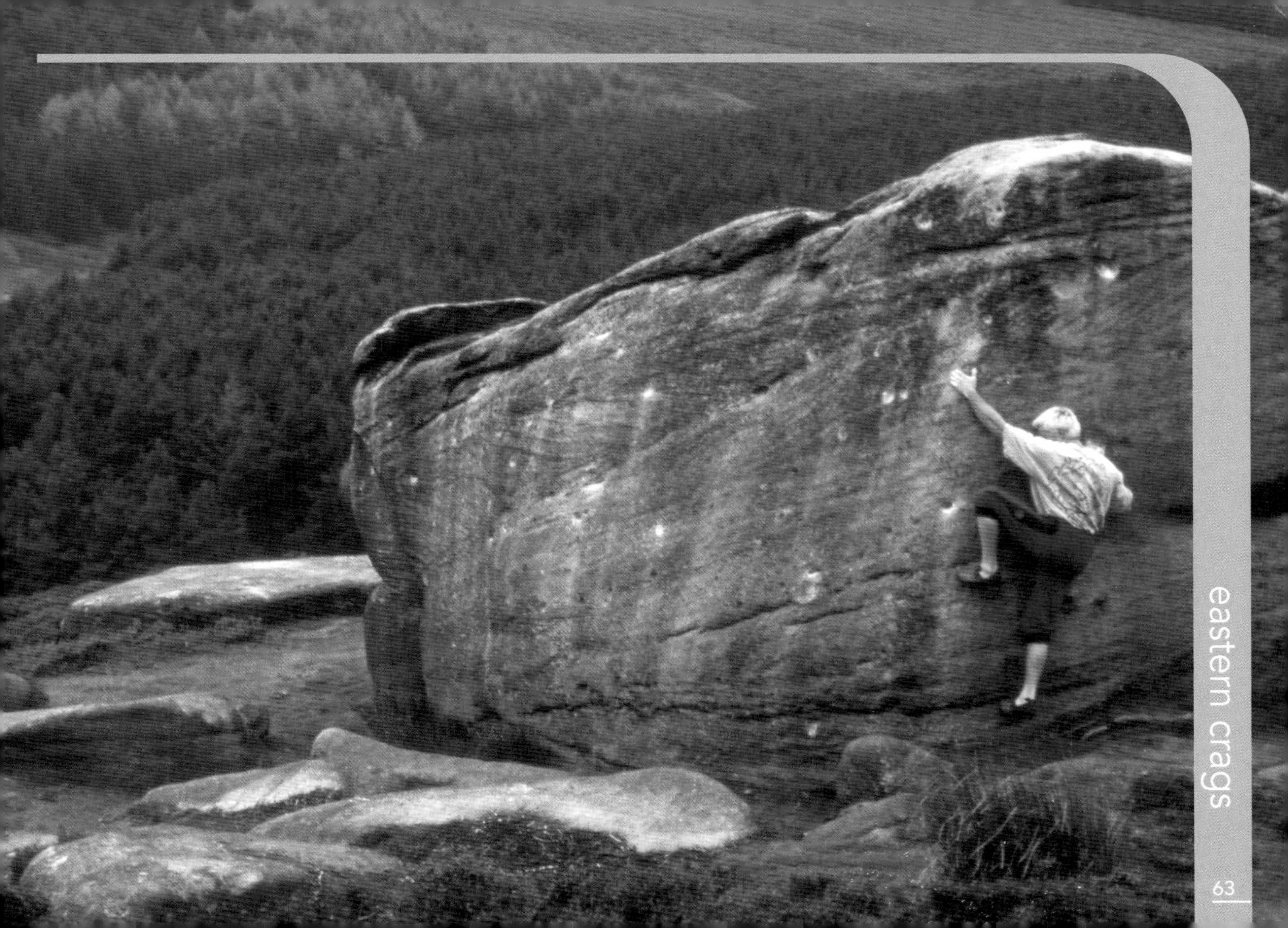

Burbage West

The hard climber's crag of choice. This series of shady buttresses of perfect gritstone, quietly facing out across to the crowds of Burbage North, keeps calling the dedicated boulderer back time and time again.

Approach

From the main car park at Burbage Bridge cross over the stile. Either walk rightwards along the top of the edge, dropping down left after about 200m, or drop down left straight away, then head slightly up right past some boggy ground – either way brings you to some world-class problems.

Conditions

A super-useful crag. There is often a wind from the west, which, in the depths of winter, can make climbing at Stanage or other areas at Burbage unbearable. In these conditions you can battle from the car in a freezing gale and climb in shelter at Burbage West with the wind rattling overhead. The wind can sometimes blow rain over the crag too.

Harry Pennells on The Famous Grouse: *Adam Long* ▲

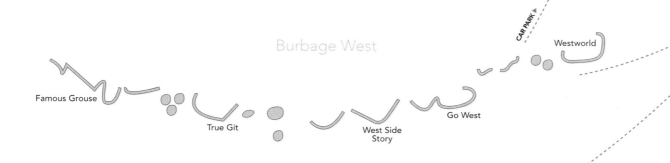

Burbage West

Famous Grouse

True Git

West Side
Story

Go West

CAR PARK ►

Westworld

Westworld

The first compact buttress reached from the car park.

1. **Right Arête** *6a*
   Easy arête, although it often has a wet streak.
   Now try it on the left.

2. **Not Westworld** *6b+*
   The wall just left of the arête, undercutting to the break - steady.
   Harder if you can't reach.

3. **Westworld** *8a*
   The wall just left again, undercutting to break – desperate.
   Possibly 7c+ for tall people. The sit-down adds a little.
   (Jason Myers)

4. **Blazing 48s** *8a*
   Bullet hole crimping on the edge of skin strength left of
   Westworld. Apparently named in honour of some strong coffee
   the first ascensionist had drunk. *(Jerry Moffatt)*

Go West Area

The next buttress has some fun warm-up circuits and…

1. **The Nose** *7a*
   The undercut nose on the right-hand side of the buttress, from low. Very hard without the toe hook. *(Martin Veale)*

2. **The Nostril** *7b*
   Hanging arête immediately to the left of the Nose. Start as for that problem before moving left using a sadly chipped hold.

3. **Go West** *6a+*
   Easy when you know how - the groove up the right-hand side of the buttress.

4. **The Traverse** *7a*
   From right to left along the vague low break. Worth being short.

5. **Western Eyes** *7c+*
   The obvious blunt overhung arête just left. Highball hugging. *(Zaff Ali)*

West Side Story

1. West Side Story *7b+*
Classic technical wall, with highball finish. Lots of methods, which incidentally all top-out. Traversing off half way up the problem is just that.
(John Allen)

2. Ron-side Force-it *7b*
This classic variation on WSS has grown a name - reach out right from the start of WSS then back left taking the flake as a press.

6b+
Traverse under WSS.

El Regallo del Mocho *7a+*
The wall to the right of Crow Man.
(Ben Bransby)

Crow Man *5*
The easy arête on the next buttress. Nice, but sometimes green.

Jason's Mono Problem *7a+*
Wall left of Crow Man, via mono.
(Jason Myers)

75m along the edge is an isolated nose on a low, insignificant looking block.

True Git *7b*
From the low break reach up to the vague pinch on the nose and slap to the top (very hard) – or use some guile and casually reach the top. Much better than it looks. *(John Welford)*

Another 75m along the edge is the excellent West End Girls area.

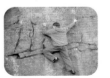     

West End Girls Area

1. **Breakfast** *7a*
   Sit start the right-hand side of the arête left of Famous Grouse (classic).
   (Mark Hundleby)

2. **Spartacus** *7c*
   A big span or a dyno or some levitation lands you on the jug high on the wall left of Famous Grouse. From here you declare loudly to the hopefully deserted valley: I'm Spartacus! Otherwise no tick.
   (John Welford)

3. **Famous Grouse** *7c*
   Small, hanging slab and arête from a sit start. Often done from standing at a grade easier. *(John Welford)*

West Side Story: *Adam Long* ▲

Harry Pennells on West Side Story: *Adam Long* ▲

Guplets Wall & Carl Wark

Two venues, two problems each. Though all of these esoteric little gems are situated in rather out of the way places, they all pack in serious levels of quality and difficulty.

Approach

Guplets wall is the isolated little buttress wall situated on the western flank of Burbage Brook, just below the Iron Age Fort of Carl Wark. It is best reached from the path that runs up from the stile by the Toad's Mouth boulder - this is next to the bend where Burbage Brook runs under the A625.

Carl Wark can be reached by taking the path opposite Burbage South. This runs up in a roughly north-north-westerly direction from the Green Drive, dropping into and out of Burbage Brook before climbing up to the fort through some soft peaty ground. Alternatively the problems can be reached by dropping down from Higgar Tor.

Andy Higginson on 'Warkin' Sit Start. *Alex Messenger*

Guplets Wall

On the opposite side of Burbage Brook, at the bottom of the valley, around 150m above the brook is an isolated little wall. Approach along the path that runs above the wall from a stile next to the toad-shaped boulder above the road at the bottom of the valley.

1. **Guplets on Toast Sit Start**   *7b+*
A sit-down start to the bulging left-hand wall, on dishes. Watch that easy top-out. *(John Welford)*

2. **Darkstar**   *7c+*
The very highball wall right of Guplets. E6 6c ish. The crux is the lower section, but the top-out was checked on a shunt before the first ascent. *(John Welford)*

Carl Wark

Opposite Burbage South and across the saddle-shaped piece of land lies the Iron Age fort that is Carl Wark. In the jumble of blocks around the base are two more documented problems:

Green Flag   *7a*
The wall left of the start of Lost World from a break and sidepulls, to undercuts and the top. *(Richie Patterson)*

J-Warkin' Sit Start   *6c*
Small wall with a rib up its left side, 30m right of Lost World, situated on a terrace. Sit start on the break and climb the rib with the assistance of some face holds on the right. *(Dave Parry)*

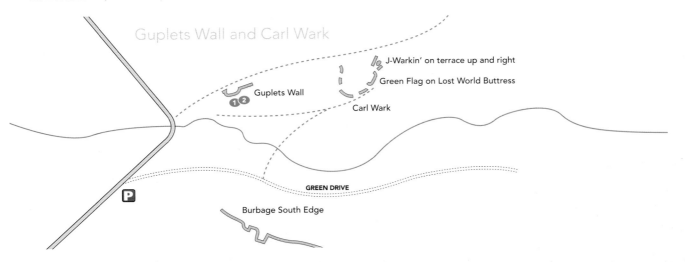

Guplets Wall and Carl Wark

J-Warkin' on terrace up and right

Green Flag on Lost World Buttress

Guplets Wall

Carl Wark

GREEN DRIVE

Burbage South Edge

Higgar Tor

Higgar Tor is yet another of the superb venues to be enjoyed in the Burbage Valley. Almost exclusively the domain of the hardcore, these tough little cookies all demand power, technique and application to achieve success. The majority of the bouldering exists on the ridge below the tourist path.

Approach

Park in the lay-bys just beyond Fiddler's Elbow. Walking up from the car, on the steps, the first climbing is reached just over the edge on the left as you reach the summit.

The main action is on/in the low, undercut cave.

Richard Williams on Piss: *Adam Long* ▲

Excreta Buttress

Just before the main buttress is
Dirty Higgar, 6c, the low prow from
a lying-down start.

1. Piss *7b*
Start on the hanging nose; finish using
sloper on the right. Well, was it?
(Ben Moon)

2. Shit *7b+*
Piss from the back of the cave to finish
up Piss (not piss, and not shit either –
actually very good). *(Richie Patterson)*

3. Hemline *7a+*
Start up Shit, finish via Sick.
(Richie Heap)

4. Sick *5+*
Dyno or mantel the ledge.

The next problems are 15m left.

5. *7c*
Right of Pooh. Sit start with both hands
in break and gain the top via a tiny edge.
Easier for the tall. *(Mick Adams)*

6. Pooh *7b*
Dyno from the low break to the top,
without using the arête.

7. Winnie The... *6a*
Left side of the arête from sitting.

Left again is…

8. The Arête *7a+*
Even the great fall off this. The obvious
arête to a slopey finish, climbed on its
right. The lower rock is unfortunately
very crumbly - be gentle. Climbed on
the other side the arête is a nice 6b.

*The ridge continues left and is home
to some lovely easy problems - none
of which is harder than 5+, with the
majority being 4 and 4+. A guide is
not necessary to enjoy this area so
explore and have fun!*

One hard problem worth seeking out is:

Krush Regime *7b*
Climb the centre of the big wall on the
buttress immediately left of The Arête.
It has tiny holds and a hard start.

*The final problem is on the famous
leaning block itself.*

Higgar Traverse *7b+*
Traverse the face underneath the Rasp.

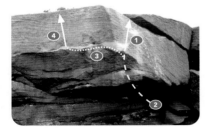

curbar

Another classic area, with problems from 4 - 8a. Once again the majority of the truly great problems are in the upper grades.

Curbar dries quickly and is close to the car, so it's a good choice of venue in 'variable' weather. Even if it does rain, you may be able to get some in on the Gorilla Warfare block.

Adam Long ▲

Access and Approach

Park by the side of the road just below Curbar Gap. Walk down the road towards Warren Lodge and take the path through the gate. Trackside is the first boulder encountered, with the rest scattered above. Ben's Wall is about 150m further on, set amongst the trees.

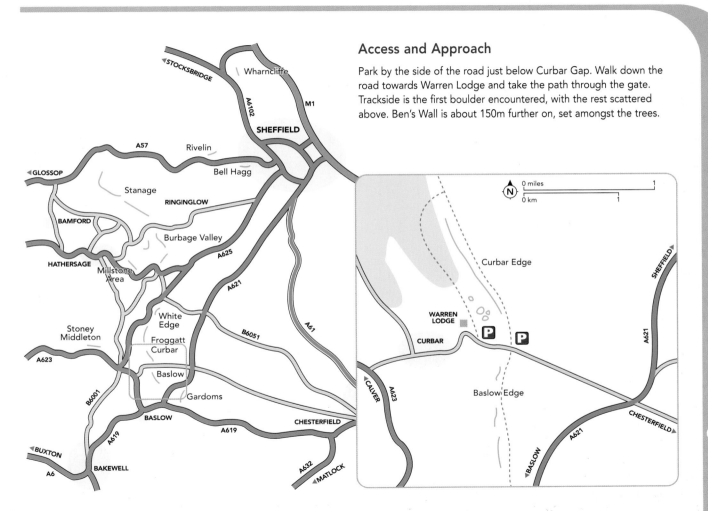

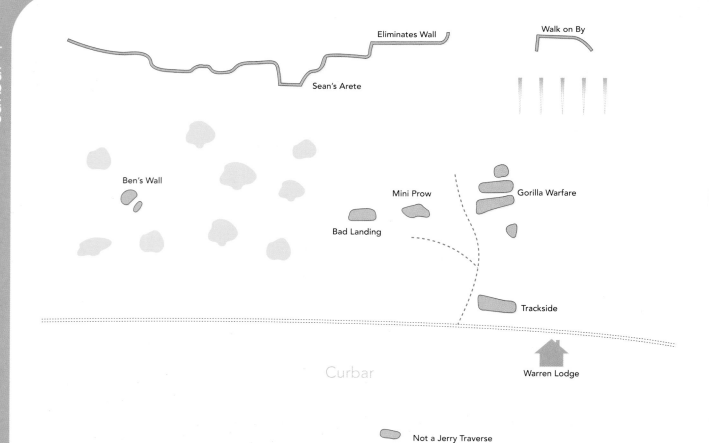

Eliminates Wall

Walk on By

Sean's Arete

Ben's Wall

Mini Prow

Gorilla Warfare

Bad Landing

Trackside

Curbar

Warren Lodge

Not a Jerry Traverse

◀ APPROACH FROM THE ROAD

Dave Buchanan on Work Hard: *Stu Littlefair* ▲

Trackside Boulder

Complete with in-situ wood-chip landings, this is perhaps the ultimate convenience boulder. The Trackside Boulder has a good spread of problems that should last most people a lifetime. It's the obvious big flat block, seen on the right as you approach along the track.

1. **5+**
   On the left-hand side of the block are a number of easy problems on excellent rock. The classic is just left of the arête, manteling up past the slot.

2. **5+**
   Climb the left-hand side of the front face using the obvious pockets. Plus: massively fun double dyno from the lower pocket to the top.

3. **4+**
   Climb the wall right of the pockets. Harder if you start on the low break, 6b ish.

4. **Strawberries** 6b
   Can feel strangely hard, or indeed trivial, depending on how you do it. Sprag/layoff the thin cracks/seam to a direct finish.

5. **5**
   The crack.

6. **Play Hard** 7c
   Eliminate – no crack. Right of the crack is a two-handed sloper. Head to the top from this via a poor hold just right of the crack and more poorness next to the top. *(Jason Myers)*

7. **Work Hard** 8a+
   Direct up the hanging slab from the sloper. A total reach problem. Morpho. *(Jason Myers)*

8. **6b+**
   The crack and various pockets and slopes land one with satisfaction on the summit. A worthwhile eliminate.

9. **Trackside** 7a
   A true Peak District classic, mostly by virtue of its proximity to the road. Reach up to grab a handful of arête, then casually reach the top with a scary knee/heel in the bottom of the crack.

10. **Sidetrack** 6c
    Can you guess where it goes? (The other side of the arête.)

Tracking 7b
Quite a nasty proposition. Traverse right from the left arête along the low slopey break, past a tricky move to exit up Strawberries, or continue to finish up Trackside at 7b+.

The next two problems are located on a large low boulder in the field below the Trackside Boulder.

PLEASE APPROACH FROM THE ROAD, AND NOT BY CLIMBING OVER THE DRYSTONE WALL.

Not A Jerry Traverse 7a+
Traverse from right to left. Kinda worthwhile and easier with a few toe bars.

Not a Problem for Jerry 6c
Up the wall on slopes from the good hold just after the crux of the traverse (towards the right of the main face). The main difficulties are due to the current amount of grittiness rather than the actual climbing. There is also another very similar problem next to it at about the same grade. *(Mark Pretty)*

Gorilla Warfare Slab

A slabby, east/road-facing boulder just below the main cluster of Gorilla Warfare boulders.

1. **The Arête** *4*
   Climb the arête on either side.

   Dan's Wall *7a*
   Sit start The Arête. *(Dan Warren)*

2. **The Slab** *4*
   The pleasant slab.

3. **The Groove** *3*
   The leftwards-leaning groove.

Chris Davies on Hurricane: *Adam Long* ▲

Gorilla Warfare

A hard-core group of problems on a superb, overhanging, partially quarried face. The big block behind also has a couple of problems/routes, but the main action is in the darkness below.

1. **Off-Width**
   No grade and very little point, but if you must we will allow you to tick it.

2. **Gorilla Warfare** *7a*
   Traverse rightwards from the off-width, move up to the slopers, then rock over the top on good small hidden edges just left of the arête. A thuggy classic. By continuing to traverse and rocking around the arête, you get to tick Extended Warfare, at the same grade. Historical Note: the original GW actually traversed the top of the block to the left of the off-width crack, dropped down the crack, and then did what is now called Extended Warfare – but it went even further right. *(Martin Veale)*

3. **Hurricane** *7c*
   A big move to the top from the slopers right of the crack. Hitting the top is reasonable – holding it is very hard.
   (Jerry Moffatt)

4. **Early Doors** *7a+*
   From the slopers in the middle of Gorilla Warfare, make a bid for the top.

6b
Climb the highball right-hand arête opposite Gorilla Warfare. Excellent.

Veale Thing *E2*
For the sake of completeness, and just in case you get confused easily, the left-hand arête is a route!

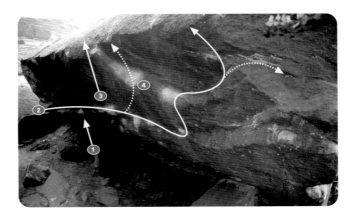

Mini Prow Boulder

25m from Gorilla Warfare is the aptly named Mini Prow.

1. **Mini Arête** *3*
2. **Mini Crack** *3*
3. **Mini Prow** *5*
   Worthwhile.

Bad Landing Boulder

Also aptly named is the next boulder along.

1. *4*
   The left arête is not very good.

2. *5*
   The right-hand side of the grooved arête.

3. *7a*
   The wall above the lip of the roof, from hanging the lip, is quite tricksome. A very low start has been climbed starting under the roof at 7c+. *(Paul Houghoughi)*

Ben's Wall

Some 100m further right and through some trees is the impressive Ben's Wall block.

1. **Pebble Wall** *6a*
   The left arête is good.

2. **Ben's Wall** *7c*
   Bounce to the large pocket. If you go with your left from the crack it is slightly harder than if you go with your right from the pocket. *(Ben Moon)*

3. **Great White** *7c*
   The wall to the right, finishing in the large pocket, has a reputation for being hard. Jump off. *(John Welford)*

4. *6c*
   Traverse from left to right under Ben's Wall to finish up ramp on the right.

   6b
   Facing Ben's Wall is a tiny overhang. Sit start from the low edge.

Ben Moon on Ben's Wall: *Ray Wood* ▲

Curbar Edge

Two brilliant problems exist on the main crag up the hill from the boulders.

Located in a quarried bay to the right of the main crag is this stunning problem, starting from the right-hand side of the platform on the left of the bay.

Walk on By   7c+
The big, blank, utterly featureless wall to the break. (Rob Gawthorpe)

100m left, on the main edge is:

Sean's Arête   7b
Left of Maupassant is a little arête. Climb it straight-on to an improbable finishing move. A classic. (Sean Myles)

Ben Moon on Walk on By: *Richie Patterson* ▲

Spray Mane   7b+
A big dyno up the wall left of Sean's Arête, starting at a pair of pockets. A pad and spotter are mandatory to avoid the boulder in the landing zone. *(Mike Gardner)*

And finally...

Follow the Trackside path for several hundred metres to where it forks, take the right fork up hill, through the trees. Almost at the end of the crag and still on the main path is an obvious block, next to the path.

The Green Mile   6c
The left arête from a sit-down. *(Dan Ogden)*

The Ultimate Gritstone Experience   6c
Climb the face of the same boulder from sitting, using both arêtes, and exit straight up. *(Dan Ogden)*

Touch Winky   7b
The right arête and faint crack from sitting has a desperate first move followed by more amenable climbing above. *(Percy Bishton)*

End of the Affair Area

Between Ulysses or Bust and End of the Affair runs a shallow gully. The west-facing wall of this has three fine problems. From left to right starting at the top of the gully:

6b+
Sidepull up to a sloping boss and then mantel the sloping top.

Down on the next block is:

6b
Arête from a sit-down start - using the big hold on the right.

Cloud Cuckoo Land   7a+
Sit-down start to good holds and then a hard move on crimps to the finishing holds. *(Allen Williams)*

Percy Bishton ▲

John Coefield ▲

froggatt

Why go bouldering at Froggatt? The problems are sprawled out along the whole crag, with the majority being part of the crag itself. The problems range from good easy-mileage material on natural grit through the full range of (mainly quarried) traverses, dynos, technical walls, starts to routes, hard highballs and, above all, slabs. Grades range from 4 – 8a. If you want a bit of this, some winter sunshine, and are prepared to ramble around between problems, you should go bouldering at Froggatt.

The edge is not as sheltered as might be expected, but the boulders beneath the edge are well protected by the trees. The main occupational hazard at Froggatt is all those people walking around with ropes to get tangled in – the ones that get annoyed as you try and boulder at the bottom of the routes they want to do.

Access and Approach

There are two main approaches:
Park in the large lay-by on the A625, take the gate on the left, and follow the path along the top of the edge. The Hairpin boulder is almost immediately on the right. Continue along the track through a couple of gates to reach the main areas.

Alternatively park around the Chequers Inn on the A625 and take a steep path - just on the left downhill past the pub - up the hill. This soon arrives at the base of the crag. A much shorter approach, but steeper.

Andy Higginson on the Pinnacle Boulders: *Alex Messenger* ▲

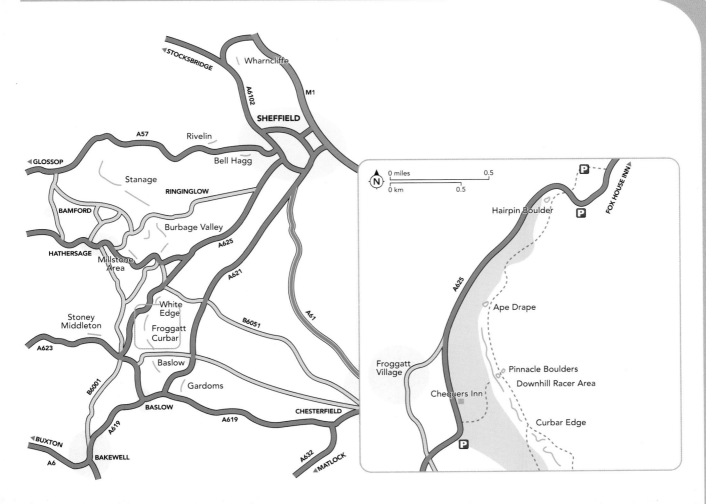

STOCKSBRIDGE

Wharncliffe

A6102

M1

SHEFFIELD

A57

Rivelin

Bell Hagg

GLOSSOP

Stanage

RINGINGLOW

BAMFORD

Burbage Valley

A625

HATHERSAGE

Millstone Area

A621

White Edge

Froggatt Curbar

B6051

A61

Stoney Middleton

Baslow

A623

Gardoms

B6001

BASLOW

A619

CHESTERFIELD

A619

BUXTON

A619

BAKEWELL

A6

A632

MATLOCK

0 miles 0.5
0 km 0.5

N

P FOX HOUSE INN

Hairpin Boulder

P

A625

Ape Drape

Pinnacle Boulders

Downhill Racer Area

Froggatt Village

Curbar Edge

Chequers Inn

P

Hairpin Boulder

An excellent if over-used boulder, with not a hold or sit-down start left unclimbed. Not unlike climbing in Yorkshire, just about every problem uses at least one chipped hold. It contains mostly easy - if a little steep - problems with one good traverse.

A few easy warm-ups and good beginners' problems can be found left and right of the steps. But the first real boulder problem is…

1. 4+
   Climb the arête using the large horizontal slot. The top-out is a lot harder if you don't find/use the chipped hold.

2. 4+
   Up the wall via a mantel on the low shelf.

3. Crash Test *6b+*
The excellent arête has no less than four main eliminates and a traverse, all are about the same grade and all well worthwhile.

a) Sit-down start from the two low cracks and climb the arête on the right.

b) Climb the arête on the left.

c) Finish up the crack to the left.

d) **Vanishing Point** *6c*
Traverse from right to left around the north-west arête to finish up the crack, and then awkwardly into the rounded groove.

4. *6b+*
From the bullet hole chip at head height on the wall left of the arête bounce up to the base of the groove and then the top – good. A sit-down start has been climbed at 7c, Jelly Bomb.
(Iain Farrar)

After heading towards the main crag, just after the gate and stream, there is a grassy track leading down between the blocks towards the impressive Renegade Master. Climbed from the back of the roof, trending rightwards up campus board edges and finishing around the arête, this is a very highball, 7c/7c+ if you are feeling strong and brave. The direct finish as per the first ascent has not been repeated to date.

Further down the path, where it abruptly meets a wall, there is a large boulder on the right, not surprisingly called the Tombstone. This boulder has been rediscovered several times over the last decade, and consequently there may be lots more problems than we've described.

1. *3*
The left-hand groove can be quite green but is a handy warm-up.

2. *6a*
Just right of the left-hand groove via a blind flake.

3. Shallow Grave *7b*
Slightly eliminate so it may be easier with a more liberal sequence. Anyway, climb the more central line. *(Percy Bishton)*

4. Tombstone *7a+*
Right of centre past an obvious pocket to the top, can be dynoed.

5. Right Arête *5*
The easy right arête.

Back on the main crag the first area of interest is the traditionally over-graded Ape Drape. The boulder is just below the edge, around 50m before Strapadictomy.

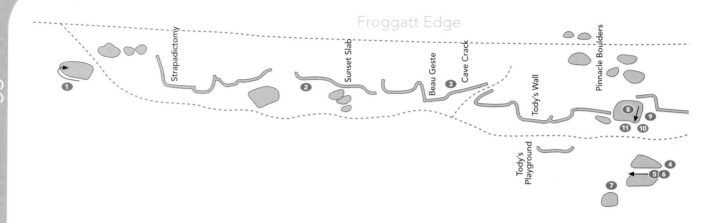

Froggatt Edge

1. **Ape Drape** 6c+
Traverse from right to left along flakes
and finish with a few upward moves.
(Martin Veale)

   Ape Drape Direct Finish 7a+
Finish via a heinous mantel over the
blob above and left of the normal finish.
(Mark Stokes)

2. **Leggit** 6b
Between Strapadictomy and Sunset Slab
is a neglected short crack in a little
sunken bay. If you do manage to climb it,
the real trick is getting back down again.

The wall just left is Cast Off, again 6b.

Pig Heart Boy 7b
The left-hand most line, starting from
the pit behind the boulder jumble and
featuring an obvious sloper. *(Adam Long)*

*Beyond Beau Geste is a large cave,
taken by the route Cave Crack.*

3. **Rambeau** 7b
Superb burly moves up the overhanging
arête to reach a break, traverse right
into Cave Crack, and then panic if you
can't jam. *(Mark Leach)*

Tody's Playground
A lot more fun than Tody's Wall.
This superb, perfectly featured
bouldering wall is just in front of
the route. It's a great beginners or
warm-up area. The top is a little high,
but it's well furnished with jugs.

We'll leave it to your imagination to
find the best lines.

*Down and left as you look out into
the valley are some large, ominous
looking boulders.*

Ape Drape: *Mike Vincent* ▲

Rambeau: *Adam Long* ▲

4. The Sound of One Foot Slipping *7a+*
Climb the right arête from the low break
on its left until a flake and a sloper
allows a precarious roll onto the slab.
(Ben Bransby)

5. Jetpack *7b*
Big, weird, steep dyno, starting off two
obvious sidepulls on the left-hand side
of the long slopey boulder in front of
Turd Burglar. *(Jon Fullwood)*

6. Pea Crab Shuffle *7c*
A 45-move traverse along the lip of
the boulder. Sit start on the left and
traverse right. *(Iain Farrar)*

7. Gibsonitus *7b*
On the block right of Turd Burglar,
looking downhill. Climb the arête from
sitting – start by hugging the obvious
steep rib. Dirty crimps and weird
heelhooks are de rigeur. The arête is
higher than it looks, but it gets easier
with height. *(Percy Bishton)*

Jessica Corrie on The Arête, Joe's Slab: *Adam Long* ▶

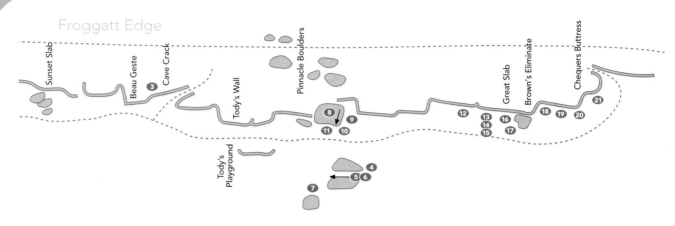

Froggatt Edge

Sunset Slab · Beau Geste · Cave Crack · Tody's Wall · Pinnacle Boulders · Tody's Playground · Great Slab · Brown's Eliminate · Chequers Buttress

Pinnacle Boulders

Back on the main path above the main part of the crag are a few lumps of millstone grit. These cliff top tors offer scores of lines, but unfortunately almost every one is about 4+ only two moves long and identical. They are ok, but a little dull for more than one visit.

Froggatt Pinnacle

The problems here are good, clean and fingery. Not everyone's cup of tea, and lacking in classic status as none of them really finishes anywhere.

8. **Oedipus Traverse** *6b*
From the cave on the right, traverse the break leftwards to its end. Now buy the route guide and finish up Oedipus (E4). Otherwise hang around for a bit and wait for someone to move your mat over so that you can jump off.

9. **Mint 400 start** *7b+*
Crimp direct through the traverse of Oedipus. Best back off at the traverse line.

10. **Oedipus Direct** *6b+*
Direct to the end of the traverse. Traversing off right would seem like a good finish. 7a for the short.

11. **Neon Dust Direct** *7?*
The thin wall left of Narcissus. The grade depends on which starting holds are used. *(Ron Fawcett)*

Pinnacle Traverse *7a+*
Start low on the left wall and swing round the arête to finish along Oedipus Traverse.

Joe's Slab Area

This perfect little slab, the main event hereabouts, gets the full midday sun, but despite this it is getting nicely polished. The slab has been climbed in every way possible. However a few classics still stand the test of time.

12. Direct Start to Downhill Racer *7a+*
You're going to have to use your common sense to know when to back off this one as it quickly stops being a boulder problem. If you find yourself at the top, well done.

13. The Arête *6b*
Harder than it looks, and better.

Two eliminate slabs take technical ground just right at 7a ish.

14. Joe's Original *6a*
The classic of the wall. From the flat edge, undercut with the right and reach up left. Superb. *(Joe Brown)*

A 7a eliminate scratches into the finishing crescent holds direct. And there is another eliminate at about the same grade to the right of the original.

15. Joe's Slab Traverse *7a*
Right to left, at head height on the obvious, various line of holds and finishing up the left arête.

Just beyond Great Slab is a collection of problems on a detached block.

16. *5*
Climb the crack, if you can jam.

17. *6b+*
From the back of the cave, pull out to a hold, then another above the lip, then grapple up the slanting crack to jugs. Excellent. Eliminates exist.

The thin slab type thing to the right is 6c.

Further right is Nutty Land, E1, a contrived route up the centre of the flake. This has a good 6c sit-down start.

Right again, and around the arête is:

18. Slingshot *8a*
The steep, highball wall right of the corner to the ledge, involves dynoing to a thin finger edge above an awkward landing. Top-roped originally by Jerry Moffatt in 1988 then soloed much later by Mo Overfield above mats.

19. Chequers Groove *7c+*
The groove right of Slingshot is again very highball and dynamic. It was soloed above a very, very large mat borrowed from the Foundry climbing wall. *(Jerry Moffatt)*

20. Sole Power *7c*
The hanging arête left of Chequers Buttress is rarely done, and quite hard. Named in honour of Jerry's new Fires, which gives you an idea of how old this problem is. No? Ok then, it was first climbed in 1983. *(Jerry Moffatt)*

21. Jankers Groove Sit Start *6c*
A sit-down start to Whillans' direct on this route. Evil fist jamming. *(Jon Barton)*

gardoms edge

Gardoms has two well-established compact circuits and a number of excellent outlying problems. Gardoms North is a great area with some classic hard lines and one of the hardest problems in the Peak. Gardoms South is smaller, but recent additions and the proximity of the highball lines at Moorside Rocks have turned this from being an esoteric venue to one well worth a visit, especially if you can climb in the 7s. Finally, the nearby Stump Hole Cavern is a neat bit of esoterica.

◄ Robin Barker on Full Power: *Stu Littlefair*

Access and Approach

Gardoms Edge lies above the A621 just to the east of Baslow. Although it's possible to walk along the top of the edge between the two areas, it's better to park differently for each – individual crag approaches are covered separately.

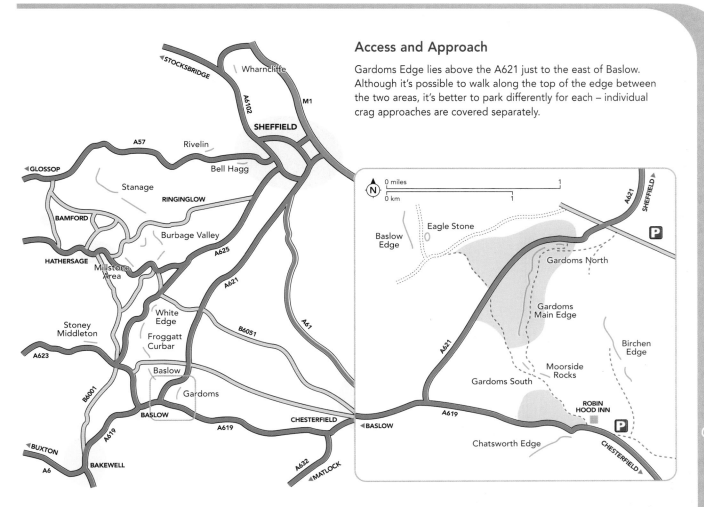

Gardoms North

The most popular of the Gardoms circuits is still rarely busy. The rock is good quality, the landings are flat and grassy, and the problems are satisfyingly powerful.

Conditions

The edge is north-facing, but most of the problems are popular enough for chalk to stop the growth of lichen. The majority of the problems are exposed to the wind and thus dry quickly. The outlying problems, scattered along the base of the edge proper, are in the trees. These take longer to dry and can become green. They are, however, sheltered on cold days.

Approach

You can no longer park in the lay-by directly below the crag. Instead, park on the extension of the Curbar Gap road, which is the first right after passing the crag if approaching from Baslow; or the first left before the crag if coming from Sheffield. Cross the stile and walk across the often boggy moor before crossing another stile to reach the first boulders.

Mark's Roof: *Stu Littlefair* ▲

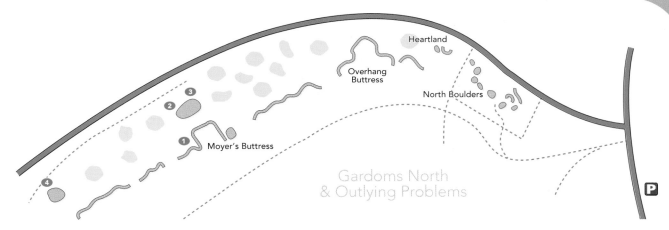

There are several outlying problems spread along and below the edge itself. They are difficult to find as negotiating the bottom of the crag is difficult, and knowing when to drop down from the top of the crag is confusing even for locals. We have used routes as waymarks – good luck with finding them. The first set of outlying problems are located around the classic E1 of Moyer's Buttress. See the above diagram for its location.

1. Perfect Day Direct Start *7b*
The superb direct start to the route right of Moyer's Buttress is quite powerful and sports dynamic moves between flatties. *(Ben Moon)*

2. Pogle's Wood *6c*
Below Moyer's buttress is a great boulder. Pogle's Wood follows the right arête of the downhill side of the block to a sloping finish. *(Allen Williams)*

3. Pogle's Wood Left-Hand *6b*
Approach the same top-out from the left arête. Not as good. The sit start is 6c.

Pogle's Wood Sit Start *7b*
The sit start is mean and frustrating but brilliant. From the low break slap up into the pinch on the right arête and make a decidedly tricky move to gain the sloping top. Not much change from 7b+.
(Rich Heap)

To reach the next outlying problem, walk downhill through the trees below Pogle's Wood to reach a path. Turn left along this, walking parallel with the edge, through the trees until an obvious problem can be seen on an isolated block on the left. This is Bin Laden's Cave.

4. Bin Laden's Cave *7a+*
The high, steep wall above the slab, with an awkward landing and a sloping top-out. Well worth finding. *(Mo Overfield)*

1. **A Tasty Graunch**   *7a+*
   A daft eliminate traverse along the lip of a roof. Traverse the low roof from right to left, using edges below the top, to gain the hanging crack, at which point you're allowed to use the top. top-out using a scoop for your left hand. The final silly rule is that no heel hooks are allowed. Don't worry, not all the problems are like this.

2. *6c*
   Another low roof. From a sit start, traverse small holds on the right side of the roof and mantel out the lip, exfoliating your chin as you go.

3. *6b+*
   As above but using bigger holds on the left side of the roof.

4. **Mark's Roof Left-Hand**   *7a*
   Now we're talking. Take the left-hand side of the large roof from a sit start, apeing along the edges, to finish up the flake on the front face. Finishing up the wide awkward crack is 7a+.

5. **Mark's Roof**   *7b*
   Uber-classic gritstone wrestling that will leave you winded. From the shelf at the back of the roof, take the centre of the roof with a spectacular cut-loose on the lip, traverse leftwards to the crux top-out slapping, matching and trying to use the sloping pod above. Traversing even further left to finish up the flake is 7a.

6. **Mark's Roof Direct**   *7c*
   Start as for Mark's Roof, but from the square-cut hold on the lip take on the short blank wall above, trying to hold onto the most marginal of gritstone ripples.

7. *6a*
   From a low start climb the nose using a flake.

8. *5*
   Seams in the wall.

9. *6a+*
   Scaryness up the prow feature.

10. *5*
    The centre of the slab on the shelf. If you're not confident, take a spotter to make sure you don't fall further than you want.

11. *5+*
    The side wall using grit-tricks to stand on the big footholds.

12. *6b+*
    Thin flakes and the hanging arête – pull on and launch or balance up by laybacking the flake. Nice. Can also be done from a sit start from a crack in the back 7b+.

13. *7b*
    The big side wall. Undercut out to the sloper using as much of the foot or leg jam as you dare. *(Ben Moon)*

14. *6c*
    The big arête.

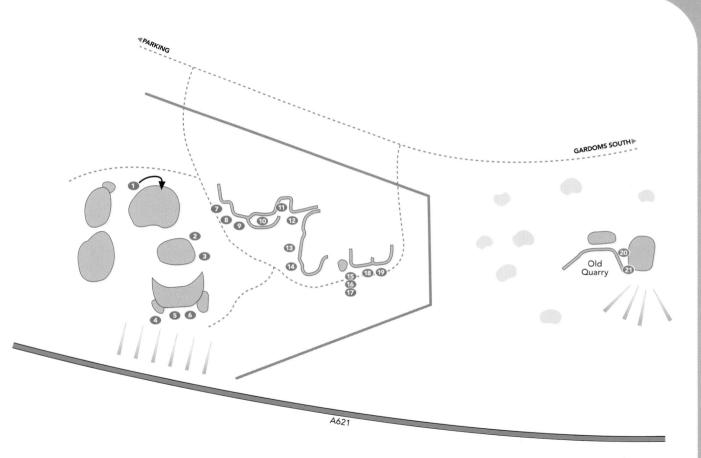

15. Soft on the G   *7a+*

The rounded undercut arête feels ridiculously easy with a bit of technique. Without it, the slopey slaps are very frustrating. Another classic.
(Allen Williams)

16. Full Power   *8a*

A low squatting or sitting (depending on how big you are) start to Soft on the G, starting with your right hand in the pocket on the lip and your left on the lowest crimp/seam on the left side of the roof. Hard slapping up ripples and slopers follows. Easy for the grade.
(Jerry Moffatt)

17. 8 Ball   *8b*

One of the hardest problems in the Peak. Sit start at the right side of the low roof and traverse left into Full Power. *(Ben Moon)*

18. Rock Hard Bishop   *6b+*

The wall between Soft on the G and the groove to the right using holds on both those problems. Pull on, hit top, that's it.   *(Johnny Dawes)*

19. *6c*

The lovely little groove from a sit start. 5 from standing.

The next problems are on a small block visible through the trees, perched just above a tiny quarried pit.

20. *7a*

Sit start on a large hold under the roof and slap up the left side of the bulge to a finger rail above.

21. Heartland   *7c*

Start on the same big hold under the roof, but exit at 90° to the last problem. Reach a high flared finger jam and use it to gain the slopers above.
(Kristian Clenmow)

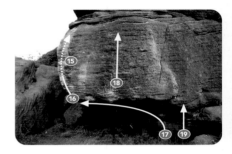

Ben Moon on 8 Ball: *Ray Wood* ▲

Gardoms South

Another compact little circuit hidden
in the trees at the opposite end of
Gardoms Edge. The rock is very
good quality, nicely featured and the
landings are generally good with only
the odd exception.

Conditions

Being in the trees it's sheltered in windy
and cold weather, however the problems
can become green in damp spells.

G Thang: *Rupert Davies* ▲

Approach

Park in the free car park next to the Robin Hood Inn on the A619 road to Chesterfield. Walk down the road towards Baslow, and cross a stile on the right. Follow the path up the hill until some rocks are visible on the right – Moorside Rocks – continue until a gate in a wall is reached. Once on the other side of the wall, head up right and the boulders are tucked away under the trees.

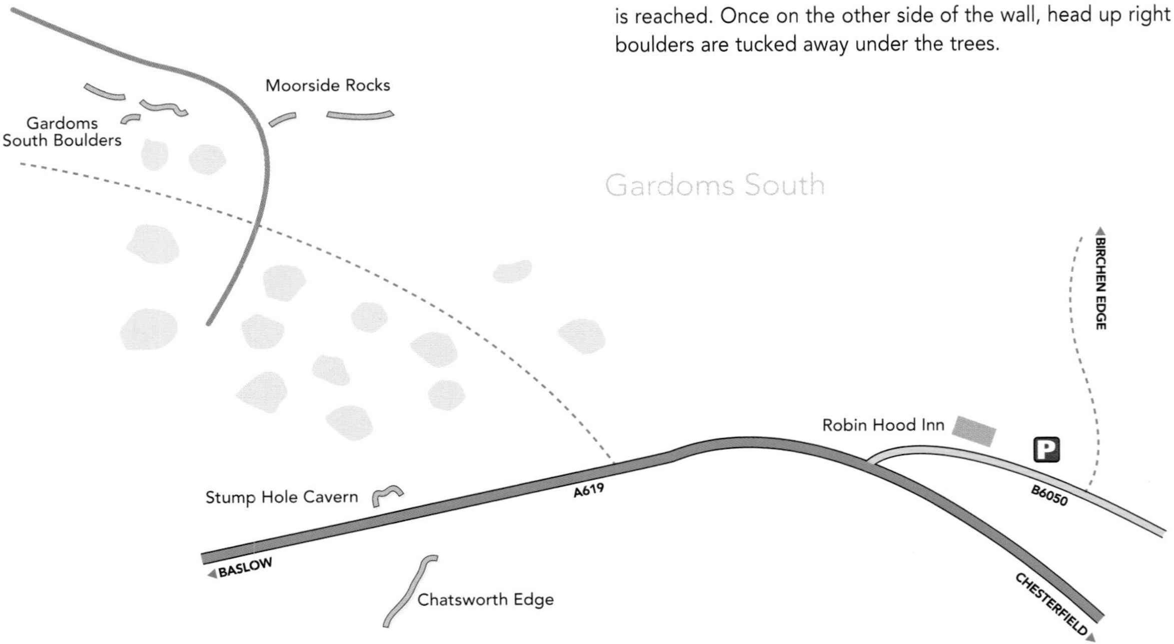

Gardoms South

Moorside Rocks

Gardoms South Boulders

BIRCHEN EDGE

Robin Hood Inn

P

B6050

Stump Hole Cavern

A619

BASLOW

Chatsworth Edge

CHESTERFIELD

1. *6b*
Climb the arête from the low hole on the left side.

2. *6a*
Hit the top from holds in the middle of the wall.

3. **G-Thang** *6b+*
The immaculate groove. At this grade, climb the groove without the arête – with the arête it's 6b. *(Allen Williams)*

4. **G-Thang Sit Start** *6c+*
Sit start the groove using the small undercut. Again, graded without the arête.

5. **Barry Sheene** *7c*
Reach and match the crimpy rail in the centre of the wall by undercutting the break. Morpho, but hard even if you can reach. *(John Welford)*

6. **China In Your Hands** *7b+*
The indirect start to Barry Sheene starting up the groove between the two boulders was briefly put out of action after someone ignored the clue in the name and pulled too hard on the pebble. Adam, however, couldn't let it go. "I couldn't have my problem forgotten so I reclimbed it. It's a bit harder, 7b+, but brilliant, honest. You bridge facing OUT then pirouette on your left foot. Way better than Barry Sheene." *(Adam Long)*

7. *6a+*
The arête just left is a bit reachy. It's also high and green.

8. *5*
The wall to the left of the arête.

9. *5+*
Arête and slab.

10. **Suavito** *7b+*
The steep highball arête gives great slappy climbing at an uncomfortable height, with a committing move to gain the top. Take some spotters and a few pads. *(Tom de Gay)*

11. *6c*
The pocketed wall just left of the overhanging left arête. Move left to the ramp to finish

12. *6c*
From a sit start do a hard slap to catch the ledge and mantel it out.

13. *5+*
The short arête and wall.

14. *6a*
The arête on the left-hand side – barely independent.

Just left there is a crap problem through the cave formed by the stacked blocks.

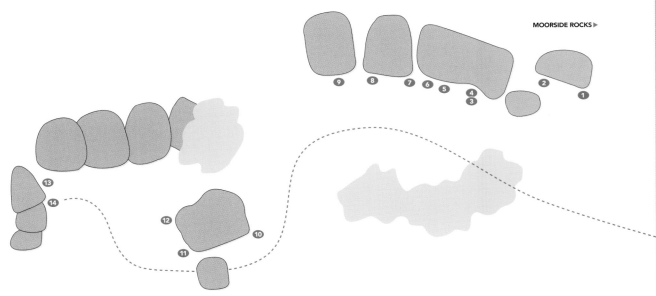

Moorside Rocks

The short buttresses of Moorside Rocks are really a continuation of Gardoms Edge. The climbing is highball and is included owing to the ease of combining a visit here with the Gardoms South boulders.

Conditions

The rocks face south-west and are good, clean, exposed and out of the trees.

Approach

As for Gardoms South. Park in the free car park next to the Robin Hood Inn on the A619 road to Chesterfield. Walk down the road towards Baslow, and cross a stile on the right. Follow the path up the hill until the rocks are visible on the right.

1. **Superbloc**   *8a (E8 7a)*
The stunning rounded arête was climbed as a route, not a boulder problem. It is however a stunning line, and may be boulderable with stacks of pads and some big hefty spotters. *(Miles Gibson)*

2. **The Jackalope**   *7a*
The bottomless hanging crack up the centre of the wall is a jamming test-piece. The flat rock-platform landing needs a pad or two. *(John Allen)*

Ben Bransby on The Jackalope: *Adam Long* ▲

Stump Hole Cavern

A hidden wall only a few metres from
the road, with a powerful problem on it.
The good news is that it's steep,
and so stays fairly dry in the rain.

Approach

Park as for Gardoms South next to the
Robin Hood Inn, and walk down the road,
past the stile on the right that leads to
Moorside Rocks. Continue for another 100m
or so until opposite Chatsworth Edge on the
other side of the road. Stump Hole Cavern
is the steep quarried wall about 10m back
from the roadside in the trees on the right.

Stump Hole Cavern   7c+
Blast up the steep wall from a sit start on
the left to the ledge. From here only a
massive five foot dyno will get you past the
blank section above to the jugs on top.
(Brian Chase)

Stump Hole Cavern (first bit)   7b+
Needless to say, most people bail out at the
ledge after climbing the lower wall from a
sit start. Powerful climbing on edges,
slopers and slots. 7b from standing.
(Percy Bishton)

Stump Hole Cavern: *Sarah Davies* ▲

millstone area

An area of small crags and bouldering spots containing many classic problems. There's a bit of everything: Millstone is a huge quarry with a smattering of smooth little classics; Owler Tor has a large number of pleasant, low, easier problems with good landings in a good setting; the Secret Garden hides a concentration of steep sloper- slapping test pieces; Mother's Pet has excellent problems on which to test your gritstone top-out skills and Mother Cap is a beautiful landmark much frequented by tourists – so have those stock witty answers ready for when you get asked the inevitable question: "What's that thing on your back for?"

Mark Hundleby on Technical Master Left-hand: *Jon Barton* ▲

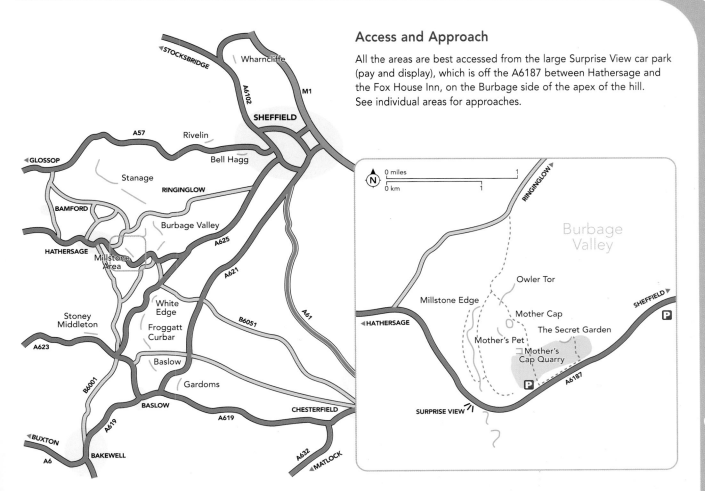

Access and Approach

All the areas are best accessed from the large Surprise View car park (pay and display), which is off the A6187 between Hathersage and the Fox House Inn, on the Burbage side of the apex of the hill. See individual areas for approaches.

Millstone

Millstone is a fantastic crag,
but maybe not for the boulderer.
However, a few good quarried classics
and one problem the likes of which
you may not have done before will
make a dedicated trip worthwhile.

Access and Approach

From Surprise View cross the stile out
of the western end of the car park,
follow the path across the moor and
drop down to the track which runs
under the crag. Head right to the
bouldering.

Jon Barton ▲

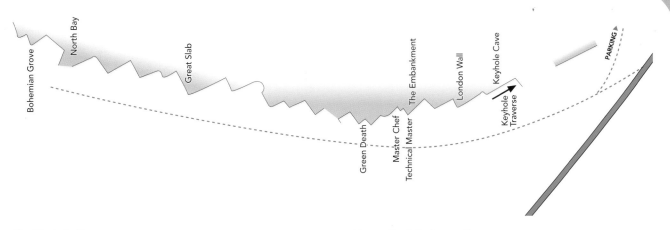

The Keyhole Traverse

A stamina exercise for those confused about their place in life; start on the left and traverse as far right and duck under as many ropes as your embarrassment allows.

Technical Master   6b

Climbed on the front face, the arête is a classic Peak testpiece. It's quite a bit harder on its left-hand side, without the crack, but 6c with.   *(John Allen)*

Technical Baiter   5c

The flake and groove just left. The way up is also the way down, which is a consideration.

Master Chef   7b

The rib/arête just left of Technical Baiter. To get down you reverse Technical Baiter for another tick.   *(Johnny Dawes)*

Master Chef Sit Start   7c

(Mo Overfield)

Green Death Super Direct Start   7b

Unique, smearing, stemming, weirdness up the corner to a good edge on the left wall. Now is most definitely the time to stop going up.

Green Death Start   6c

Edges in the wall left of the corner leading rightwards to good sloping holds. If you don't know when to jump off, you're too stupid to be bouldering.

Over in the far north bay of the quarry is a small wall to the right of an arête.

Bohemian Grove   8a

The fingery wall, which eliminates the arête.   *(Mo Overfield)*

Mother Cap

Mother Cap is the squat, square tor of rock that can be seen from miles around on the hill behind Millstone Quarry. Most of the problems were originally climbed as routes (some with gear) that finished over the capstones on the top. Climbed as boulder problems they finish on the ledge below, so shuffle/jump off as best you can.

Access and Approach

Follow the walkers up the path that exits north from the centre of the Surprise View car park, straight up the hill, after which Mother Cap will be unmissable.

1. **Milk Cap**   *4+*
   The wide crack right of centre on the south face.

2. **Conan the Librarian**   *6b+*
   A contender for the best-named problem in the Peak.
   A classic; climb the centre of the south face. Shuffle right at the ledge or switch into route mode and go over the capping block.
   (Johnny Dawes)

3. **David**   *7b*
   The wall to the left on tiny holds.   *(Richie Patterson)*

4. **Oyster Cap**   *6a+*
   The left arête of the south face.

5. **Elf Cap**   *6a+*
   The centre of the west face. Harrowing

6. **Blue Cap**   *5*
   The left arête of the west face.

Conan The Librarian: *Simon Richardson* ▲

Mother's Pet

A low-slung slug of perfect gritstone with a range of great problems all characterised by the mother of sloping top-outs. It's hidden down to the left of Mother Cap as you approach from the Surprise View car park. You're gonna be glad you got your 200m badge 'cos we're going swimming.

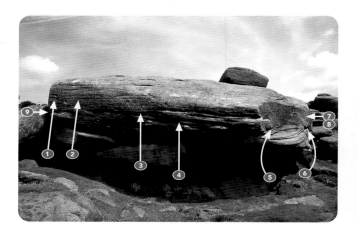

1. *6b*
   The right-hand side of the left-hand arête.

2. *6c*
   Climb the front face using sloping pockets, finding these with you feet proves to be the crux.

3. **Mother's Pride**   *7b+*
   Climb the centre of the wall to the sloping top; get your armbands out now. Harder for the short. *(John Welford)*

4. **Pet Cemetery**   *7a+*
   Don't let the big starting holds make you complacent. Advice: keep the armbands on and blow up the rubber ring. *(Jon Fullwood)*

   Just right is a project. Want to try? Armbands – check; rubber ring – check; now notify the lifeguards.

5. *6a+*
   Move onto the ledge from the left. To date all of the suitors that have tried to mantel onto the ledge directly have been found wanting. Starting from problem 4 is a classic.

6. *6b*
   Move onto the right-hand side of the shelf from the low break. Direct from flakes under the roof is harder, 7a. *(SS Simon Weill)*

7. **Proper Grit**   *6c+*
   Attain the 'proper grit' finish from a low edge and small pocket. Proper bo. *(Jon Fullwood)*

8. **Pets Win Prizes**   *7b*
   Sit start. Clever footwork may assist in climbing the right-most wall, just left of the quarry. Very good. *(Jon Fullwood)*

9. **Pet Whale**   *6c*
   The mid-height traverse, from left to right, finishing up problem 5. Curious moves with your legs stuck deep into the break.

Mother Cap Quarry

Not as good as any of the other bouldering spots in the area, but an interesting bit of esoterica none the less. The tiny quarry is down to the left of the approach path before Mother Cap is reached.

The quarry has a prominent natural boulder balanced on the edge and the first problems are on this. The keen will also get excited at the prospect of sit starts.

1. *6b*
The wall left of the arête.

2. *6c*
The bulging arête just right.

3. *6c*
The right wall.

Meanwhile, down in the quarry itself…

Flat Cap   *6a*
The wall starting just left of the arête and trending left. 6a+ for the direct start.

Dog Brush   *6a*
Start on the arête and drift rightwards up the ramp features. The crack just right is not worth the effort.

Night Cap   *6b+*
Tackle the centre of the wall right of the cracks.

Simon Richardson on problem 2: *Stu Littlefair* ▲

Owler Tor

Follow the track past Mother Cap. Owler Tor is the jumbled edge on the left. The bouldering is in an open bay just south of the main pinnacle.

From right to left as you look at the crag, the obvious clean arête and crack of problem number 4 is a good base camp.

1. *3*
Arête just right of problem 2.

2. *4+*
An excellent problem up the arête – a bit bouncy.

3. *4+*
A right-hand variant on the previous problem.

4. *6b+*
A superb problem up the arête and crack to finish on the arête. 7a+ from a sit-down start, eliminating the arête.

5. *3+*
A good one move wonder, up the wall, left of the arête.

6. *4*
The short arête is good if you just use holds on the arête. Has a good sit-down start.

7. *3+*
The crack using everything (but the crack).

8. *3*
The left arête.

9. *6a*
A roof problem. If it feels harder than 6a, you are missing out some footwork. Start at the back of the low roof, reach out to the slopes and mantel to glory – good climbing.

10. *6b*
Traverse under the roof from the right round the corner to the obvious top-out – ugly for all but the very short.

11. *3+*
Another arête with lots of holds.

12. *5*
Good climbing which turns into a route after the break.

13. *6a*
The little crimpy wall is quite good up to the gritty top-out.

14. *3*
More good holds on an arête.

15. *6b*
A good problem, which might need a few tries.

The wall above the cutaway to the left is dirty.

In front of the all these fine problems is a free standing block with a number of easy problems. However, 50m to the left, under the main crag is a square-cut block with an overhanging face. On this is a mean flake and small pocket, to a crimp and top ...7a.

Secret Garden

Hidden away in the trees above Surprise View is the Secret Garden. No longer quite as much of a secret as it once was, all the remaining gaps have now been plugged to give a brilliant venue with a fantastic circuit. The climbing is brutal – roof starts with sloper-slapping above – so bring your spare skin.

Approach

Park at the Surprise View car park on the A6187 and follow the path that leaves the car park on the right (east) and runs parallel with the road. As you reach the end of the wooded area on the left, the path goes left and up into the trees, just opposite a metal milepost. The main area is visible up and left of the path after 150m or so.

◀ Pat King on Zaff's Problem: *Adam Long*

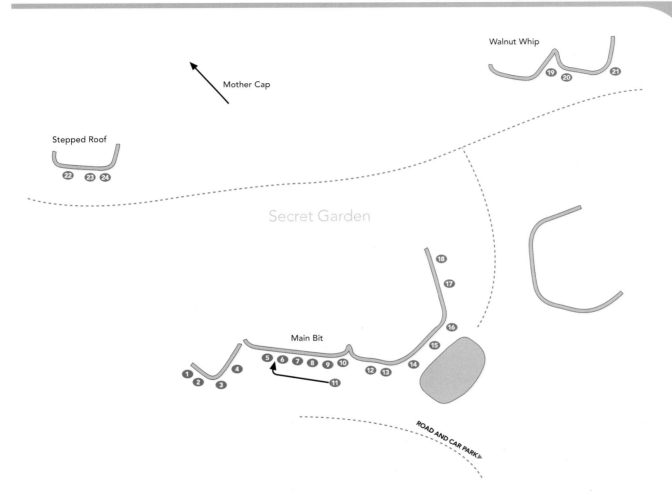

Walnut Whip

19 20 21

Mother Cap

Stepped Roof

22 23 24

Secret Garden

18

17

16

Main Bit

15

1 2 3 4 5 6 7 8 9 10 11 12 13 14

ROAD AND CAR PARK

Main Bit The first area of rock reached, on the left of the path.

1. *6b*
Sit start, and move left, or direct slightly easier.

2. *6c*
A great little problem. Sit start the bulging arête, slappety slap. The eliminate up the wall to the left will be very hard.

3. *5+*
Pockets and crack up the wall. Also good as a sit start and with eliminates – crack only, just pockets etc.

4. *6b+*
Pull up and leftwards after starting with one hand under the roof and one on the lip.

5. *7a*
From the back of the roof use assorted slopes to gain the sloping top-out.

6. Zaff's Problem *7b+*
From the back of the roof move out to the lip and try and match the sloper above (using a big bag of hip flexibility) before taking the small divot/pocket over the bulge to top-out. Neo-classic.
(Zaff Ali)

7. *7a+*
Again from the back of the roof, bail out to the lip and move left to take the rounded pocket with your left hand. An even further left-hand variation takes the pocket/rib with the right hand - 7a+.

8. Beach Ball *7a*
Another classic, just right of the previous problem. Start as for that problem, and slap direct up slopers to finish.

9. *6b*
Just right of Beach Ball, with a big move from the holds on the lip to a hidden pocket over the bulge. Also known as 'Not Zaff's Problem', 'cos it's not.

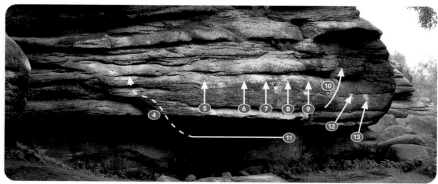

10. *5+*
The right-facing crack.

11. *6c+*
Traverse the lip break/sloper leftwards
from the crack to finish up problem 4,
with your feet on the back wall.
Completing this traverse footless is
the almost mythical 'Zippatricks';
grade, Very Hard.

12. *6c*
The faint groove from a sit start.
Probably better as a stand up,
as the top-out is the best bit.

13. Nigel's Problem *7a+*
Sit start left of the arête, reach up and
right for a pair of poor slopers and slap
into the flake.

14. Left-Hand Man *7c+*
A brilliant sit start problem with two
methods. Using holds on the arête to
reach the top pocket with your right
hand is 7b+. The original method used
these holds as intermediates, going
again to the top pocket with the left
hand - 7c+. *(Ian Fitzpatrick)*

Left-Hand Man Direct *7c+*
Climb direct from a sit start, with no
arête holds. Eliminate. *(Rupert Davies)*

15. Middle Man *7c*
A diagonal line starting at Dick Williams
and crossing the face leftwards to join
Left-Hand Man at the top pocket.
(Ian Fitzpatrick)

16. Dick Williams *7b+*
One of the best problems of its grade
on grit. From a sit start on the shelf
ascend the rounded bulging arête to a
scary sloping exit. *(Zaff Ali)*

17. *4+*
The left-hand pocket line.

18. *4+*
The right-hand pocket line.

Patch Hammond on Dick Williams: *Adam Long* ▲

Walnut Whip

20m up and right of the main area is another block containing some good sit start problems.

19. *7b+*
Just left of the gap in the boulder is a short wall with some tiny pockets. Climb the wall from a sit start. The grade depends on where you allow yourself to put your feet. Obviously bridging behind yourself will make the problem about 3+, but cunningly letting your feet drift around to the right will also reduce the grade. Being *very* strict may make it harder. *(Tim Hulley)*

20. Fireball *7b+*
The slanting, rounded arête from a sit start. *(Mick Adams)*

21. Walnut Whip *6c*
The right undercut, rounded arête from a sit start on ripples. Nice moves, but not many of 'em. Top-out over the funny egg thing.

Stepped Roof

Up and left of the main area is a great stepped roof with body-tension dependant problems on good and interesting holds. To some extent the problems described are a little arbitrary as the roof is covered in close-together holds, so all the problems mix and match a little. The following seem as good a selection as any.

22. *6c*
The left-hand line. From jams move out to match the great sloping edge of the block, pop to a good hold in the break and top-out. *(Richie Patterson)*

23. *6b+*
The middle line. From a sidepull (right hand) and undercut or jam (left hand) move out to good slots in the break using a big span or other holds in the roof – top-out. *(Richie Patterson)*

24. *7a+*
The right-hand line. Start as problem 23, out to a slopey rib in roof (right hand), small holds in the roof (left hand) then again (left hand) to holds in the break right of the good slot. Control the swing and top-out.

7b+
Traverse below the lip on edges, pocket and slopers to top-out around the right-hand arête. *(Zaff Ali)*

rivelin

The bouldering at Rivelin is a combination of the old and the new. Several problems are really routes, while others (the hard ones) are the work of a few dedicated modern explorers.

Generally shady and clean, the crag is often in good condition. South-facing and sheltered it can be a good alternative on cold windy days.

Please note Rivelin is situated in an environmentally sensitive area, no tree cutting and no climbing right of Altar Crack.

Ryan Pasquill on Master Kush (1st ascent): *Chris Doyle* ▲

Access and Approach

Rivelin is located just off the A57 about 2.5 miles outside of Sheffield. Park on the south side of the dam in the Water Authority car park, walk back across the dam and up the footpath, over the stream and head up to the crag, bearing left at the fork. Follow the vague path up and then down beneath the crag. Master Kush is the obvious undercut block 50m right of Cool Running Buttress.

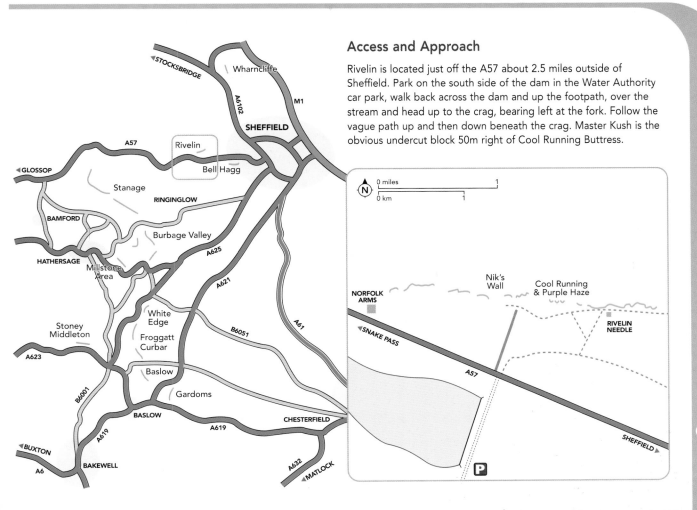

STOCKSBRIDGE

Wharncliffe

A6102

M1

SHEFFIELD

A57

Rivelin

Bell Hagg

GLOSSOP

Stanage

RINGINGLOW

BAMFORD

Burbage Valley

A625

HATHERSAGE

Millstone Area

A621

White Edge

Froggatt Curbar

B6051

A61

Stoney Middleton

A623

Baslow

Gardoms

B6001

BASLOW

A619

A619

CHESTERFIELD

BUXTON

BAKEWELL

A6

A632

MATLOCK

0 miles 1
0 km 1

N

NORFOLK ARMS

Nik's Wall

Cool Running & Purple Haze

SNAKE PASS

RIVELIN NEEDLE

A57

SHEFFIELD

P

eastern crags

125

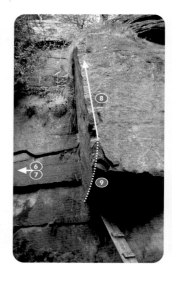

1. **Purple Haze** *7a+*
Traverse the lip from left to right.

2. **Master Kush** *7c+*
The undercut right arête from the low jug.
(Ryan Pasquill)

50m to the left is the neat little buttress of Cool Running.

3. **Cool Running** *6b+*
Really E1, but a good highball. Start in the centre of the wall and head left to finish. Traverse off left at the break. *(John Allen)*

4. **Faze Action** *7b*
The direct finish to Cool Running. *(Andy Crome)*

5. **Cool Running Left-Hand** *6b*
Climb the left arête.

From Cool Running follow a vegetated path left below the crag, heading up almost to the top of the crag. Cross a stream, then head back down again to meet a quarried yellow wall. This is Nik's Wall.

6. *7a+*
Dyno arête left of Nik's Wall. *(Iain Farrar)*

7. **Nik's Wall** *8a*
A thin crimp-fest up the centre of the yellow wall.
(Nik Jennings)

8. **Happy Campus** *7b*
The arête right of Nik's Wall. *(Paul Houghoughi)*

9. **No Class** *7b+*
Motör up Happy Campus from a sit-down start.
(John Welford)

Further along to the right, Rivelin offers up a few other gems that blur the distinction between bouldering and soloing – consult your definitive BMC guidebook and then try to decide if the following qualify as boulder problems: Face Climb 1 and 1.5 and Fumf (all in the easy-4 category), Wobbly Wall 5+, Europe After Rain 7a+, the start of Sparks 7b, Acid Reign 6c – the short squared quarried arête behind the needle. Also try Trivial Pursuits 2, 6b+ and Boulder Club, 7a.

John Welford on No Class: *Mark Hundleby* ▲

stanage

Nearly 3 miles of fun-packed gritstone blocks,
neatly arranged into a handy line.

Not To Be Taken Away: *Adam Long* ▲

Access and Approach

From Sheffield, head along Ringinglow Road past Burbage bridge and fork right down to Hooks Car. From Hathersage, take a left just outside the village, uphill past The Scotsman's Pack. Turn left past parking at Hooks Car and take next right fork in the dip to reach the Plantation pay & display parking. Continue below the edge to park for The Buckstone & Far Left. Far Left can also be accessed directly from the A57 - park in a lay-by near the county/city boundary sign and take the footpath opposite Moscar Lodge.

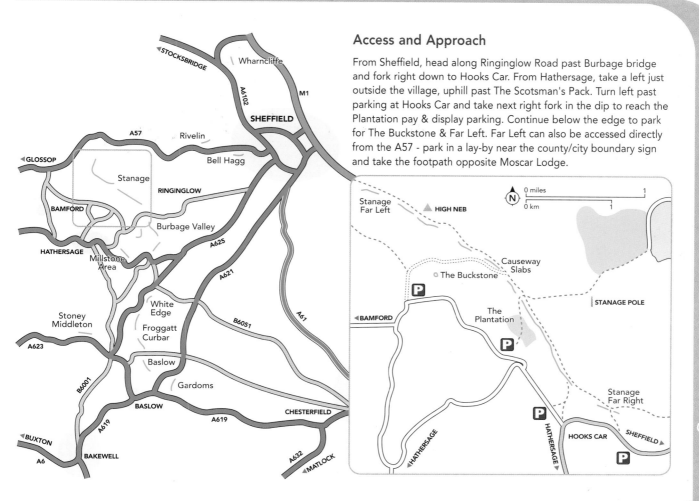

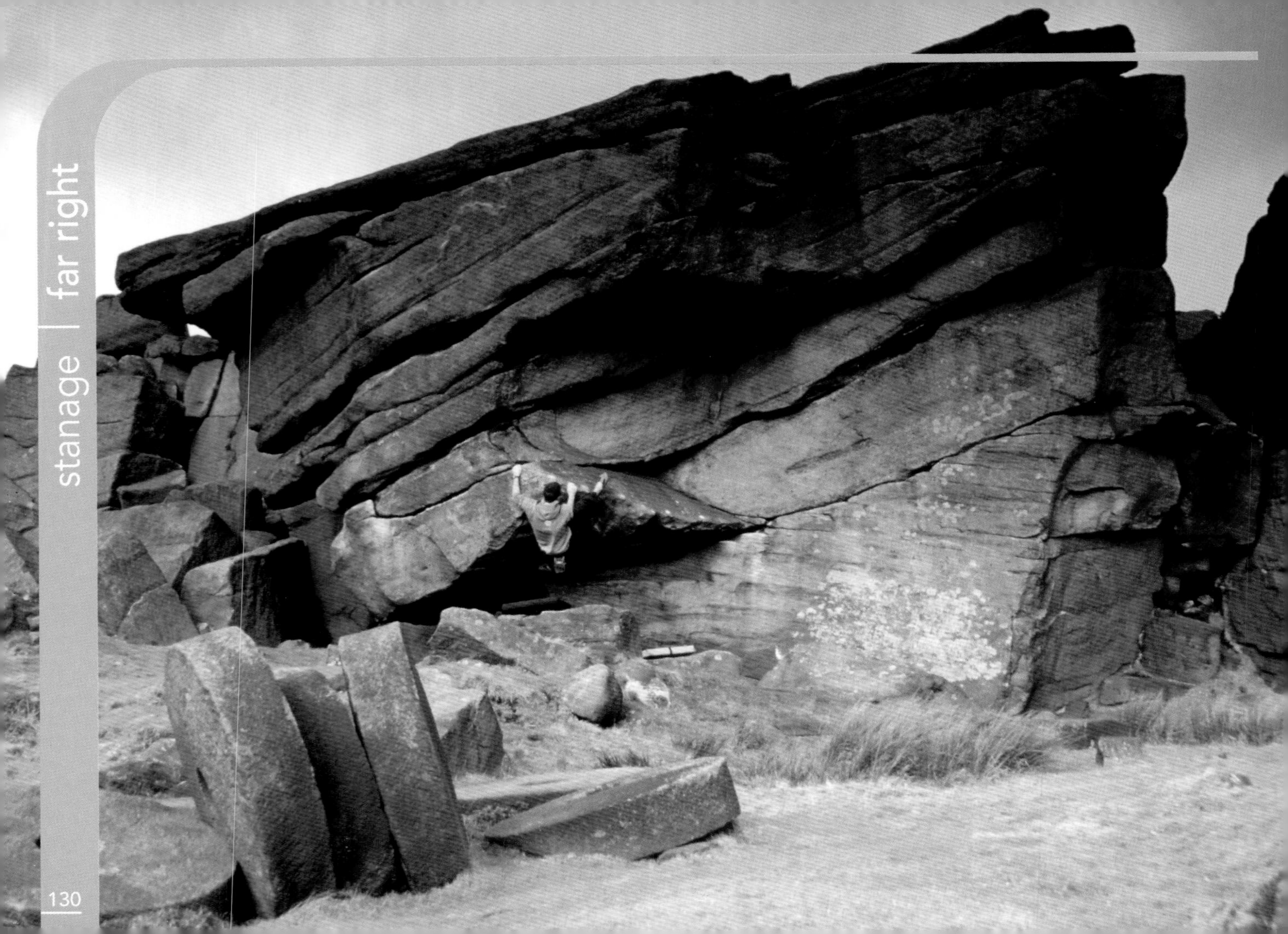

Stanage Far Right

Stanage kicks off at its eastern extremity in great style with a wonderful globule of grit called the Cowperstone. It then continues with a number of small, spaced-out blocks and buttresses for some distance before it really gets going. There are some interesting up type problems and a number of good traverses in this area.

Conditions

This end is slightly more sheltered than the rest of Stanage, but it still catches the breeze. With the exception of the Cowperstone, the area is very quick-drying after rain.

Approach

Park on the road in the large purpose-made lay-by and follow the path up to the rocks. The Cowperstone can also be approached by parking at the Burbage North car park and then walking directly over to it.

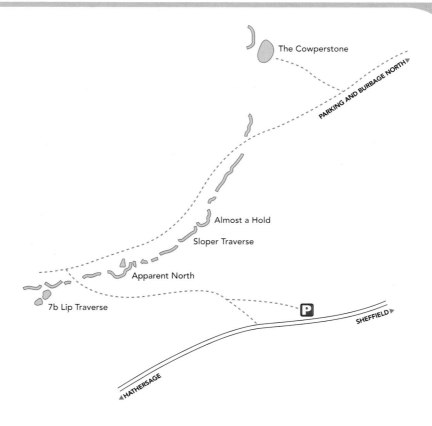

The Cowperstone

PARKING AND BURBAGE NORTH ▶

Almost a Hold

Sloper Traverse

Apparent North

7b Lip Traverse

SHEFFIELD ▶

◀ HATHERSAGE

◀ Hamper's Hang: *Simon Richardson*

Chippy Buttress

It would be nice if this was a fish and chip shop, alas, it just looks like one. Apparently.

1. **Pudding** *5*
The wall left of the arête, heading towards a crack.

2. **Chips** *5+*
The arête taken on the left.

3. **Peas** *6c*
Another problem that's really a route. The problem is the mantel, but if you top-out then you will think otherwise – E4 5c.

The Cowperstone

4. **Zippatrocity** *7b+*
Fist jamming masochism in the form of a traverse from extreme left, round the arête and finishing at the extreme right. Actually illegal in some states in America. Can seep (blood) in winter.
(Mark Pretty)

5. **Leroy Slips a Disc** *7b*
A hard wall via an undercut to a high, rounded top-out. Hard for the short. *(John Allen)*

6. **Headspin** *6b*
The wall right of Leroy, with a hard, scary, rounded top-out.

The Cowperstone: *Simon Richardson* ▶

Grand Theft Area

6c

The cave a hundred or so metres right of Almost a Hold,
climbed from the back using a painful lip hold.

1. **Almost a Hold**   *6c+*
   Whilst you can shuffle along all of the breaks on this wall,
   the best problem traverses the low break rightwards from the
   arête with a morpho crux reach. No Cigar adds a move by doing
   a sit start from the ledge at the bottom of the arête.

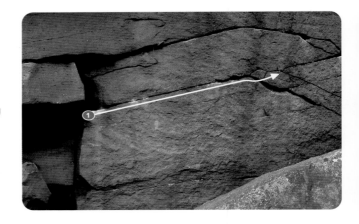

2. **Sloper Traverse**   *7a*
   The appealing line of slopers from left to right finishing up
   crimps. Climbing direct through the traverse line is a very slopey
   and condition-dependant 6c, while the sit start line of edges
   leading into the end of the traverse just right is 6b.

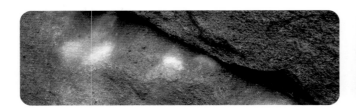

Apparent North Block

1. Hamper's Hang *7a*
The traverse. From the back of the niche on the left, traverse right, down the sloping undercut shelf – crux – and along the break in the right-hand wall.

2. *7a*
Direct through the overhang from a ledge at the back to an awkward mantel.

3. Skinless Wonder *7a+*
A hard start to a route, up the wall on pebbles to the break. Reverse, jump or traverse off. Topping out via a horrendous skin-grinding mantel is very hard and E6, even with gear.

4.
Immediately to the left of the buttress is a short wall, with a couple more good problems. The right arête just left of the gully, tackled on its left, is 6b. The wall left again on pebbles is 7a.

Left again and the approach path is reached. Just before this is an undercut arête on an isolated block – climb the arête from a low, hanging start – 6b.

On the slope below this is a large boulder consisting mainly of a large, easy-angled slab.

5. *7b*
A classic slopey traverse along the bottom of the huge slab - clearly visible from the road. *(Rich Heap/Andy Harris)*

The buttress just behind this has a couple of problems

6. *6c*
The undercut arête from an extremely low start is harder for people with legs.

7. *5*
The lovely wall to the right, which can be done from a sitter. It's got a great hold on it formed by a seam and a perfectly placed pebble.

The Plantation

A world-class bouldering venue, the Stanage Plantation is home to a concentration of historic and unique problems of all grades. The only downside is the 5-minute slog up the hill to get there. Unfortunately, the inevitable popularity is having its effect. The grass is gone from below the Face of Business, the landing below Deliverance is wearing lower and lower and the paths are getting wider each season. The boulders themselves are suffering too. Please read our environment notes and help to preserve this superb but increasingly fragile crag.

Jon Barton on The Green Traverse: *Chris Plant* ▲

Conditions

South-facing, the Plantation catches the sun throughout the day, and dries relatively fast after rain. When it's really cold the Plantation can catch too much wind to be bearable – if this is the case you could try Burbage West which is sheltered from the predominant Westerlies.

Access

Park in the large pay and display car park and follow the path up to the edge. For the Plantation bear right after the second gate up to the boulders or carry on up the path for the Grand Hotel area.

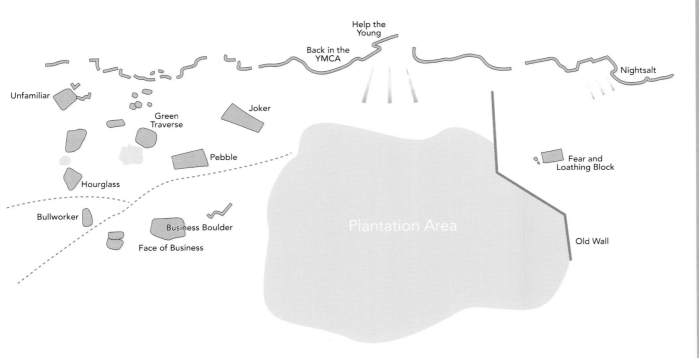

Unfamiliar

Help the Young

Back in the YMCA

Nightsalt

Joker

Green Traverse

Pebble

Hourglass

Fear and Loathing Block

Bullworker

Business Boulder

Face of Business

Plantation Area

Old Wall

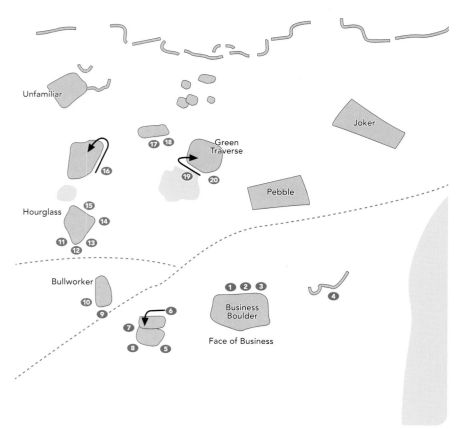

1. *4+*
   A vague arête.

2. *4*
   Climb the middle of the overlapped wall.

3. *4+*
   The left arête.

4. **Victorian Overmantel** *(>7c)*
   A very powerful, footless mantel that has got much harder since a pebble broke. Hang the lip and start manteling. Keep manteling. Now hernia. Those with long arms may be able to rock to a crimp first – obviously much easier than the pure mantel. *(Johnny Dawes)*

   Left of the Face of Business are two boulders leaning against each other.

5. *5*
   The crozzly slab on rough holds.

6. *5+*
   Traverse the low lip from left to right to a mantel out. Thuggy.

7. *6a+*
   The awkward wall just right of the groove.

8. *6a*
   Climb the arête on the left, with a pop for the good sloper. Easier but not as good on the right-hand side reaching in from the block.

9. **Bullworker** *6b*
   Bullwork up the arête.

10. *6b+*
   Just left of the Bullworker arêtes, the short flakey wall from a sit start.

11. *6c+*
   The left side of the arête, but it doesn't climb like an arête.

   Born Slappy *7a*
   Crouching start on slopers just left of 11, with a really tricky slopey slap. A good one-move wonder.

12. *7a*
   The same arête, climbed on its right-hand side. Cunning and satisfying.

13. **Born Snappy** *7b+*
   The thin, snappy wall between the hourglass arêtes has gotten harder since holds eroded. Extremely hard for those under 6' ish. *(Richie Patterson)*

14. **Hourglass** *5+*
   The arête on the right starting on the right-hand side. Harder on the left-hand side all the way.

15. *5+*
   The lovely little wall on the right, climbed on pockets

16. *6c*
   The steep traverse from the shelf; a Plantation classic. Finish around the arête. Climbing direct through the middle of the traverse is a tricky 6b.

17. **Bentley's Gonna Sort You Out** *7b+*
   Of all people. Start low, hanging the biggish hold, then finish by rocking back left using the pebble scar (left hand) and dish (right hand). Awkward. *(Neil Bentley)*

18. **Captain Hook** *7b*
   From the start of Bentley's stay under the roof. Get an undercut under the roof then slap to the nose and exit. *(Mike Lea)*

19. **The Green Traverse** *7a*
   From the rounded blob on the arête traverse leftwards displaying as little technique as possible. Once you've done this, do it again missing out the holds of your choice. Endless fun. Reversing it is slightly harder.
   (Martin Veale/Mark Stokes)

20. **Full Green Traverse\
    Dope on a Slope** *7a+*
   Extend The Green Traverse by doing a sit start in the middle of the sloping shelf to the right. For yet more fun, mantel out the start. 6b+. *(Martin Veale)*

   7a
   The fun just doesn't stop. Dyno from the crimps on The Green Traverse to the sloping top and mantel it out. Eliminate, but too good to miss. Locking the dyno statically (feet on smears) will earn you the respect of your peers.

The Pebble

This is the house-sized block that dominates the Plantation.

1. **Twister** *7b*
   Sit start in V-slot, move up to undercuts, then left to more
   undercuts to reach the high ledge. The low ledge on the right is
   out. A bit of an odd eliminate but good moves.

2. **Original Sloper Traverse** *6b+*
   From ledge on Twister, traverse left on massive slopers
   with big slaps.

3. **Boston Mess** *6c-7c+*
   Tiny undercuts and smears for feet, but the hard problem is an
   eliminate. The original method started from a very low undercut
   (not quite sitting), pulled on, moved left hand to the left-most
   undercut, moved right hand to catch the middle undercut – the
   crux – and then up to the ledge via a couple of other holds.
   Since then it has been done by pulling on and jumping straight
   for the ledge (7b), by pulling onto the left-hand undercuts and
   then up (7a+) and from a standing start (6c).

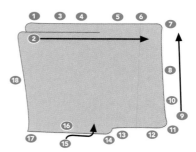

4. *5*
The flakes in the centre of the wall.

5. *4*
The big holds just left, often used as the way down.

6. *4+*
Climb just right of the arête.

7. *6a+*
The right arête of the Deliverance face, climbed on its left from a sit start on undercuts, is very pleasant but still not totally straightforward. 5+ from a stand-up.

8. Deliverance *7b+*
The superstar dyno, named due to the imminent arrival of Dr Fisher's child. Morpho and almost ungradeable. The direct start is harder. *(Quentin Fisher)*

9. Deliverance Traverse *7a+*
A very thin exercise in smearing from the start of Deliverance to the right arête.

10. Andy Brown's Wall *7c+*
The direct up the wall above the crack from the start of Deliverance is even more morpho and even more ungradeable. *(Andy Brown)*

11. Pebble Arête *5+*
Classic easy arête. It has been done from a sitter, but really, have you nothing better to do? Direct on the left-hand side it's harder, 6a+.

12. Ron's Slab I *7b*
The thin slab immediately left of the arête. If it feels anything but very thin you're on the wrong holds. *(Ron Fawcett)*

13. *6b*
A squeezed-in problem up the slab.

14. *4+*
The beckoning rampline approached from flakes on the right.

15. Pebble Face *3+*
Approached from the left the ramp is much easier. You can even do it without using your hands, the crux is retaining your dignity and ribs as you jump into the belly flop top-out. Gratifyingly however, you get a new name (The Design Award) and therefore a new tick.

16. *6b*
Direct up the thin face above the start of Pebble Face.

17. *6b+*
The left arête is a touch intimidating.

18. *6b*
The excellent thin end wall starting up the groove, and of course a complete girdle traverse is worthwhile. Hard 7b.

In the jumble of boulders behind the green traverse is...

19. The Deep End *6c+*
Hop on the block at the right-hand side, shuffle left for about three moves, or until you run out of rock, then mantel out the slab and arête above. *(Allen Williams)*

20. Badger *6c*
The overhanging arête from a sit start.
(Richie Patterson)

21. Sit Start to Unfamiliar *7a+*
More a rumour than a problem.

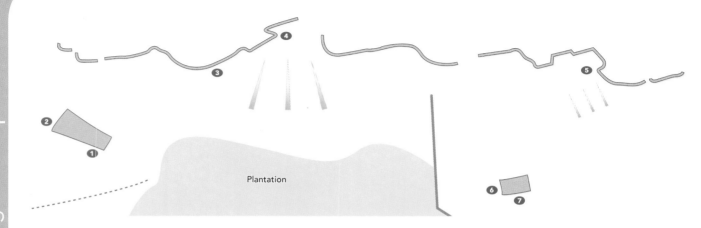

Plantation

1. **The Ace** *8b*
   One of the hardest problems in the Peak looks really hard, but is actually harder than that. Start on a jug on the left side of the cave and then levitate past the two pathetic holds to the top. *(Jerry Moffatt)*

   The Joker *8a*
   The original problem reached into the 'crimps' on the Ace from the adjacent block. *(Jerry Moffatt)*

2. **Honorary Caley** *7a*
   So named because it's pebbly and it's often green. *(Richie Patterson)*

3. **Back in the YMCA** *7b*
   The steep pocketed wall to the break. *(Neil Travers)*

4. **Help the Young** *7a+*
   This modern classic arête is climbed initially on the gully side with a French start, before rocking back left to the shelf at the top. The difficulties are all within jumping height. *(Paul Mitchell)*

   Help the Young Sit Start *7c+*
   Powerful leg hugs lead into the standing start. The foot block at the back is IN at this grade. *(Adam Long)*

5. **Nightsalt** *7a+*
   The tricky, reachy and slightly worrying arête above the drop opposite Telli. Finish at the break (to go to the top is E4 but you have done the hard bit) and reverse the chimney to get down.

Simon Richardson on The Rose and the Self-employed Business Man: *Stu Littlefair* ▲

The Joker: *John Coefield* ▲

6. Brass Monkeys *7c*
The powerful roof starting from the detached block at the back. Morpho - the initial reach is practically impossible for the short, but it may be possible to contrive something using the various slopey pods in the roof instead.
(Iain Farrar)

7. Fear and Loathing *6b+*
More high than hard. The centre of the highball slab feels a little gritty, and has a nasty landing. The climbing eases with height. A pad is probably not really going to help much. *(Mark Stokes)*

Blair Witch Project *6c*
The Blair Witch Project hides in the spooky woods below the approach path. It's a low blunt arête climbed on its left. Half the fun is finding it.

Face of Business

Slightly eliminate some of the problems may be, but if you like going sideways there's over a hundred feet of superlative, super-hard, lateral pedantry squashed onto this boulder.

1. **Jerry's Traverse** *7c*
    Traverse left from the centre of the shelf, keeping low around the vague arête, and do a big finishing rock-over (without the large jugs). A Peak rite of passage, slightly spoiled by an eliminate last move. *(Jerry Moffatt)*

2. **Ben's Extension** *8a*
    A hard extension to Jerry's featuring the infamous drop-down move. Every young lad's and lass's ambition, or it should be anyway. *(Ben Moon)*

3. **Danny's Problem** *7c*
Brutal crimping from a sit start. Easier if you get the lower edge with your left and rock for the top hold using the higher crimp as an intermediate, although the 'proper' way uses the holds in the obvious order and is more powerful. **H Top is the superb stand-up version at 7a. *(Danny Brooks)*

**Ben's Extension
into Danny's Problem** *8a+*
A ridiculously hard connection. The grade is guessed and unconfirmed.
(Steve McClure)

4. **Ben's Reverse** *7b*
From the centre of the shelf, traverse right to the arête and then the top. Essentially a reverse of the drop-down section on Ben's Extension, but using a different sequence.

5. **Rose and the Self-employed
Business Man** *7a+*
An easier alternative to Jerry's Traverse. From the end of the shelf, move up to holds beneath the top and finish using a totally unnecessary rose move to reach the jugs.

6. **Zippy's Traverse** *7b*
Traverse from the good slot to flakes around the arête – tricky. *(Mark Pretty)*

7. **Jason's Traverse** *8a*
Do Zippy's Traverse, but keep low at the end. Now reverse Jerry's Traverse and then dyno to the top from the middle of the shelf at the end. Not quite as hard as Ben's Extension. *(Jason Myers)*

8. **Close of Business** *8b?*
The final test of endurance. Link Jason's Traverse into Ben's Reverse.
(Steve McClure)

9. *6a+*
A nice, easy problem from a sit start on the low slot via the flake. Also, why not try and go from the same start to the top of the slab using only the slot for your hands - stupid, but fun.

10. *4*
The groove line.

The Lone Boulder

On its own, stuck between the Plantation and The Grand Hotel areas. Problems are described anti-clockwise

1. **The Lone Slab** *5+*
A hard step-up onto the slab just right of the arête.

2. *5+*
The vague grooveline just right.

4+
Reach from the ledge to the top, hard for those with short arms.

6a
Odd little groove in the next arête right.

4+
Arête. A fun sit start is 6b.

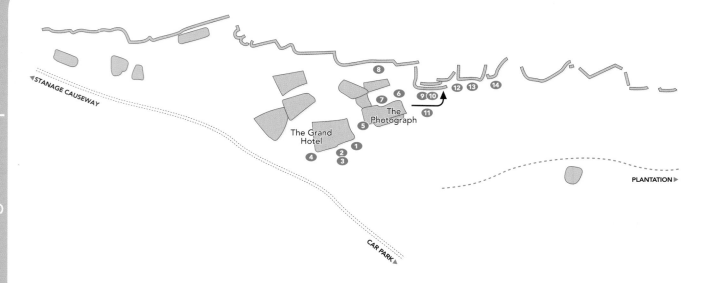

STANAGE CAUSEWAY

8

7 6
5 9 10
The Photograph 11 12 13 14

The Grand Hotel

1
2
4 3

CAR PARK

PLANTATION

The Grand Hotel Area

The cluster of boulders 100m or so left of the first Plantation boulders are also often called The Grand Hotel area. The Grand Hotel is the huge block taken by Not To Be Taken Away, and refers to the once popular bivi that can be found if you scurry into the slot (with all the sheep poo) that is underneath the boulder.

Brad Pit: *Davies Coll.* ▲

1. *6c*
   The flakes on the right-hand side of the face.

2. **Not To Be Taken Away** *6c*
   The ramp line is perhaps the best problem on grit at its grade. *(John Allen)*

3. **To Be or Not To Be** *7a+*
   The direct dyno finish to NTBTA from crimps in the middle of the wall. Quite committing. *(Mark Leach)*

4. **Careless Torque** *8a*
   The stunning left arête is guarded by a blank undercut start. To date (autumn 2004) it has not been climbed without top-roping first. When this is done it will be a major achievement. *(Ron Fawcett)*

5. **Adults Only** *6c*
   Climb out to the arête from slots and move up to a high finish.

   The Hit Man *7b+*
   Extend problem 5 around the arête, traversing the thin crease rightwards to finish up a short groove. *(Simon Wheil)*

6. *6c*
   Dyno from the sloping shelf to the top.

7. **Brad Pit** *7c+*
   Down in the pit is this famous and unique groove. *(Jason Myers)*

Brad Pit Sit Start *8?*
A massive span into the start of Brad Pit is steady if you can reach, but otherwise impossible. *(Thomas Willenberg)*

8. **Gnome Man's Land Direct Start** *6c*
   The groove in the wall below Fairy Steps (VS) is an ignored classic with a bad landing.

9. **Left Spur** *7a*
   Start at the low jugs. If you're wondering how to do this, you use the pebble that's now snapped off. *(John Allen)*

10. **Right Spur** *6c*
    Starting again from the low jugs, move up and right using the square-cut rib.

11. **Spur Traverse** *6c+*
    Traverse the low flakes from left to right to a crux exit left of the arête.

12. **Pressure Drop** *7c*
    The very hard slab left of Satin.
    (Adam Long)

13. **Satin** *7a*
    The overlap and thin slab up the centre. Traverse off at the first break.
    (Johnny Dawes)

14. **Pullover** *4+*
    Climb the overlap via the flake.

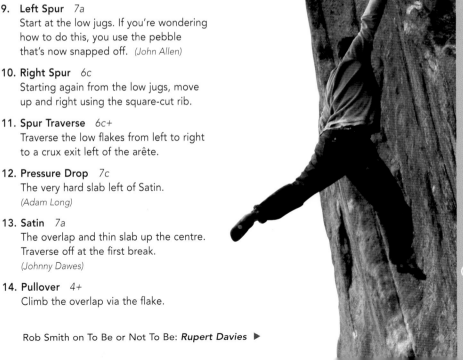

Rob Smith on To Be or Not To Be: *Rupert Davies* ▶

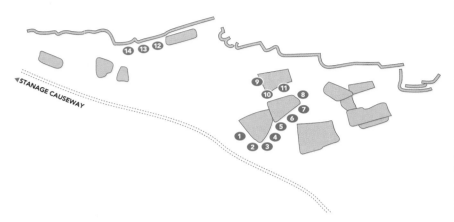

Jvan Tresch on Careless Torque: *Adam Long* ▲

1. **Ron's Slab II** *7b+*
   A hard highball slab, trending up and left from the start of Crescent Arête. Not to be confused with all of the other Ron's Slabs. The direct start just left is a very do-able project. *(Ron Fawcett)*

2. **Crescent Arête** *5+*
   The classic, curving, highball arête on the left-hand side. On its right it's a tenuous highball 6b+. *(Gabe Regan)*

3. *7a*
   The thin slab just right of the arête.

4. *7a*
   Superb slab just right again using a small pocket.

   5+
   Right again is a nice short problem using the sloping ledge.

   Just behind Crescent Arête is another large boulder in a cluttered gully.

5. *6c+*
   Sit start the arête. Just left is a crimpy 6c+ up the brittle wall

6. *6b+*
   Up the wall on pockets

7. *5+*
   The steep side of the photogenic arête.

8. *4+*
   Wall right of arête stepping in off a block

9. **The Storm** *7b+*
   The modern, classic, massive rock-over. Possible even for the short – just rock further. It feels very hard until you get it right. *(Jerry Moffatt)*

Deadline *7b+*

From the start of The Storm continue traversing right to the arête via a large pocket and slap up. *(Richie Patterson)*

10. Beneath the Breadline *7b*

The highball right arête and slabby top. *(Pat King)*

Breadline *6c*

Gains the upper arête from the block on the right. Classic highball smearing.

Baseline *7c*

Start up Beneath the Breadline, span left into the pocket, finish up The Storm. *(Pat King)*

11. *6a*

Groove with a reach to a pocket

4+

Scooped wall, just right.

4

Right again the arête on left-hand side.

12. Help the Aged *7a*

From poor slopers to jug; Cortomaltese comes to Stanage. Much easier in good conditions. There are some even poorer slopers just right which yield an identical, but harder, problem. 7b. *(Johnny Dawes)*

13. *7a+*

The bulge just right of the crack.

14. Silk Start *7a+*

Awkward mantel onto the bulge – jump off. *(Johnny Dawes)*

Sit Start to Silk *7c*

A smattering of crimps, smears, heel hooks and the arête lead into the mantel of the stand-up problem. *(John Welford)*

Just right is Wall End Slab with a range of easy, polished problems with grades from 4 – 5 at its base. Up and right again is a nice little wall with rounded slopey holds – the most obvious line is 6a, with possible eliminates. Behind this, further right still, and part of the edge itself is a great little groove, 6b.

The Hippo *7a+*

Directly below the DIY Buttress (see BMC guide) is an overhung prow. Climb out to its right edge and top-out on the apex. Not really worth the walk over. *(Iain Farrar)*

Stanage Causeway

The path leading to The Grand Hotel area rises up to meet the Roman Road that crosses the edge and continues over the moor. On the edge itself, just above the Roman Road is a low, quarried area that yields some good esoteric sport. Central Buttress Direct (see BMC guide) is 6c and Iain's Prow 6c+.

About 200m left, past Count's Buttress, is a dry-stone wall that rises up to meet the edge. At the top of this is a small arête – Cock 'o' the Rock.

Cock 'o' the Rock *7a*

A strange little arête whose grade is anywhere from 6a-7b, depending on exactly where you pull on. As such it's a bit annoying.

Rupert Davies on The Storm: *Stu Littlefair* ▲

The Buckstone

The Buckstone used to form part of the wall of an inn of the same name and there are still stones and bits of wall remaining in evidence. These days, however, there's less drinking but a whole lot more dyno action going on.

Conditions

The block is in an exposed position on the moor below the edge. It catches the breeze and sun, and as such it dries quickly. The huge holds of the Buckstone Dyno mean that it is possible when warm, or even when a little damp, but you will need better conditions for the problem to the right and for Spring Voyage.

Access

Continue along the road from the Plantation car park and park in a lay-by on the left. Cross the wall via the gate and follow the vague path to the block. It's the big, obvious one in the middle of the field.

◀ Ben Moon on the dyno: *Jerry Moffatt*

1. **Spring Voyage** 7c
Undercuts to slopes to sloping top.
Morpho. *(Ben Moon)*

2. **The Buckstone Dyno** 7b
A big dyno using holds that were
originally a structural part of the boozer.
Obviously morpho, the real grade is
between 7a and 7c depending on
your size. *(Jason Myers)*

3. **7c**
Sit start on obvious jugs and then
contrive a sequence up the rubbish
slopers. Hard and reachy. *(Ron Fawcett)*

4. **6b**
The bulge just right. Right again,
the bulge can be manteled at 6c.

*The opposite side of the block has
some lovely easier problems:*

5
The attractive groove.

5+
The blunt nose/rib just left.

6a
The hard, sloping shelf left again.

*The block 50m nearer the edge
contains a few more easy problems.*

Solomon's Seal

Back on the edge, a small east-facing
wall contains two hard problems.
Directly above the Buckstone are a
series of large buttresses and the
Solomon's Seal wall is on the right-hand
side of these buttresses, facing right,
starting from a grassy terrace.

5. **Solomon's Seal** 8a
A very hard, crimpy wall – potentially
impossible to start for the short.
The arête is not used. *(Kim Thompson)*

6. **The Jester** 7b
A little one-mover, from two poor,
slopey edges. *(Iain Farrar)*

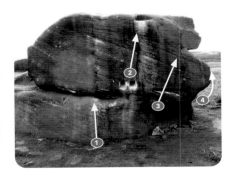

The Buckstone groove: **Simon Richardson** ▲

Stanage Far Left

Some superb problems are spread out along the edge to the north-west, some of them very hard and most very good. There's a bit of walking involved, but it's considerably quieter than the rest of Stanage and you get to enjoy the views over the fabulous, desolate moorlands below.

Conditions

Exposed to most of the wind that's going, it can be cold here in winter. The advantage to this is that in summer it is cooler and less midgy (important) than the Plantation, and because the edge curves round to face west, it is shady in the mornings.

Access

Continue along the road past the Plantation car park. After about 3/4 mile there is another car park on the right – Denis Knoll. Park here, follow the Roman road (the track), then take the first stile on the left and follow paths up and leftwards below the crag.

◀ Jon Barton on Green Room Slap: *Rupert Davies*

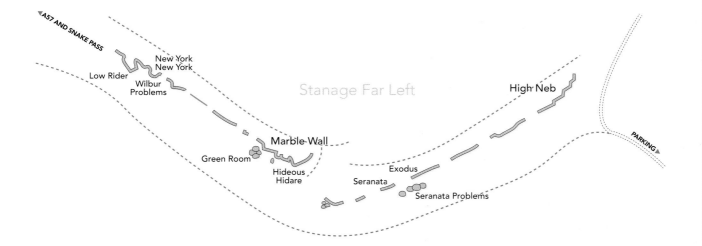

A57 AND SNAKE PASS

New York
New York

Low Rider

Wilbur
Problems

Stanage Far Left

High Neb

Marble Wall

Green Room

Hideous
Hidare

Exodus

Seranata

Seranata Problems

PARKING

Seranata Problems

There are three isolated problems in the cluster of boulders down and right of the route Seranata, which is on the last buttress before the edge curves out of sight to the west.

1. **Beauty** *6c*
   The blank slab with two pebbles just left of the arête. Nice smearing.
   (Kim Thompson)

2. **The Beast** *7b*
   The grim mantel just right (no arêtes), starting from the break under the roof. Oof. Hard, isn't it? There's a small scallop in the slab that you may not have noticed – doesn't help much, does it? *(Jon Fullwood)*

Dowager's Hump *6c*
A similar mantel on the next block right, but much easier as it's not undercut.
(Jon Fullwood)

The next problems are situated around Marble Wall, which is the obvious second set of buttresses reached once the edge re-starts after it has curved out of sight. Keep following the path round from the Seranata problems. Hideous Hidare is on a short buttress 10m right of Marble Wall itself, just over some boulders and sandwiched to the left of the buttress containing the route Slap 'n' Spittle, left of the gully.

Hideous Hidare *6c*
Smart moves off the sloping ledge to the break are followed by a shuffle right and a troubling exit onto the sloping top. Highball. *(Paul Mitchell)*

Green Room Problems

The Green Room is an almost subterranean chamber formed by the large pile of stacked boulders at the left-hand side of Marble Wall. It's dry in the rain and can be cool and shady in hot weather.

Green Room Slap *7a+*
At the back of the Green Room is this fantastic problem. Hang the sloping rail and power up to the holds above. It's about 1-5, but with your feet on, if you catch the drift. Escape left.
(Kim Thompson)

Green Room Slap Sit Start *7b+*
The sit start is even better. The last move is still the crux, but you're going to be lacking a bit of oomph by the time you get there. A well-hidden classic.
(Kim Thompson)

Soft Top Beetle *6c*
The rib in the sidewall of the entrance tunnel from a sit start. Try not to get irretrievably wedged as you top-out, as you'll spoil the problem for others.
(Ian Barnes)

Stanage End

Further still. You have informed someone at home where you're going and what time to expect you back, I hope. The very last block with the flying right arête contains Chip Shop Brawl and Low Rider, whereas the Wilbur problems are on the edge before this.

1. **New York New York** *6b*
   Classic highball arête. Bail out at the break or put your soloing goggles on.

2. **Wilbur's Wall** *6a*
   The wall left of New York New York from the low break, slapping to the top.
   (John Welford)

3. **Wilbur's Rib** *6a*
   The rib just left again, from the low break, again slapping to the top.
   (John Welford)

4. **Low Rider** *7c+*
   This wicked traverse along the lip, then up slopers to the break, is well worth the (repeated) walk. *(Jon Fullwood)*

5. **Chip Shop Brawl** *7b*
   Another route that has been promoted to a highball with pads, although it's worth noting that once you're past the crux it's still about 6a and you're too high to safely fall off. *(John Allen)*

   Opposition *7a+*
   Bridge and undercut up the centre of the scooped wall right of the Chip Shop Brawl arête, in the crevasse, behind Low Rider. Traverse the break left to finish below the hanging arête. The grade according to the first ascentionist is 7a+ or there about, but it's massively morpho and unrepeated at time of press. *(Kim Thompson)*

wharncliffe

The year that Foot and Mouth disease closed many crags had an unexpected benefit - many neglected crags were developed as they were the only ones left open. It was in Foot and Mouth year that Wharncliffe was converted from a routes-only venue that nobody goes to, to an extensive bouldering crag with many quality problems…

…that nobody goes to.

The bouldering is spread out along almost a mile of edge on small blocks and buttresses, there's a fairly high legwork to problem ratio, but on the positive side there are still first ascents to be bagged.

The bouldering here was mostly developed by Jon Fullwood, Kim and Yan Thompson and Iain Farrar, and much of the original information comes from the subsequent documentation by Jon Fullwood. The credit should go to him if you find yourself here and have fun. Of course, if you hate it and waste a day's climbing, that'll be his fault.

Wharncliffe can be divided into five main areas: The Belle Vue Boulders, Long John's Stride, The Upper Tier, The Outlook and The Lodge/Dragon's Den areas: the best climbing is at the Dragon's Den and Outlook areas.

Jon Barton on Problem 4a, Dragon's Den: *Matthew Coutts* ▲

Access and Approach

Leave Grenoside along Woodhead Road, past the public parking for Wharncliffe Woods on the left. Continue, passing a large farm on the left after emerging from the trees. A small, unsurfaced lane heads left, after a small quarry. Limited parking on this lane before Chase Lodge. Follow the track, through a gate, on foot, to Wharncliffe Lodge. A vague path leads off under the edge to Lodge Buttress and the Dragon's Den. Follow the overview map to reach the other areas.

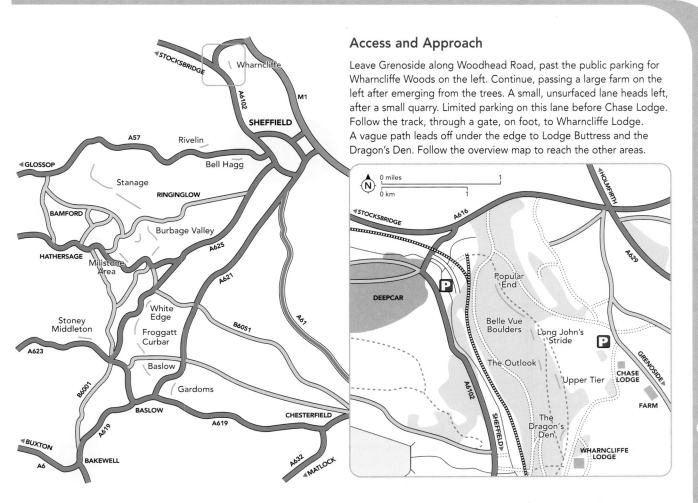

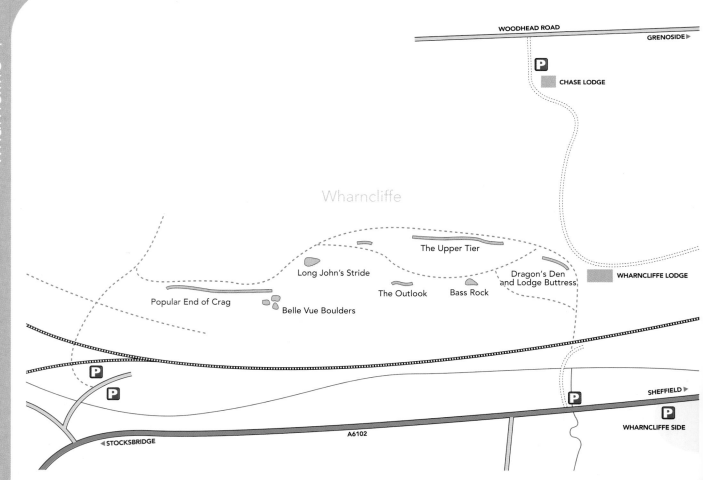

WOODHEAD ROAD

GRENOSIDE ▶

CHASE LODGE

Wharncliffe

The Upper Tier

Long John's Stride

Dragon's Den
and Lodge Buttress

WHARNCLIFFE LODGE

The Outlook

Bass Rock

Popular End of Crag

Belle Vue Boulders

SHEFFIELD ▶

◀ STOCKSBRIDGE

A6102

WHARNCLIFFE SIDE

Jon Barton on Blunted: *Matthew Coutts* ▲

Lodge Buttress Right

Lodge Buttress and the Dragon's Den have the best bouldering at Wharncliffe.

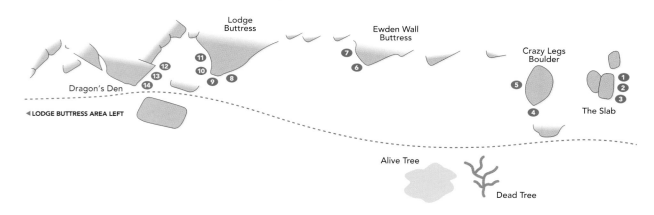

◄ LODGE BUTTRESS AREA LEFT

The Slab

1. *4*
   The right arête of the slab.

2. *4+*
   The narrow slab left of the arête.

3. *3*
   The centre of the slab.

Crazy Legs Boulder

4. **The Parson's Finch**   *7a+*
   The rounded prow climbed directly on slopers, starting with feet in the back.

5. **Crazy Legs Crane**   *6b*
   The left wall starting from the slot and trending left to an exciting top-out.

Ewden Wall Buttress

6. *4*
   The steep finger crack.

7. *5*
   Climb the steep arête to the ledge – escape left.

Lodge Buttress

8. *6a*
Climb the slab leftwards, starting from the boulder, to the sloping ledge.

9. Curvaceous *7a+*
A brilliant, double arête feature – slopey hugging and a slap to a blob lead to the sloping ledge. *(Jon Fullwood)*

10. Ogilvie's Direct *6b+*
Climb the finger crack from a sitting start, with a special bonus mono move. *(Terry Hirst)*

11. Ogilvie's Corner *4+*
Traverse pockets into the direct. *(Alan Clarke)*

12. *3*
The right arête of the slabby wall.

13. *3*
The centre of the slabby wall.

14. *3*
Flakes and left arête of the slabby wall.

Dragon's Den

1. The Dragon's Den *6a+*
Start on undercuts in the back, reach out to the lip and climb the wall above. *(Jon Fullwood)*

2. *4+*
Climb the big flake from undercuts.

3. Dragon Slayer *7a+*
An eliminate line. Start low (left of the Dragon's Den) and climb the flake as a prow, avoiding the right wall. *(Iain Farrar)*

4. A number of problems climb the centre of the wall, with varying degrees of eliminatiness.

a) *6a+*
The easiest way, starting on the rib and moving right to the big hold.

b) Jorge *7b*
A direct finish to **a)** missing out the hold. Fantastic. *(Kim Thompson)*

c) Jorge Jr *6c*
A half-way house. Start as for a) but span right to the slopey pocket.

d) Crouching Tiger *7a+*
Direct dyno start to a), jumping to the big sloper from the thin break. *(Kim Thompson)*

5. Blunted *7a+*
From a low start sharing the edge, climb to the break and then up the rib above.

6. Sweet Release *7c*
Start up Blunted, traverse the thin break left, make a shoulder-busting span into the flake and finish up the Dragon's Den. *(Jon Fullwood)*

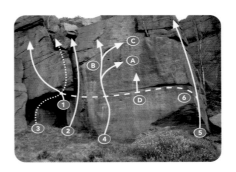

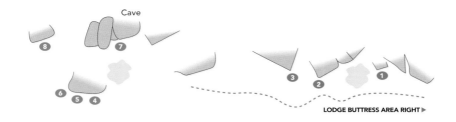

Cave

LODGE BUTTRESS AREA RIGHT ▶

Lodge Buttress Left

1. *3*
   Arête

2. **The Bear Pit**   *7b*
   Start in the pit left of the crack, cross the roof on pockets and finish up the wall above. *(Iain Farrar)*

3. *6a+*
   Arête - can be wet.

4. *5*
   The groove.

5. **Jellyeyes**   *7a*
   Climb the wall left of the groove. Can be done as an eliminate dyno which is harder and better if you avoid undercutting the break – 7b+.

6. *5+*
   The left arête.

7. **Fishboy**   *7a*
   Climb out of the cave starting from the good hold near the back. Bridging, kneebars and a bit of struggling are all required.

8. **Blu Wig Sheep**   *5*
   The slabby graffiti-covered block, without the arêtes.

The Outlook Area

A compact little area with many roofs and highballs.

1. *6a+*
   Traverse the lip from left to right into problem 3.

2. *6b*
   Hard mantel. *(Jon Fullwood)*

3. **Outlook Roof**   *6a*
   Climb through the roof from the low break to a rockover.

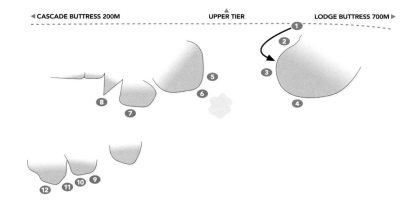

Upper Tier Boulders

More problems have been done on the boulders around and below the upper tier, with much more left to be done.

Long John's Stride

There are several good problems here, some getting quite high. Grab a BMC guide and check out the slab on the buttress left of Autumn Wall, starting in a niche – 6a+. Three good problems are to be found on the small buttress right of the pinnacle. The scary arête is 6b, the thin crack is 4, and the wall between the two is 6a+. Another good problem here is the sharp arête of the next buttress right, climbed on the right from a sitting start – 6b.

Belle Vue Boulders

These are a disappointing cluster of boulders below Belle Vue Buttress at the right-hand side of the popular end of the crag. The best bit is the large boulder just beneath the buttress, with several up problems with grades up to 6b, and a 6c+/7a traverse starting in the crack, with a section of weird climbing to move around the arête.

4. Pete's Route *6a*
Climb out through the roof, via a horn. Highball. *(Pete Hoy)*

5. *6b*
Through the roof – needs a clean.

6. Kim Span *7a*
From a sitting start, climb the small leaning wall and make a massive span to an edge near the arête of the roof, and hence the top. Note: Kim has a BIG span. An easier finish goes leftwards.
(Kim Thompson)

7. Lembas *6c+*
The big, scary, highball wall. E4-ish.
(Kim Thompson)

8. Pixie's Arête *4*
Good moves up the overhanging arête.
(Jon Fullwood)

9. *6b*
Pockets. The sit start is 6c+.
(Kim Thompson)

10. *6b*
The problem just left.

11. *6b*
Slappy moves up the steepness from a low start. *(Kim Thompson)*

12. *7a+*
Sit start the face and then climb it using the arête on the right. *(Kim Thompson)*

eastern crags

163

white edge

The few slightly dysfunctional and bullet-hole riddled rocks of White Edge look not unlike a product of American foreign policy. If, however, you want to do some really rather good roof problems, or one slightly eliminate undercut wall, then White Edge could be the place for you. The potential for more problems is marred somewhat by the quality of the rock, some of which has a structural integrity that is only slightly better than cake.

It can be pretty breezy, which is nice in summer but less so when it's cold.

Rupert Davies ▲

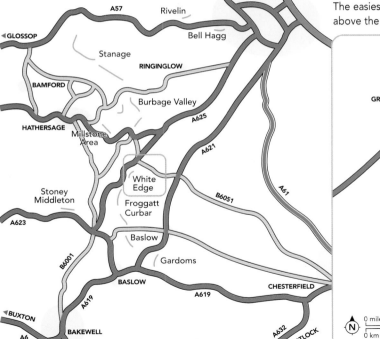

Access and Approach

Park in the lay-by on the Froggatt side of The Grouse Inn on the A625, and take the signposted bridleway on the other side of the road across a field, through a gate, and up a bit more path. Where the path forks there's a handy sign – turn right (or left for Lodge Block). The edge is surprisingly small and soon appears on your right. The easiest way to access the problems is to take the path that runs above the edge then drop down when you are above the blocks.

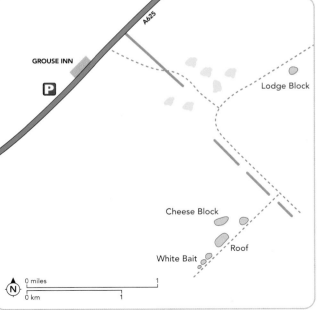

GROUSE INN

A625

P

Lodge Block

Cheese Block

Roof

White Bait

0 miles   1

0 km   1

N

The roof and prow feature yields a surprisingly good problem, with a couple of useful variations. The rock, which is slightly crumbly in places, is the only thing that prevents this from being a classic - that and the fact that there's no true line through the roof.

1. **Diamond White Left-Hand**   *7a*
   From the back of the roof, move left via a flake and various scoops and edges to a reach out to a bullet-hole pocket on the hanging left arête with your right hand. Graded for avoiding the ledge on the left with your feet. *(Jon Barton)*

2. **Diamond White**   *7b*
   The original line on the roof takes a slightly more convoluted path to the same finish, i.e. it takes on the roof at its full length. Start at the back of the roof and move out to the flake. From here, make a bid for the mono pocket on the lip of the lower prow and use this to move back left for the holds on the left side of the prow - finish as for DWLH. *(John Welford)*

3. **Cream**   *7b*
   Another variation, which would be a worthless eliminate in anyone else's guide. Climb DWLH until the edges on the left side of the prow are reached, then slap for ripples on the headwall. Use these to reach left to the bullet hole on the arête, as used on the previous problem. *(Rupert Davies)*

4. **Whitebait**   *7b*
   The undercut wall 5m right, eliminating the right arête. A tricky span from an undercut to a sloping feature and a tentative/powerful step up. *(John Welford)*

Diamond White Left-Hand: *Jon Barton* ▲

Lodge Block

From the junction of the path at the finger post, head left along the bottom of the vague edge through a gate. After 200m the block can be seen on the right, just before the spooky house.

1. Lodge Arête 5
From the lowest point, traverse up left and rock over to finish.

A good sit-down start to this exists, starting from the lowest point at about 7a.

2. Mantel 6a
A straightforward mantel onto the block.

3. White Rose 7c
A steep proposition, climbing out from the undercut end of Lodge Arête. *(John Welford)*

4. 7a
Head up and right. *(John Welford)*

Rupert Davies ▲

yarncliffe quarry

Despite the fact that this area has been padded out by including the start of an E6, and by optimistically highlighting a warm-up area, this is really only a one-problem venue. Luckily it's a future classic.

In the trees and sheltered.

1. **Crème de la Crème** *7a+*
   The left-hand side of the arête, above a poor landing, is the problem start to the E6 route. *(Ron Fawcett)*

2. **THEM!** *7c*
   The right-hand side of the arête has a hard jump-on start that favours the tall and lucky. This is followed by powerful pulls to the ledge above. It has been done without the aid of the dubious ancient bolt head used on the first ascent, which is harder. The name refers to the large ants that continually lap the problem. *(Mo Overfield)*

◀ Andy Banks on THEM!: *John Coefield*

Access and Approach

Park in the obvious lay-by on the B6521, cross to the gate and follow the track to a clearing. The problems are on the striking sharp arête that can be found through the trees on the left. The warm-up area can be found in the main part of the quarry through the trees and down the slope to the left. It consists of a steep stepped wall on which some very easy juggy problems can be found to get the blood flowing.

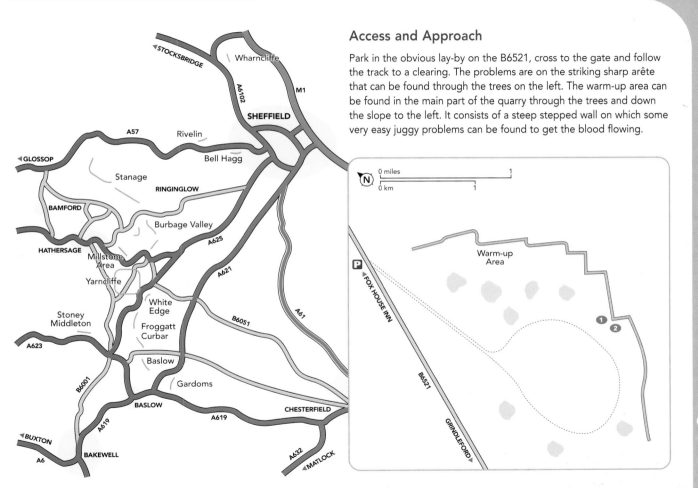

southern crags

Matthew Coutts ▲

clifftop boulders

A nice block in a nice place with some nice problems. The climbing is all straight-forward pulling between mostly positive holds and there's nothing harder than 7a+ – so you could probably clean up the place in an hour or so if you climb at this grade.

As access to this crag might be sensitive, please see **www.thebmc.co.uk** for the latest access information.

Stuart Littlefair on *Boing Boy*. *Rupert Davies* ▲

Access and Approach

Leaving the village of Elton going west, take the first road on the right. Follow it round a few bends and park just after a corner with a bench and gate and water trough. Follow the path after the gate, walking beneath the quarry and keeping to the left-hand path. Take a stile into a field and follow the path towards the obvious blocks up on the right, to the left of a large wooded area. Vault the wall beneath them with care.

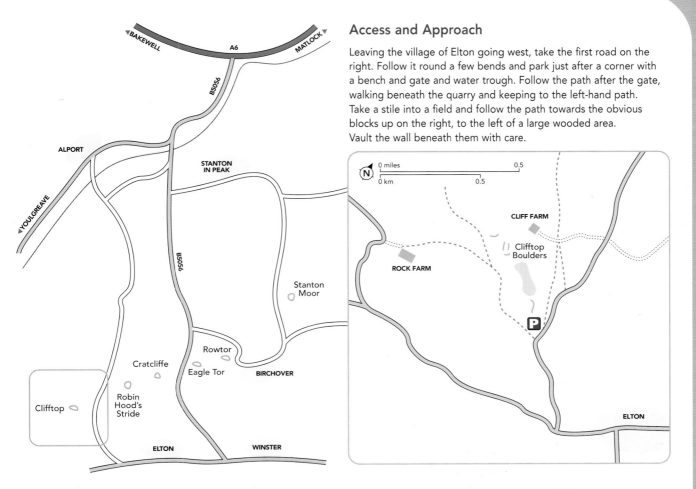

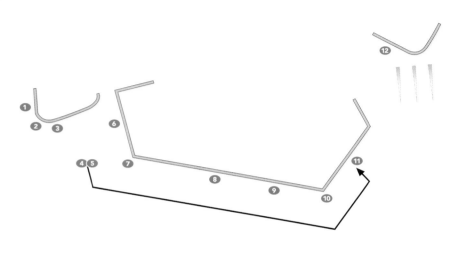

The first problems are on the block on the left.

1. *4*
Climb the nose on the left, padding up the slab.

2. *5*
The nose direct.

3. *5*
The nose approached from the right via the obvious hold.

The main block has a number of good up problems and two good traverses.

4. Brad's Block Traverse *7a+*
Start on the juggy break on the extreme left of the block, drop down onto crimps and traverse the low line rightwards, into and out of the scoop to finish up the wall in the gulley using the arête right round the corner. *(John Bradbury)*

5. *6c*
The higher level traverse – start as above but continue along the upper break.

6. Emergency Room *7a*
Squeezed in left of the arête is this dyno. From the juggy break at the start of BBT spring for the top with your feet smearing on the triangular bit of wall below.

7. *7a+*
The left-hand arête from a sitting start down and right is very good and offers up some crispy pinches at the top.

8. *6b*
The central line up the face from sitting has a stretch for the top.

9. Original *6a+*
From low in the scoop, climb through the centre of the feature using the protruding crimp, then move out to the arête and up using the thin flake.

10. Boing Boy *7a*
A direct start up the arête from sitting - jugs, edge, pinch on the arête, jump to jugs, finish up the arête above.
(Andy Crome)

11. Cracker Block *6b*
Sit start on the jug and then up using the grippy sloper.

Up and right is an arête –
the final problem.

12. *5+*
The arête on the left-hand side.

cratcliffe

Often combined in circuit with Robin Hood's Stride, Cratcliffe is a fantastic bouldering venue. Grades extend from 3 through to the mid 7s, and the crag offers a superb combination of problems from technical offerings that smear up rounded scoops and blobs to steep, powerful climbing on incuts, slopers and some gratton-type crimps that are peculiar to the local gritstone.

Cratcliffe also harbours more than its fair share of must-do Peak classics.

The grattony crimps and incuts mean that there's a lot to do in warm weather when you just can't hold the slopes, especially in the shade given by the trees. The circuit below the crag can be dirty and damp after wet weather, but the exposed top boulders dry extremely fast.

◀ Paul Worsdale: *Rupert Davies*

Access and Approach

Park in the lay-bys on the side of the B5056 and take the obvious track up the hill. Where the track goes right to the farm, continue up the hill and take a small path into the wooded area on the right next to a bench. Cratcliffe Middle is up on the left, continue along the path to the right to reach the main area. When you can see the Egg boulder on the left, continue up the hill to reach the top boulders.

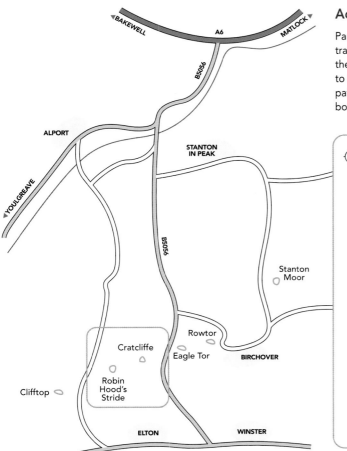

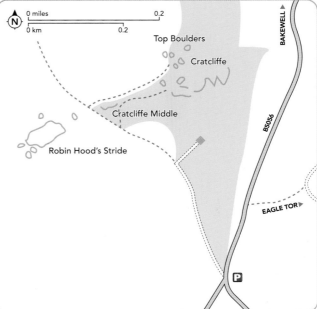

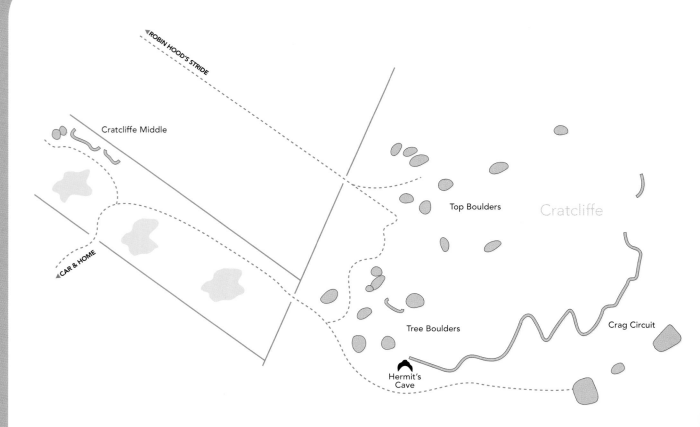

ROBIN HOOD'S STRIDE

Cratcliffe Middle

CAR & HOME

Top Boulders

Cratcliffe

Tree Boulders

Crag Circuit

Hermit's
Cave

Cratcliffe Middle

The first area is midway between Cratcliffe and Robin Hood's Stride. The best feature is the roof, which has some very good lines on it. Some problems have been climbed further right and on a slab below, but these have got dirty through lack of use and are slowly returning to nature.

Just to the left of the roof are two boulders stacked against each other and forming a roof crack.

5
Climb the left side of the slab on the left face of the left block.

5
The right side of the same slab.

Look at Me! *7a+*
Superb chimneying/jamming weirdness through the roof-crack/cave.
(Adam Long)

5+
The double arêtes on the right-hand boulder, facing the roof. Can be done with left arête only at 7a.

1. *6c+*
   The left arête of Razor Roof using cunning but slightly worrying footwork. Nice.

2. **Razor Roof**   *6c*
   The central line of the roof. Pull out from the jugs on the left side of the cave and use razor-sharp crimps to slap the top.

3. *6b*
   Low start on jams, then use small protruding crimps to reach the break up and right.

4. *7a+*
   Starting up 3 and finishing up Razor Roof is the classic link up.

Paul Worsdale: *Rupert Davies* ▲

Top Boulders

A nice selection of low, easy problems, a great place to learn the grit art of smearing and a nice spot for a picnic in the sun. Virtually every inch of these blocks is climbable, so defining individual problems is somewhat arbitrary. We have pointed out some of the best features, but the most fun to be had is just messing about with some mates and seeing what you can find.

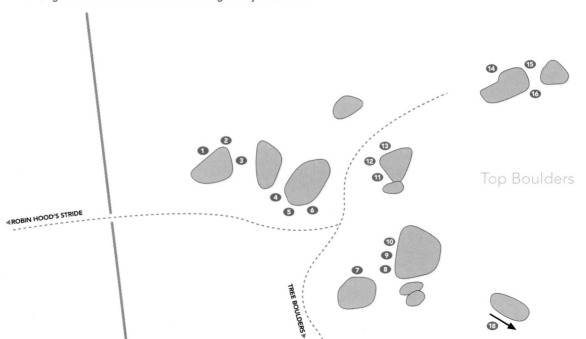

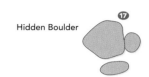

Hidden Boulder

Top Boulders

ROBIN HOOD'S STRIDE

TREE BOULDERS

1. *3+*
   Scoop.

2. *4+*
   Arête on the left-hand side.

3. *4+*
   Into the runnel thing.

4. *4*
   Short flake.

5. *5+*
   Arête on left-hand side.

6. *5+*
   Climb the rib using the lovely pinch. The grade is for eliminating the arête on the left, 4+ if done with the arête. Best in cold conditions when the pinch stops being random chalk marks and starts being a hold.

7. *4*
   Pad up the left-trending rampline.

8. *5*
   Right arête and pocket.

9. *5+*
   Pockets up the wall.

10. *5*
    The left-hand side of the slab.

11. *4+*
    The slab is straightforward using the chip. Without, it is a good exercise in smearing that will improve footwork confidence (if you can do it).

12. *3*
    The chipped arête is elementary.

13. *4*
    Another chipped slab that's better without the chips.

14. *6b+*
    You'll either walk up this groove or struggle like hell.

15. *6b*
    Sit start the chipped arête. The grade of this one changes by the month as footholds wear out and some idiot chips new ones. Currently it's easy as there's a big new chip at the bottom to stand in.

    You can also traverse the top of the boulder on slopes from the groove to the arête, 6c ish.

16. *4*
    Up the back wall. The block just right also has lots of good slabby problems at the same grade.

17. *5+*
    Included for esoteric value. Hidden in the bracken is a rarely found boulder. Start the obvious steep arête from the low shelf via slopes.

18. *7a*
    Sloper shuffling. Sit start at the left end of the low block, make crux moves up and right, keep traversing and exit up the scoop.

19. **Tit Traverse** *7a*
    More sloper shuffling. Left to right traverse using the pair of intimate features.

T Crack: *Stu Littlefair* ▲

Tree Boulders

Down in the trees the problems get harder and steeper.

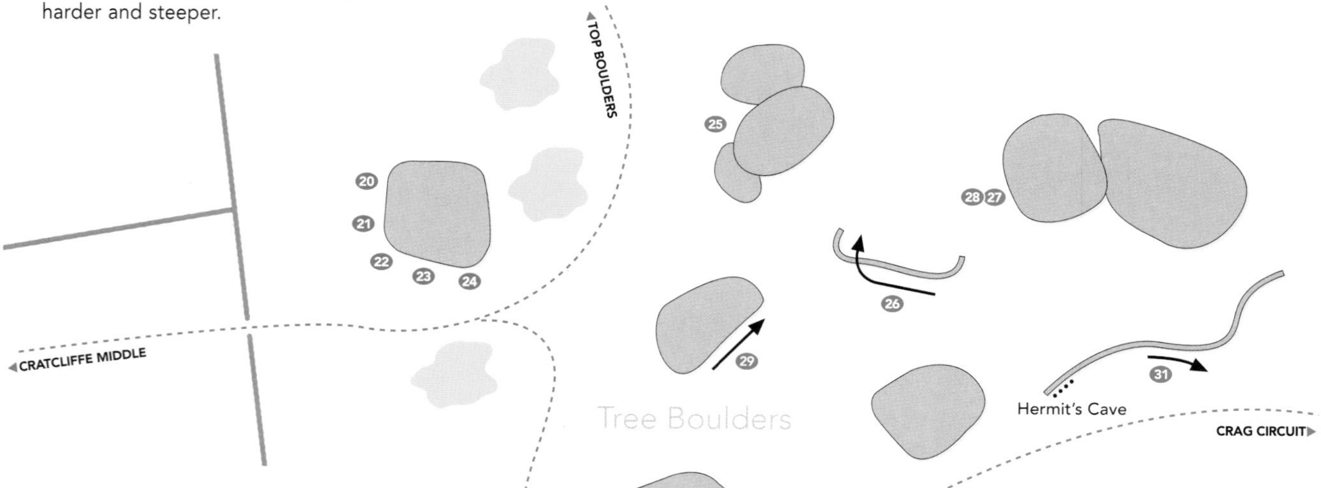

◀ TOP BOULDERS

◀ CRATCLIFFE MIDDLE

20
21
22 23 24

25

28 27

26

29

Tree Boulders

Hermit's Cave

31

30

CRAG CIRCUIT ▶

20 21 22 23 24

The Egg Boulder

The big green grit blob is covered in big green grit slopers.

20. *5+*
The left-hand slab line.

21. *5*
The central slab line above the scoops.

22. *6a+*
The blunt arête is a classic grit thing. Pull on the slopes? Press off your palms?

23. *7b*
Suction onto the slopiest of slopers using all of your gritstone 'feel'.

24. *5+*
The right arête using the high flake.

25. T Crack *7b*
A powerful grit classic. From the detached block under the roof, gain the sloping break via hard pulls on rippling undercuts and the pod-like crack. Then use strength or cunning to turn the final bulge. The foot-block on the right is out, and using the chip in the break is similarly not cricket.

26. Jerry's Traverse *7b*
Classic a-technical traverse with powerful sideways campus moves. Traverse the slots from right to left, to a final lunge for the slanting shelf at the extreme left. An alternative exit is just right: throw for good holds over the top from the jugs. Finally, the strong can do a there and back, finishing up the next problem - 7c. *(Jerry Moffatt)*

6c+
The wall above the start of Jerry's Traverse. From the low slots head up the steep wall on good edges.

Up above the traverse is a low roof.

27. Serpico *6c*
Span out from the back via a pocket on the lip. The problem has also got a harder extension that traverses the lip left before topping out.

28. Shunting Biscuits *7a+*
Does Serpico, then traverses left up obvious ramp to nasty mantel.

29. *6c*
Traverse the top of the block down and left of Jerry's traverse, from L-R. Sloper shuffling at its most boring.

30. *6c+*
R-L traverse. Another exercise in sloper shuffling, but crossing the wide crack/gap using knees and whatever provides some interest. Fun.

The Hermit's Cave

A hermit lived here until at least 1549 when local records show payments being made to him. Inside, on the wall, is a 4ft high carved crucifix that is thought to be contemporary with a 14th century rule requesting that all hermits have an image of the crucified Savior. The rule doesn't mention traverses, however, so it is likely that the next problem was climbed later.

31. *6b*
Traverse rightwards from the bars, along an assortment of natural and hermit-made features.

The path now continues below the crag, here we find the final part of the Cratcliffe circuit.

Crag Boulders

A mini-circuit below the crag. Contour below the crag until the huge v-notch gully containing the route Fern Hill is reached. The boulders around here are just being opened up and they will need more attention before they clean off properly.

The first feature on the left is the obvious arête – a last great bouldering project. Just below this, on the left wall of the gully is a small low cave/roof.

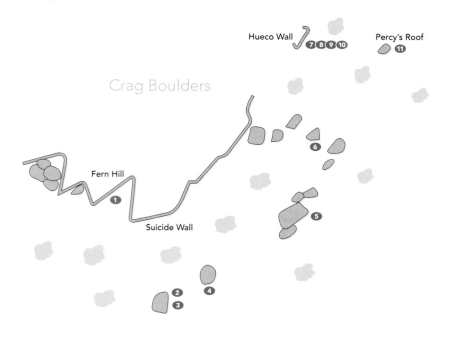

1. *7a+*
   Sit start on a jug on the right-hand side of the low roof and climb the wall above to the break. *(Percy Bishton)*

   Below this, in front of Suicide Wall, is a detached block with an arch feature.

2. *6a*
   The arête from a sit start.

3. **The Arch** *6c+*
   Sit start, and climb the arch. *(P Bishton)*

   Right of this block, looking towards the crag is a smaller block with PRIVATE written on it.

4. **Brian's Private Arête** *7b*
   Sit start the right-hand arête – left hand undercut, right hand arête – pull on and launch for the top. Using pretty much any other features to climb the same face is much easier – holding the right arête seems to add grades. *(Brian Chase)*

5. **Brain Dead** *6c*
   The big, square-cut, sharp, highball arête. 7b from a low start. *(Martin Veale)*

6. *6a+*
   A lost arête up behind Brain Dead, with a good hold halfway up.

Hueco Wall

Approximately 30m further than the right-hand end of the crag is an attractive wall with some obvious huecos. It seems to stay dry even in the most foul of weather.

7. Chapel of Rest *7a+*
Gain the left hueco and undercut it to reach the sloping top. *(John Allen)*

8. Wish *7a+*
Gain the right-hand hueco/pod and leave it via undercuts and edges to reach a hidden hold over the top. *(John Allen)*

9. *6c+*
Traverse the deceptive break-line from right to left.

10. Percy's Start *6c+*
Start low at the left-hand side of the wall and use edges to gain the higher traverse, which is followed rightwards. Finishing up Wish or Chapel of Rest is 7b/+. *(Percy Bishton)*

Percy's Roof

Some new problems have recently been freed from the moss beneath Hueco Wall.

11. 72 *6c*
Climb leftwards through the roof from a sitting start with both hands in the big hole to gain the boss on the lip. Traverse left along the slopey rail and mantel. *(Percy Bishton)*

72 Direct *7b*
Start as for 72 but continue straight up the hanging arête from the boss on the lip. *(Percy Bishton)*

P Crack *7b*
The central line through the middle of the roof. Sit start in the pocket at the back of the roof then head out via the pockets to a sloper under the lip. Gain the hanging crack in the head wall using toe hooks in the big hueco under the roof and climb this to the top.
(Percy Bishton)

eagle tor

Eagle Tor sits quietly on the hill, hiding its jumble of boulders behind a veil of trees and shrubs and waiting for the initiati. Subtle holds, improbable moves and problems from 5 – 7c+ are to be found on the sculptured pink chunks that litter the woods on the less popular side of the valley from Cratcliffe and the Stride.

Access and Approach

Eagle Tor is privately owned, but climbing is kindly allowed. Please keep noise to a minimum, be respectful to the landscape and if the Tor is busy with other parties consider climbing elsewhere. Please also avoid carrying bouldering mats past the farmhouse as they distress the landowner's dog.

Eagle Tor can be approached either from the roadside parking below Cratcliffe or from the village of Birchover. From below Cratcliffe, walk back up the road in the direction of Bakewell and cross a stile on the right after a few metres into a muddy field. A path rises up the hill and through a gate. Double back and follow the path round to the right of the tor until the remains of a stone building are reached. The blocks of the tor lie up the hill on the left. From Birchover, follow a track past the side of the Druid Inn to a gate marked Rockingstone Farm. Turn left up the path to reach another gravelly track. Then turn right and head down this track for 40 metres until a small path (below a wall) runs up the hill to a gate leading onto the Tor.

◀ Jerry Moffatt on Autumn: *Moffatt Coll.*

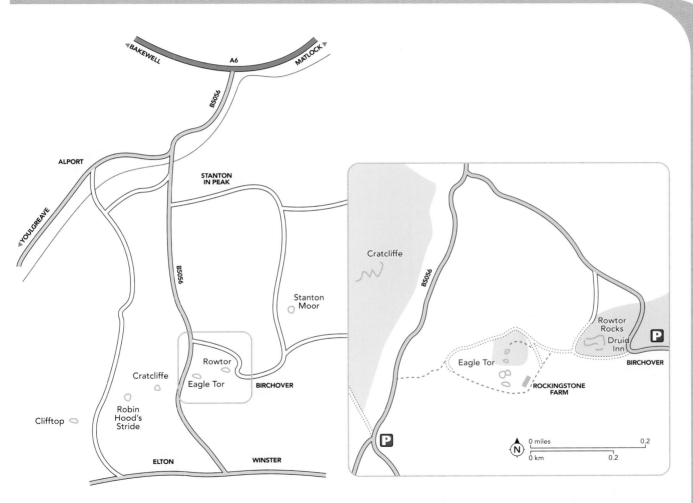

BAKEWELL ◄ A6 ► MATLOCK ►

B5056

ALPORT

YOULGREAVE ◄

STANTON
IN PEAK

B5056

Stanton
Moor

Rowtor

Cratcliffe

Eagle Tor

BIRCHOVER

Clifftop

Robin
Hood's
Stride

ELTON   WINSTER

Cratcliffe

B5056

Rowtor
Rocks

Druid
Inn

P

BIRCHOVER

Eagle Tor

ROCKINGSTONE
FARM

P

0 miles   0.2

N

0 km   0.2

southern crags

187

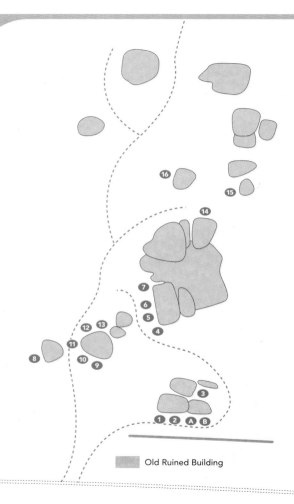

Old Ruined Building

1. **Knuckle Duster** *6a*
   The left side of the wall.

2. **Invisible Touch** *6a+*
   The wall to the right.

a) *5+*
   Nice arête/slopey ledge problem. *(John Bradbury)*

b) *7a+*
   Direct up wall right of 2a on very grim undercuts and ledges. *(John Bradbury)*

3. **Tourettes Arête** *6c*
   A brilliant problem situated on a little terrace above a drop. Although it looks about 7c+ the steep little arête cum prow starting from the shelf just works. Nicer with a spotter. A left-hand start is the same grade but misses out all the good bits. *(Percy Bishton)*

4. **Heart Arête** *6b*
   The blunt arête is a little gem.

5. **Feel Good** *7c+*
   Tiny crimps to a sloping top. Use pads or a stone to reach the crimps, and the coldest weather possible to hang them. *(Jerry Moffatt)*

6. **Autumn** *7b+*
   Jump left to razor crimps from the start of Feel Good. Harder if you pull on first before jumping (7c). A direct start 'Fall' jumps straight to the better crimps and is allegedly easier. *(Jerry Moffatt)*

7. No Mercy *7c+*
The left arête was originally climbed by jumping right to the crimps on Autumn. It has since been repeated straight up the arête, which makes for a better problem. Very morpho. *(Thomas Willenberg)*

8. *5*
The slopey shelf - often dirty.

9. *6a+*
Up from undercuts.

10. Boeing *6b*
Sit start. Up the arête from the massive undercut.

11. *6b*
The rib arête and slopes up the front face.

12. Brush *5*
The short crack line is brilliant.

13. *6c+*
Pockets and small features up the wall from sitting.

14. Rollin' Pat *7a*
Sit start, then make fingery moves out to and up the arête left and back right to the arête. Mini classic.

15. *6c*
A little sit start up the pinches and crack. *(Percy Bishton)*

16. Scaramanga *7a+*
Used to climb via three nipples, hence the name, now it climbs the two remaining ones. Dirty through lack of traffic. *(Percy Bishton)*

Jules Copnall on Heart Arête: *Stu Littlefair* ▲▲

17. *7a+*
Sit start. Onto the curving hold then press up to the top.
A good left-hand variation matches the hold and reaches left
to slopers and up, 7a.

18. Bulb Sit Start *6c*
The unusual gritstone tufa feature from the sidepull down and
right. A sit start directly beneath the tufa is easier but much less
satisfying as you can just miss out the tufa altogether. A direct
finish from the sidepull via a big dyno is also brilliant, but much
harder – 7a+ish.

19. Shroom *7a+*
The roof on the left via a poor pocket and sloper.

20. I'm With Stupid *7b*
The small rib. Start sitting and launch for the top as your
spotters sympathise with the name. *(Percy Bishton)*

21. Brad's Arête *7a+*
A technical classic. The sitting start is 7b, but the hard bit is still
on the original. *(John Bradbury, Thomas Willenberg (sit start))*

22. Angel Falls *6c*
Excellent smearing up the centre of the slab – no arête.

23. *6a+*
Smearing and palming up the right-hand side of the slab.

24. *4+*
The centre of the slab.

25. *4*
The crack and arête on the left side of the slab.

26. *5+*
More friction work up the slab.

27. *6b*
A recently unearthed gem. Sit start the leftwards trending arête.
(John Bradbury)

28. Parachute   *6a*
The ramp feature is started by a tenuous rock onto an
obvious foothold.

29. Face Arête   *7b+*
Sit start the hanging arête from low jams, eliminating blocks on
the left. A great problem. 6c, or thereabouts, if you use the left
block for your feet.   *(Percy Bishton)*

*The final problems are on a hidden wall on the other side of the
plateau. Cross the fence via the barbed wire gate and jungle
bash rightwards until you find it.*

30. Mona   *7c*
The wall is climbed using the small sidepull, a jump and some
finger strength. Scary and high in the grade.   *(Dawid Skoczylas)*

31. *7c*
From low finger dishes campus up the wall to the left.

Simon Richardson on Brad's Arête: *Stu Littlefair* ▶

robin hood's stride

Robin Hood's Stride is an ancient site that is thought to have been held sacred by prehistoric man: a theory supported by the presence of 'Nine Stone Close', a stone circle in the field below, of which only four standing stones remain. 'Robin Hood' refers not to the famous outlaw of Sherwood Forest, but is instead another name for the Green Man, the pagan god of fertility - a big man hereabouts.

The Stride has great value, mainly very friendly, bouldering with grades from 4 – 8a+. Hundreds of problems and variations have been climbed here over the years in the spirit of exploration and experimentation – the problems detailed below take the strongest lines with the least amount of eliminates possible, and avoid those boulders that have been covered with a cloak of lichen and moss after years of (usually well justified) neglect.

Open in aspect, with bouldering on 360° of the tor, the Stride gets any weather coming at it. Having said that, the ancient gods have ensured a very special microclimate for this gathering of stones and the weather is often better than on the Eastern Edges – i.e. it's often possible to climb here when the weather has closed in further North.

◄ Problem 34: *Alex Messenger*

Access and Approach

Park in the lay-bys on the side of the B5056 and take the track up the hill. The Stride is the obvious twin monoliths and the boulders are scattered beneath.

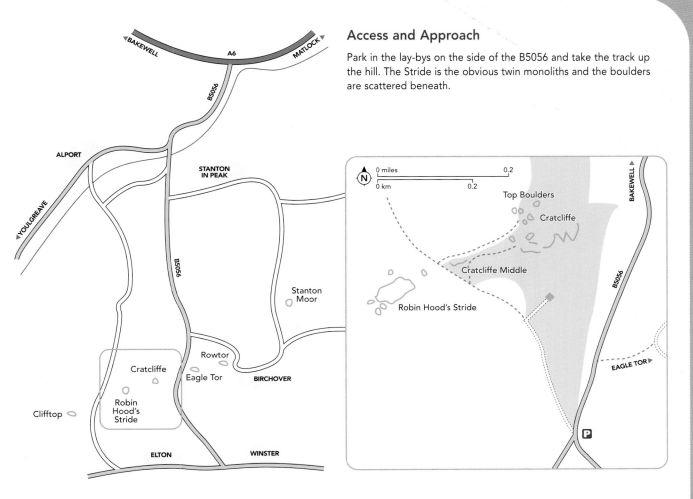

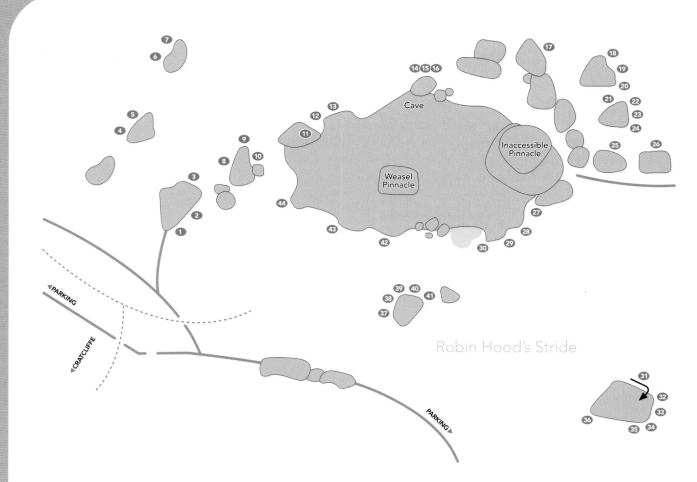

Cave

Inaccessible
Pinnacle

Weasel
Pinnacle

Robin Hood's Stride

PARKING

CRATCLIFFE

PARKING

Robin Hood's Stride is unfortunately covered in carved graffiti, and some of the easier problems use chipped holds. This has, in the recent past, encouraged inexperienced climbers to chip further holds, a practice that is wholly inappropriate. Please refer to the notes at the front of this book. However, there is one large (50cm) circular carving on a horizontal ledge, behind the Eastern chimney, that, although of uncertain age, is allegedly very old indeed and may relate to druidical practices in the area. It was uncovered in the 1970s and may have been preserved by the vegetation that covered it.

1. *6b*
   The rounded arête just right of the fence is great.

2. *7a*
   Hard smearing up the wall to the right.

3. **Boysen's Crack** *6c*
   A classic tussle up the offwidth.

   On the other side of this block is a green face, with a good rightwards trending line from a seam – about 6c but the difficulty will depend on how clean the face is – it hasn't had much traffic for a while.

4. *5*
   Slab and cracks.

5. *3*
   Slab and bulgette. Eliminating the holds on the left arête makes for a nice padding problem too - 5.

6. *4*
   Climb the centre of the nice slab via a slopey ledge.

7. *5*
   Flake and slab.

8. *3*
   The chipped slab.

9. **Sweet Arête** *6c*
   The left side of the arête from a sit start.

10. **Sweet Thing** *8a+*
    The short wall is ultra hard. Sit start on undercuts (bit cramped) and use a poor two-finger dish and an edge to slap the sloping top. *(Ben Moon)*

11. **Dry Wit in a Wet Country** *7a+*
    The wall up to the hanging crack direct is barely highball with a good pad and some spotters. *(Johnny Dawes)*

12. **Grizzly Arête** *7a+*
    The high arête using the gradually decaying undercut. *(John Allen)*

13. **The Growler** *7c*
    Sit start under the right side of the sloping pod, climb up to it using edges and exit with a big span from the undercut. The top moves were originally climbed on Martin Veale's Mock Beggars Wall. *(Percy Bishton)*

    No Regrets *7b+*
    Starts as for The Growler but traverses the pod left, to exit stepping onto the blocks on the left. *(Percy Bishton)*

The Cave

14. *7a*

The right edge of the cave from low undercuts.

15. *7a+*

Start in the back and work back right to the lip pinching the roof blobs.

16. *6a*

Lock from the pocket on the left hand wall to the top. A poor problem climbs the wall to the right from a hanging start.

17. *4+*

The chipped slab.

18. *6a*

The awkward bulging arête.

19. *6c*

Summon your manteling skills and use 'em to get onto the nose.

20. Jerry's Arête *7a*

The classic arête on the left-hand side using a finger jam to start. The arête on the other side is also good at 6a.
(Jerry Moffatt)

21. *5*

A rising line on the side of the block.

There are three tasty classics all based around the scoop feature.

22. *6b+*

Enter the scoop and use the right arête with a little trepidation.

23. *6c+*

Enter the scoop again and head straight on up the slabby wall with more than a little trepidation.

24. *6a*

Enter the scoop for the final time and trend left up the arête with less trepidation than the other two.

25. *6a*

Grattonny type crimps up the slab

26. *6c*

Grovelling mantel onto the block.

27. Picalli's Pickle *7a+*

The roof crack, hear it growl.

28. *5*

Slab and flake.

29. Nobody Knows *6b*

Into the scoop using a bit of route mentality. Finish over the steep juggy nose.

30. Big Al Qaeda *7b*

The left arête was a last great problem at the Stride for quite a while – it's now a modern classic. *(Michael Duffy)*

31. *5*

Hop on the slab on the right and smear leftwards to top-out up the arête - only use the top to finish.

32. *4+*
Short arête.

33. *7a*
The thin, tenuous slab between the arêtes, willing your feet to stick.

34. *5*
Classic stepped arête on the right hand side. On the left it's 6b.

35. Ben's Wall *7c*
The wall left of the arête – undercut to the high sidepull and use it to exit direct or rock over leftwards into the scoop – it's hard either way. No arête. *(Ben Moon)*

36. *6b+*
The nose approached from the hole, wriggling onto the top.

37. *6a*
More eroding chips. It is easier (5) if you jump for the top chip, rather than pull on first.

38. *6c*
The hanging crack used to be approached from the chip that has now worn away – undercut the left wall and reach to the crack, share and up. 6a if you use the left arête as well.

39. *4*
The wide crack.

40. *4+*
The wall.

41. *4*
The wall and arête.

42. *6b+*
The high scoop requires more survival instinct than skill – reach into it and start swimming.

43. *6a*
The little arête.

44. *5+*
The sharp arête on the left-hand side.

Adam Long on Big Al Qaeda: *Rupert Davies* ▶

eastwood rocks

The most salient feature of Eastwood Rocks is that YOU ARE NOT ALLOWED TO CLIMB HERE. Furthermore, the inclusion of this crag in the guide does not imply that you have a right to climb here either.

The problems are few but of great quality and mostly in the harder grades. Eastwood Rocks also features one of the best traverses on grit. Allegedly.

Cave Buttress, around which most of the problems are centred, is steep and can stay dry in wet weather.

Access and Approach

In case you skipped the introduction, YOU ARE NOT ALLOWED TO CLIMB HERE, so obviously the approach details are only included for completeness – and in case the farmer at Eastwood Hall ever changes his mind and decides to allow access in the future.

Approaching the village of Ashover from Kelstedge (on the A632 Matlock to Chesterfield road) take the first left turn, past a school, and turn right at the top. Take the second left past the pub and the next left again up a steep road. The road rises over a hill, at the top of which is a rough lay-by on the right. Continue past this until a T-junction is reached shortly afterwards – turn left and park. The crag is accessed from the lay-by – cross the fence and follow a vague track through undergrowth, over a wall until Cave Buttress is reached.

Corpse Crack · ▲

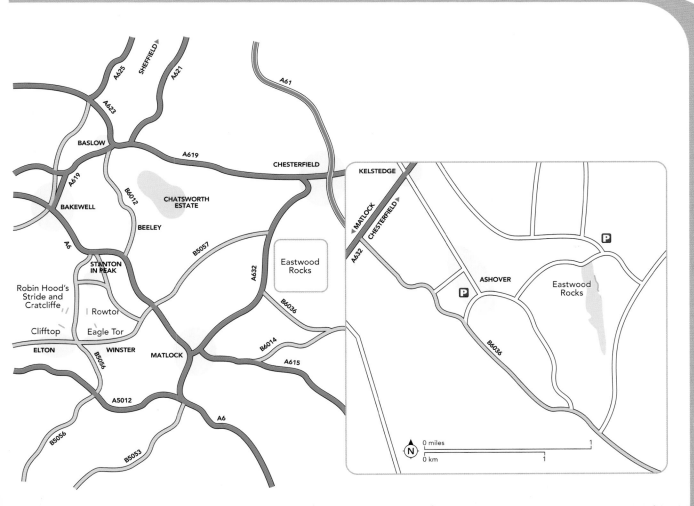

SHEFFIELD ►
A625
A623
A621
A61
BASLOW
A619
CHESTERFIELD
A619
B6012
CHATSWORTH ESTATE
BAKEWELL
BEELEY
A6
B5057
STANTON IN PEAK
Eastwood Rocks
A632
Robin Hood's Stride and Cratcliffe
Rowtor
B6036
Clifftop
Eagle Tor
ELTON
WINSTER
MATLOCK
B6014
B5056
A615
A5012
A6
B5056
B5053

KELSTEDGE
◄ MATLOCK
CHESTERFIELD ►
A632
ASHOVER
P
P
Eastwood Rocks
B6036
0 miles   1
N
0 km   1

The problems are centred around the left-most Cave Buttress.

1. **Hats for Clowns** *7b*
   Just right of the left arête. Gain a layaway at the base of
   the steep finger crack from the flake/crack on the right via a
   jump-start. A hard move using a flared jam and a sloper gains
   jugs on the arête. A quality Kyloe in the Woods esque problem.
   (Jon Fullwood)

2. **Hats for Percys** *7b*
   A left-hand start has been climbed, which avoids the jump-start,
   but is unfortunately a bit eliminate due to the proximity of the
   arête. Gain the layaway as a gaston from edges on the left
   (avoiding holds on the arête), and then work back leftwards to
   the high jugs on the arête. *(Percy Bishton)*

Hats for Weasels   *7c+*
A sit start to HFP's starting from underneath the roof.   *(Ian Vickers)*

3. The Eastwood Traverse   *7b+*
The Powerband (or should that be Powerbanned?) of grit. Originally done from right to left sit starting at Corpse Crack and traversing left to finish in the big break of the green slab right round the corner. It's also been done t'other way, to finish on the ledge beneath Corpse Crack. Done in reverse opens up possibilities for links – finishing up Ten Inch Zombies is perhaps 7c+.   *(Rich Heap)*

4. Corpse Crack   *5*
The crack is a great feature, and as a boulder problem is climbed from hanging the ledge to finish at the vegetated break.

It all sounds great so far, doesn't it? Remember:
YOU ARE NOT ALLOWED TO CLIMB HERE.

5. Jon's Traverse   *7a+*
Traverse right from Corpse Crack to finish up the groove problem. Also awaits a link with the Eastwood Traverse.
(Jon Fullwood)

6. Ten Inch Zombies   *7a*
The wall on chicken-heads right of the crack, finishing at the break.   *(Jon Fullwood)*

7.   *4+*
The slabby groove right again.

7a+
Right of the slab (on the far side of the tree) is a brushed wall climbed on crimps past an overlap.   *(Percy Bishton)*

Percy's Highball   *7b+*
Further right still is another buttress with a 45° prow and an arête above. Climb this. Highball.   *(Percy Bishton)*

Beyond Percy's Highball is a buttress with a couple more problems on it. A L-R diagonal traverse of the finger break is easy, and the arête just to its right is a superb 6b from a sit start.

The Eastwood Traverse ▲

rowtor rocks

Rowtor is another local curiosity with many strange rooms and shapes carved into the rocks, maybe by druids. So, more history: Rowtor takes its name from the two huge rocking boulders found at the east end of the top terrace. From these came the name Rootor, from the localism 'roos' which means anything that moves to and fro. At least one of them doesn't rock anymore after someone tried to push it over.

The climbing is mostly steep and powerful with plenty of roofs and hideous sloping mantels.

Rowtor is covered in trees, slow to dry, and can get green. Once dry though, it's pretty sheltered and some of the steep problems stay dry in the rain.

Rupert Davies on Raw Deal: *Jon Barton* ▲

Access and Approach

Park sensibly in Birchover village and take the track past the Druid Inn. Just after the Druid, turn right along a path that goes behind the pub and wanders up and left to the rocks.

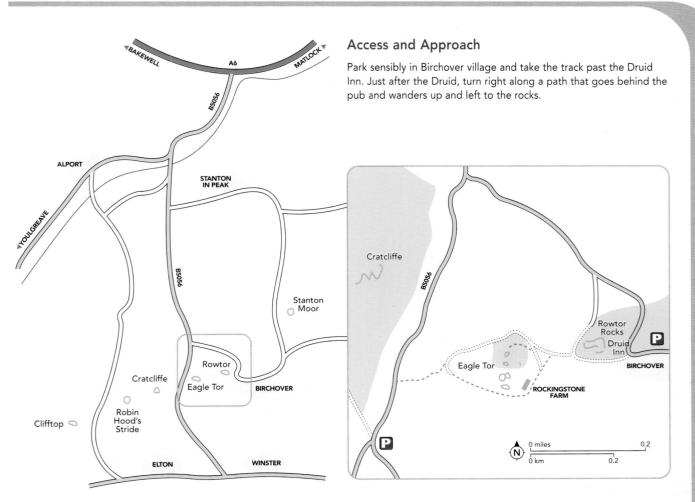

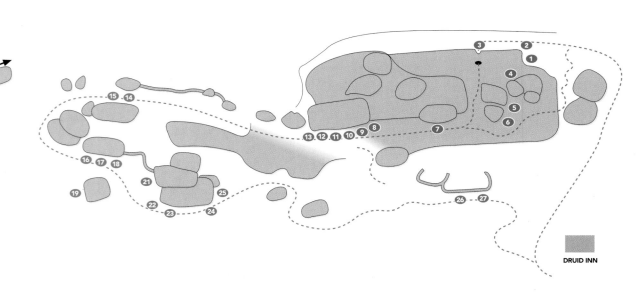

DRUID INN

Walking up from behind the pub, the first problems are on the long, carved canopy.

1. **Chip Shop Mantel**   *6b*
Hand-traverse the rain gutter around the corner then mantel up.

2. **The Yoghurt Hypnotist**   *7b*
The overhanging arête/rib below the rain gutter is climbed from a sit start, without the use of the gutter on the left wall, to top-out up the arête above.
(Percy Bishton)

Continuing under the canopy, a door is reached on the left that provides access via a tunnel to the terrace above. There are also two large chambers carved into the rock under here. According to the druid theories, the smaller one was perhaps a High Priest's room, lit by candles sunk into the many holes drilled inside. The larger room supposedly had a much darker purpose. Anyway …

3. **Abyss**   *6c*
The horrendous looking, but brilliant, off-width above the tunnel door. Overhead knee bars and undercutting, or get in and squirm.   *(Percy Bishton)*

On the top terrace:

4. **Humpty Dumpty**   *6c+*
One for the keen. Sit start with feet in the recess under the roof and move up on slopers.   *(James Pearson)*

5. **Blood Falls**   *7b*
The prow and pockets from a low start on slots under the roof. A frustrating reach to gain the pocket line is followed with a powerful move to the top. There is some crumbly rock, so please treat it with care.

6. *6a+*
The little nose on the left, from the break.

Continuing along the top terrace, a carved seat is reached with a sloping canopy above. Have a nice sit-down or attempt…

7. **The Bus Stop Mantel**   *7a*
Mantel out the canopy roof. This problem has seen failure by some of the best boulderers on the planet and has been flashed by others, so the grade could be anything really. Back on the historical note, it's unlikely that the original purpose of the carving was either a) a bus stop or b) a boulder problem.

Matt Birch on The Yoghurt Hypnotist: *Rupert Davies* ▲

8. *6c+*
The right arête

9. Dissolution *7b*
Start on edges left of the right arête, move up and left on edges and slopers. Has been done from a sit start on the jug below the arête – a bit harder.

10. *7b*
The line of the block. Sitting start on the flakey crack and proceed upwards using the tiny fragile crimps and a heel jam to mantel out the scoop. Brilliant.

11. Raw Power *7a+*
Jump to, and mantel out the highest point of the block. Again, the grade depends on your ability to mantel.

12. Raw Deal *7c+*
The hanging slab, using a shallow pocket for your right hand and a rib.
(Mike Lea)

13. *4+*
The left arête, 6c from a sit-down start.

A traverse of the whole block starting up this problem would be a great project.

Further on, and down some steps with sculpted chairs on the left (history bit: believed to be more modern than the rooms) is a low boulder with a very steep wall/roof. Neither of these two problems use the rock underneath the boulder for your feet.

14. Quine   *7c*
Power out to the lip from a sitting start on the sidepull/pinch. There are two totally different methods: the original undercuts the pod, but most subsequent repeats dyno for the lip using a foothold out right. *(Rupert Davies)*

15. *6b+*
The little arête just right from sitting, using a sidepull. Nice move.

The path now goes down and left, to some boulders beneath the terrace.

16. *6a*
The crimpy flake in the wall.

17. *6a+*
Sharp crimps up the wall, to a sloping top.

18. *5+*
Just left of the arête, using a flatty.

19. *6a*
The slab above a funny landing.

The next problem is on an isolated block below the main action on the other side of the ridge – check out the topo and get to it as best you can.

20. Hang 'em High   *7a*
R-L lip traverse, using heels.

Back on the main path.

21. Domes   *7a*
The hanging prow above the cave formed by the stacked boulders.

Domes Sit Start   *7c+*
Starting on the ledge on the right-hand wall, move out to join Domes using some fancy footwork. *(Percy Bishton)*

22. *6b*
A high line reaching into the left arête features of the large roof. *(Percy Bishton)*

23. Pat's Roof   *7a*
A big line through the left side of the roof, starting in the break and reaching out to the lip from big undercuts, before moving left to finish up the previous problem. The landing is poor, and a long way away. *(Pat King)*

A traverse starts at the same point, moving right under the roof to finish up problem 24 – 6b. Finishing up Short Sean's is 7a+.

24. *6a*
Start on the right arête under the roof and then pull out and up the nice rounded runnel.

25. Short Sean's Reachy Roof   *7a*
The right side of the roof. From the break in the back undercut out to the break on the lip, move right and lock or slap for the top. The block to the right for feet is in at this grade, 7a+ without.

Further on is a final block, tucked into the hillside.

26. *7b+*
A hard pull on crimps to the top.
(Kim Thompson)

27. *6a+*
The right arête on the left. An eliminate dyno from the flake to the top is 7a.

stanton moor

You could easily go for a stroll over Stanton Moor without seeing a single problem. They are there though, hidden behind trees, down slopes and behind bushes. The problems range from 4 – 7c, but the best problems are 7a and harder and a trip may well be disappointing if you cannot climb at this grade or above.

Lucy Atkinson on My Left Foot: *Percy Bishton* ▲

Access and Approach

To access the moor drive up the road through the village of Birchover. At the top of the hill the road veers left, and a smaller road appears on the right. To access the Andle Stone and the Cork Stone, follow the road left and then back right to finally park in lay-bys by the road after a few hundred metres. The best parking for the other areas is to be found by taking the small right-hand road to Stanton Lees, soon reaching some small lay-bys on the left.

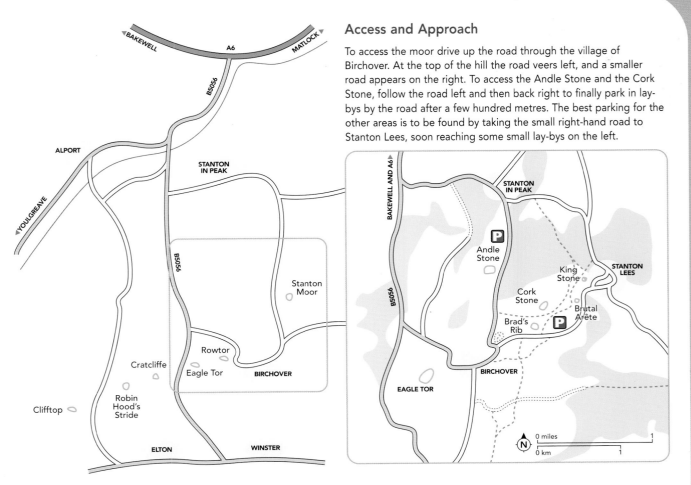

Although the small blocks on the plateau above the village of Birchover have been climbed on for years, the development that resulted in many of the problems described below occurred around the years 2000/2001. Rumours quickly spread about stunning hidden problems and virgin rock, and many people wasted days wandering over the moor with only vague descriptions to guide them, without finding anything.

When the initial rush for first ascents finished, and everyone came clean about what had been done, it transpired that many problems had been climbed and claimed more than once, and many of the amazing walls/ribs/arêtes turned out to be the same problems with different descriptions. Indeed there are not a lot of problems here, but one of the rumours was true - a few of these elusive little gems are truly great.

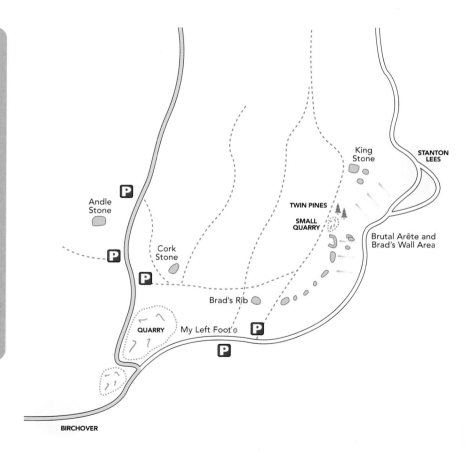

The Andle Stone

The Andle Stone is situated on the left-hand side of the road, just after the main parking for Stanton Moor, in a copse of rhododendrons in the middle of a cow field and is currently guarded by a big bull. The problems are described anti-clockwise, starting from just left of the handy rungs.

1. *7c*
Climb the wall just left of the rungs and right of the next problem. It's a bit squeezed in and the grade depends on which holds you allow yourself. If you keep a very tight line it is 7c+. Reachy. *(Ron Fawcett)*

2. *7b*
The steep slab right of the arête is a real classic in the same mould as L'Impossible at Roche aux Sabots, Fontainebleau. Technical moves gain good crimps in the middle of the wall, after which the crux trends up and right on poor holds to the top. Don't veer left to the arête.

3. *6b*
The arête climbed on the right.

4. *6b+*
The arête climbed on the left.

5. *6c+*
A big reach from jugs gains the sloping top. Those under 6' will find this much harder.

6. *5*
Traverse leftwards under the roof, and then move up to a slopey top.

7. *4*
Crack and wall.

8. *4+*
The arête.

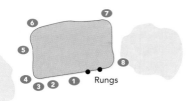

The Cork Stone

Park on the road just before the Andle Stone (as approached from Birchover) and cross the stile on the right. A path leads out onto the moor from here, and after 100m or so the Cork Stone becomes obvious on the left – an isolated pinnacle with yet more carved steps and rungs. The problems are described anti-clockwise, starting just left of the rungs.

1. **The Mammoth Book of UFOs** *7b*
   From a sit start under the arête left of the rungs (on poor rock – please take care and do not brush). *(Percy Bishton)*

2. *6c*
   The arête on the right-hand side.

3. *6a*
   The arête on the left-hand side is very good.

   5+
   The rest of the boulder consists of yet more arêtes. Climbed on their left, or on their right, they are all around 5+.

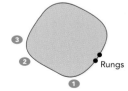

Jon Barton on The Mammoth Book of UFOs: *Rupert Davies* ▲

Brad's Rib Block

Obvious coming from the road, but hidden from view as approached from the Cork Stone.

1. **Mike Tyson** *7b+*
   The wall, climbed from sitting via double fist jams in the cheese-grater break - much more painful than having the top of your ear bitten off. *(Justin Critchlow)*

2. **Brad's Rib** *7a+*
   The arête is technical, but the main difficulty is in topping out. It is the same grade from sitting. *(John Bradbury)*

3. *6a+*
   The wall to the right of the arête.

My Left Foot

An isolated but convenient problem, just next to the first path to be found on the left if you take the right-hand turn at the top of the hill after leaving Birchover. *See overview map for location.*

1. **My Left Foot** *6b*
   The vague arête and hanging scoop/crack. A nice little find. 6c from a sit-down start. *(Lucy Atkinson)*

Brad's Rib: *Rupert Davies* ▲

Brutal Arête Area

Following the path along the edge of the moor, many blocks are visible on the right. These are good fun to play on but there are no problems of note. Instead, continue along the path until two pine trees are reached on the right. In front of these is a small hidden quarry. With the quarry on your left, walk to the edge of the moor and start dropping down the slope – hidden in the hillside is the stunning Brutal Arête.

1. **Brutal Arête** *7b*
   A beautiful piece of rock, an elegant arrangement of ribs that fades out into a rainbow of shockwaves. A technical sequence on sidepulls up the ribs is made more tenuous by poor footholds until all holds disappear and only the final jump to the top remains - with the floor way below. Highball. Often mistakenly called Spare Rib. *(Jason Myers)*

2. *6b*
   Around the corner to the right, on the next block along, is a mini prow. Climb the front face using both arêtes.

3. *7a*
   Climb the arête on the left from a sitting start.

   Directly down the slope below Brutal Arête is a cluster of boulders containing some good problems.

4. **Wonder Bra** *6c*
   Climb the left arête from a sit start and rock onto the wall. *(Lucy Atkinson)*

5. **Big Brother** *7a+*
   The highball arête – get a good spot. Sit start. *(Percy Bishton)*

6. **The Cresta Run** *7b*
   A very low problem. Sit start under the arête and cross the wall on slopers and a tiny undercut to finish up Little Brother. *(Percy Bishton)*

7. **Little Brother** *6b+*
   Climb the arête from a sit start.

8. **The Toboggan Run** *5+*
   Climb the middle of the wall from a sitting start. *(Percy Bishton)*

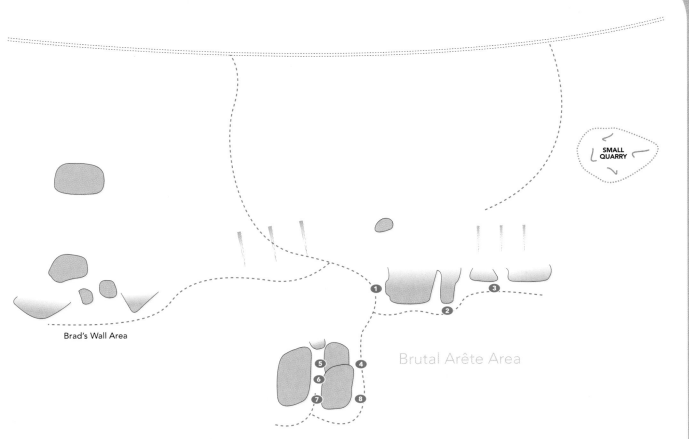

Brad's Wall Area

SMALL QUARRY

Brutal Arête Area

Brad's Wall Area

A pair of small, clean buttresses 30m right of Brutal Arête (looking into the valley) give some more good problems.

1. *6a*
   Climb the short wall on undercuts, to a hard top-out.

2. *5*
   Climb the wall from the low break – nice.

3. **Brad's Wall**   *7c*
   The wall left of the arête, climbed from a sitting start, is a mini classic. Sadly the foothold is crumbling - please be careful. *(John Bradbury)*

The slabby boulder below has two very good problems:

Chicken Ninja   *6a*
Very smeary padding up centre of the slab. *(Yan Thompson)*

Chicken Ginger   *7a*
Steep right arête. *(Jon Fullwood)*

Rupert Davies on Brad's Wall: *Stuart Littlefair* ▲

The King Stone

Continue along the path across the top of the moor above Brutal Arête, and The King Stone soon becomes obvious on the right, easily identifiable by a plaque carved into the boulder.

1. **The Plaque** 6c/7a+
   Climb the arête starting from undercuts in the roof.
   7a+ if the cracks on the left are eliminated. (Al Williams)

2. **The Green Man** 7b+
   Jump out right from the plaque itself to a sloper, then up.
   (John Welford)

   6c+
   Classic break-to-top dyno on wall 10m behind and to the right, as you look at the Plaque.

   Some good easy problems are to be found round the back of this block.

Rupert Davies on Brutal Arête: *Stuart Littlefair* ▶

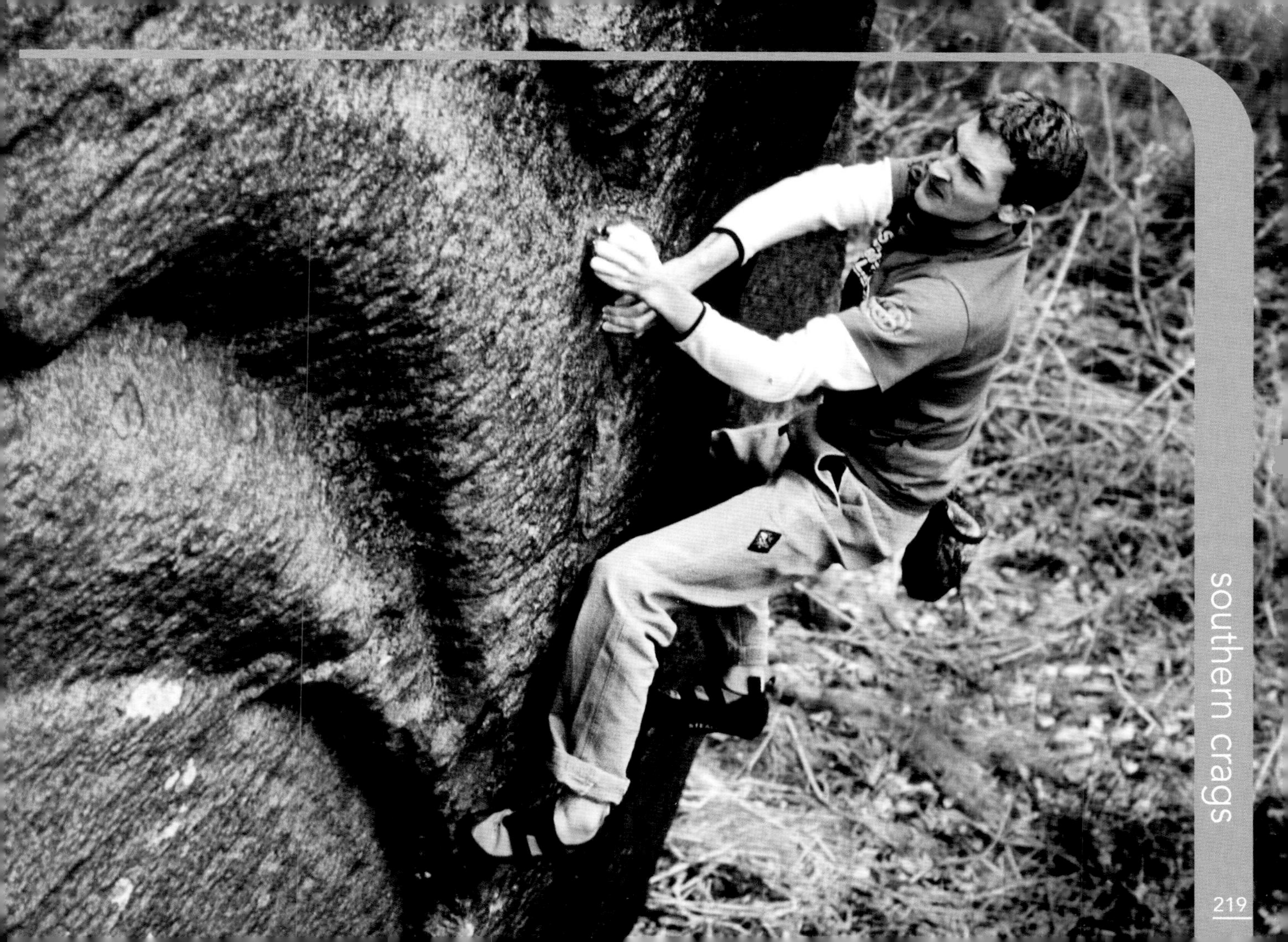

western
crags

Matthew Coutts ▲

churnet valley

The Churnet gets less esoteric with every new guidebook,
and should really be a prime venue on any Peak boulderer's map.
Lovely crags on two sides of a river; easy walking from the car park
on good tracks; a strange café where seemingly everything is for sale
(and some of the tables are in garden sheds) and pockets of sound
where the quiet is punctuated every 10 seconds by screams from the
nearby Alton Towers. The climbing is brilliant – a number of classic
long traverses and good up-problems that range from the very easy
to the kinda hard. The rock in the Churnet is a sandstone
conglomerate – some of which is fantastic, with solid pebbles,
nice flakes and deep pockets - but in other parts it's like flapjack.

Happily, almost all of the bouldering takes place on the former sort.

The Virgin Wall Traverse: *Sarah Davies* ▲

Access and Approach

From the village of Alton take the Red Road (to be found ⋯
pub if you take the first right after the bridge, after passing th⋯
entrance to Alton Towers) and park at the Rambler's Retreat café ⋯
the left. Follow the track behind the café into the dale – then see
approaches for the individual crags.

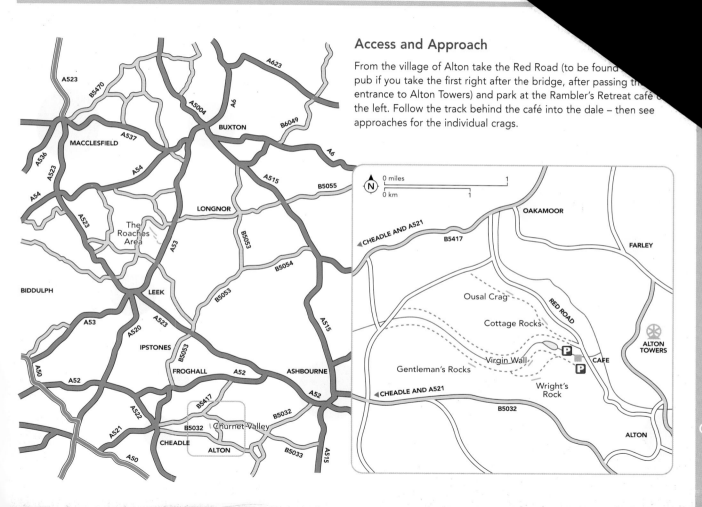

...-hand
...at Cafe,
... about half
... this track
...couple of zig
...little spot
...sy problems on
.... The trees offer
...and the right-
...s steep enough to
stay dry in sno...

The first problems are situated on a small buttress 10m right – Pine Buttress. All the problems start low to make the most of the good rock and then stop about 4 moves higher in flapjack land.

1. **Left Pine** *6c*
   Start on the obvious flake hold and pull through the bulge.

2. **Pine Wall** *6a+*
   The central groove feature from sitting.

3. **Right Pine** *6b+*
   Vying with the foliage a bit here. Move right from the same start as Pine Wall.

The quality climbing at Cottage Rocks starts 10m further left, set just above the path.

1. 5
   The wide crack at the right-hand side of the buttress.

2. **The Wafer** 5+
   The initially fingery wall using the wafer feature. 6a from a sit start.

3. **Pocket Wall** 5
   The central line up pockets, with a final move to the break using the big square pebble. A sit start is 6b.

4. 5+
   Pull up pockets right of the arête.

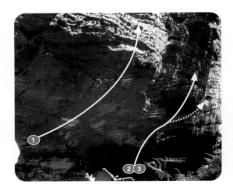

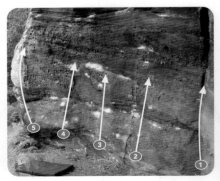

5. Tufa *5+*
Use the pinchy feature on the arête.

6. Sapling Bulge *6b+*
Climb just left of the arête, using the fingery ramp feature for your left.

7. *6b*
The line just left using the finger ramp for your right hand.

8. *5+*
The wall just left to a hole.

9. Sid the Sexist *4*
Slab and pockets.

10. Crusty *3+*
The cracks.

11. Billy Bunter *4+*
Use the big pebble. A variant shares the same finish from a start just left.

6c
A right to left traverse starting at the crack on the right, then heading round the corner to finish up Billy Bunter.

Bizarre

12. Bizarre *7c*
Continuing up the path from Cottage Rocks to Ousal Crag, this is the obvious path-side steep wall. Bizarre is probably the hardest problem in the Churnet since some holds broke.

Sit start on the flake, lurch up for the crimp in the break and then slap for the top. The move to the break goes static - and the last move to the top is a heartbreaker.

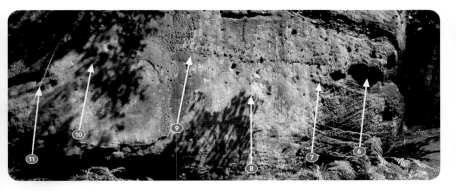

Ousal Crag

A crag covered in pebbles with two more Churnet-style classic traverses and a couple of up problems.

Continue up the path from Cottage Rocks, passing Bizarre on the right - Ousal crag is up in the trees on the right.

1. **Ousal Low**   *7a*
   The low traverse, starting on the blunt arête on the right then traversing left and finishing by pulling up to the jugs above the bulge at the left end.

2. **Ousal High**   *6b*
   The higher traverse line is good too.

3. *5*
   Reach the end of the traverse line through the bulge from a low start.

4. *4*
   The vague arête.

5. *4*
   The blunt arête at the start of the traverse.

Long Wall/Virgin Wall

From the left-hand track behind the café, continue until opposite a small bridge on the second leftwards bend. Scout up the hill as best you can and make for the rock.

Virgin/Long Wall Traverse   *6b+ - 7b*
An awesome traverse – at least 25m long I would have thought. The full thing – starting from the extreme right via technical pebble pulling, through the juggy central section, and regaining the higher pebble line to a redpoint crux continuing left to finish on the ledge is 7b. The central section alone is 6b+ (normally done from the large tree on the left), and the central section plus the excellent puzzling sequence along the higher pebble line at the left-hand end is 7a.

Gentleman's Rock

Continue on the left-hand track, around a series of bends until opposite the first small waterfall. Gentleman's Rock can be seen in the trees on the left.

1. **Jill the Traverse** *6b*
The low-level traverse line to the central crack. It's not as good as the other long traverses in Dimmings Dale as it's just a line of crimps with big footholds on often damp rock. Finishing up The Nose is better and harder at 7a.

2. *6c*
From the juggy ledge, climb the vague arête using a high pocket.

3. *6c*
A big reach from the traverse line to the two-finger pocket in the middle of the damp green crud, and a big lock to jugs.

4. **Gentleman John** *6b*
Steep finger crack nastiness. Finish at the high jugs.

5. **High Speed Imp Act** *7a+*
From low edges attack the leaning wall with final committing lobs between good pockets. Finish on the high jugs.
(Martin Veale)

6. **The Nose** *6c*
Start low and climb the good edges/slots through the steepness. Can be started from the very low shelf on the right for an extra grade.

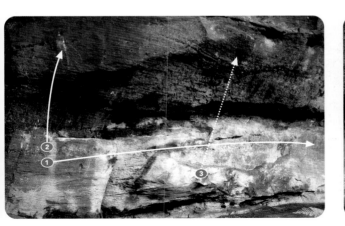

Wright's Rock

Whereas the other crags are enclosed in the trees, Wright's Rock overlooks an open meadow above the valley. Wright's offers a good burly traverse and lots of powerful problems that cross steep bulges. Grades from 4 – 7b+.

North-facing, the crag gets no sun. It stays dry in the rain and is great in hot weather, but the lower section of rock can become green after damp periods – such conditions will also bring out the midges.

Take the left branch of the track behind the café, then take a smaller track that scouts up and left into the trees after about 50m. The track comes out into a meadow, from where Wright's Rock can be seen up on the left.

Just left of the main crag is a pebbly wall in a niche – a left to right traverse is 6a.

The Main Crag

1. **The Traverse** *7b*
   From the niche on the left, to finish up problem 11. Jugs, pockets and plenty of steep, positive pulling.

2. **Thorns** *4+*
   Climb jugs up the left side of the niche.

3. *6a+*
   Climb direct up the wall of the niche and through the roof on sidepull flakes. Very good. An extension – Fireman Indirect – continues traversing right to gain the curving ramp.

4. **Simple Simon** *7b*
   Gain the jug on the lip (jump, or climb from the back – 6b in its own right, but no increase in overall grade) and continue with steep pulls on reasonable crimps and flatties to gain the curving flake. 7b - but this may be in part due to the unnerving height. *(Andy Brown)*

5. *7b+*
   From big pockets under the roof reach over to a two finger pocket and traverse left on edges into Simple Simon and finish up this.

6. Fingers *7b*
The nose/arête/prow just right.
Gain good holds over the lip and
continue on slopes and edges to the
break. High.

7. Alternative Three *6b*
Good, steep, juggy pulling through the
bulges just right, then cross the roof
using the flake underneath it to finish at
the break.

8. The Undercut *7a*
Good pockets get you established on
the pinchy undercut, from where a
powerful pull gets you established on
the blocky pinch above – unfortunately
that's it.

9. *7a*
Another good problem that again
finishes too soon. Cross the bulge on
awkward diagonal crimps to share the
sloping break (in control) then drop off.
The grade is correct for cunning
sequence meisters.

10. *5+*
The little groove just right.

11. *6a*
Pulling through the square bulge.

12. The Crack *7a*
Gain the crack from a sit start using
slopers and climb it to a dirty top-out.
The grade may drop with a cleaner top.
An eliminate – No Crack, 7b+ - climbs
the same line without the crack. Lots of
mauling with one of the most aesthetic
slopers in the Peak.

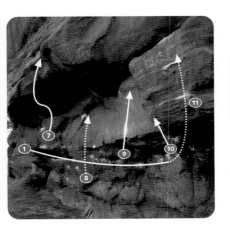

The Undercut: *Sarah Davies* ▲

newstones
& baldstones

Newstones and Baldstones are really two parts of an intermittent line of outcrops spanning along a secluded ridge. Combined, they make a good day out. On their own the Newstones have a great selection of easy problems and a couple of highball frighteners that make it a good evening venue or a nice place to warm up if you are planning on progressing to some fierceness elsewhere. The eliminate potential is massive, so the problems listed are the most independent lines only.

The landings are flat and grassy at both venues and the rock is of good quality. All grit is prone to local peculiarities and Newstones has got a sprinkling of weird veins and protruding armour plate things that makes much of the climbing that bit different and interesting. However, under the hard skin, the rock around here is very soft, so please brush any problems with great care or preferably not at all.

Both areas are exposed to adverse weather along the ridge. Both areas dry fast, but the Fielder's Wall area of the Baldstones can get a bit green if it's been wet or after an access restriction, especially on the top-outs. Nine times out of ten, however, it's fine.

The rocks to the east of the Baldstones ridge area an important wildlife area so no climbing please.

…and remember no wire brushing.

◀ Harry Pennells on Ripple: *Adam Long*

Access and Approach

Park in the lay-by opposite the house and take the small path that runs to the right of the house along to the crag. The house owner is very tolerant of climbers, so please behave. There may be occasional access restrictions on this estate due to nesting birds – please respect any bans. Also please note that the land between the Baldstones and Gib Torr is a protected SSSI, so please do not walk directly between the two.

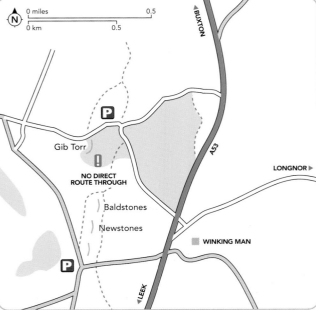

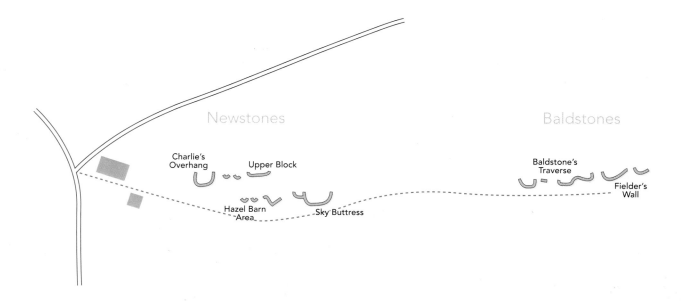

Newstones

Baldstones

Charlie's
Overhang

Upper Block

Baldstone's
Traverse

Fielder's
Wall

Hazel Barn
Area

Sky Buttress

Charlie's Overhang

When walking along the path past the house, this is the large overhang that is encountered on the first block.

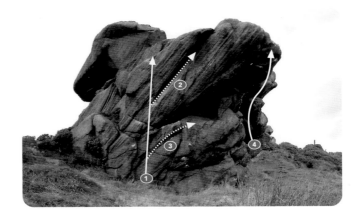

1. **S & M** *7a+*
   The flake/cracks up the left side of the wall lead to a very distressing top-out. Finish direct to get 7a+. Only 6c if you cop out leftwards.

2. **Leather Joy Boys** *7b*
   Start up S & M and grimly slope or jam rightwards along the break. Or climb something pleasant instead. Strictly speaking you don't get the tick if you do this though. *(Mark Stokes)*

3. **Little Traverse** *6a*
   Starting at the same point as S&M, traverse rightwards on rounded holds until they stop. Finish as you like.

4. **Charlie's Overhang** *6b*
   The big roof direct. It's easy until you think you're at the top.
   (Tony Barley)

5. **Moonshine** *6a*
   The steep wall right of the crack right of Charlie's.

6. **Praying Mantel Sit Start** *6c*
   Sit start the little low prow.

7. **Wraparound Arête** *6c*
   The steep undercut arête.

Upper Block

A low, rounded barrel of rock above
and right of Charlie's Overhang
contains a concentration of fun sit starts.
The problems all take independent
lines but are quite tightly packed.

1. *6a*
Sit start, the steep left face.

2. *5+*
Sit start the arête on the left side.

3. *6a*
Sit start, and climb the wall using
slopers and mono just right of the arête.

4. Varicose *6a+*
Sit start the vein feature.

5. The Grinding Sloper *5*
Sit start the wall on slopers right
of Varicose.

*The slabs to the right have some nice
easy problems on them, all around the
3s – 4s, with the right arête being a nice
5+. A decent traverse also starts just
right of problem 5, does a 'Ben's
Extension' drop down onto the sloping
shelf and then traverses left to finish up
any of the above problems.*

Hazel Barn Area

The outcrops below the Upper Block have yet more good easy stuff and one Staffordshire classic.

1. **Left Twin Arête** *3+*
   Arête of the left-most (looking up) of the three blocks beneath the Upper Block, climbed on the left-hand side.

2. **Right Twin Arête** *3+*
   The arête on the next block to the right.

3. **Flake Slab** *4+*
   The slab just right gives delicate padding. A sit start is a nice 6b.

4. **Ripple** *6b*
   The aesthetic ripple/vein feature gives a superb problem. Totally classic.

5. **Martin's Traverse** *5*
   The rightwards trending lower break. If you climb until halfway before breaking out up the wall above it is 6b.
   (Martin Boysen)

6. **Crack and Arête** *6a+*
   The overhanging flake/crack to a final rock onto the slab to the right.

   There are two routes on the face to the right (to the immediate left of the next problem). These are Hazel Barrow Crack (HS) and Hazel Barn (S). Although these are routes, they are also good highballs at 4+.

7. **Hazel Groove** *6b*
   The nice looking slopey scallops are slightly tricky to climb.

8. **Nutmeg** *4+*
   The armour plate jugs. Highball.

9. **Nutmeg Groove** *5+*
   The slight groove right of Nutmeg.

10. *5+*
   From a low start on the shelf pull up to the hanging arête.

Scratch Buttress

Just left of Sly Buttress is this scarred collection of problems. Preventing further damage may involve not climbing them.

1. *5+*
   The eliminate left wall.

2. **Scratch Crack** *4*
   The crack. The 'sitter' is 6b off an undercut.

3. *6c*
   Climb the steep arête trending left from a sit start on the right, below the start to the next problem. A bit squeezed in.

4. **Itchy Groove** *6b*
   The groove is a bit tricky.

5. **Itchy Fingers** *6a*
   The thin slab on the right, approached from slightly right.

6. **Bridget** *3+*
   The set back slab on the right.

Sly Buttress

7. **Stallone Arête** *6c+*
   A classic steep trip on big fat slopers up the left arête.

8. **Sly Stallone** *6b+*
   Dyno from the finger holds to the top. 7a if you don't stand on the ramp. An extension starts up this and traverses left to finish up the arête – Char's Traverse, 7b.

9. **The Sly Mantelshelf** *5*
   Traverse the vein from the left and mantel it at its highest point. Finish up the slab above.

10. **Sly Super Direct** *5+*
    Gain the centre of the daddy vein using the mini vein that has sprouted beneath.

11. **Captain Quark** *6c+*
    Just right, use two small ripples to reach a blind pocket and thus the vein.
    (Rupert Davies/Jon Barton)

There's more stuff around the back if you're keen but the best bet at this stage is to walk onwards to Baldstones.

Jason Pickles on Charlie's Overhang: *Adam Long* ▲

Baldstones

Continue along the ridge from Newstones and you will reach the Baldstones. Do the classic Elephant's Ear, get pumped on the traverse, puzzle about how to climb Fielder's Wall with its single hold and try the classic arête Clever Skin until your fingers bleed. It's also traditional to muse at how Ray Jardine climbed Ray's Roof and deemed it to be only 5.11c, but that's not mandatory. Yet more good landings.

1. **Baldstones Traverse**   *7a+*
   A right to left traverse from the corner along the rail. Dip lower at the end, then pull up to big chips. A couple of good hard, low eliminate variations have been done at 7b+.

2. *6b+*
   Dyno from jugs on the rail to the holds above.

◀ The Baldstones Traverse: **Matthew Coutts**

Fielder's Wall

The undercut block left of Fielder's Wall and right of Ray's Roof has a little arête climbed on the right-hand side. On the left-hand side it's a totally artificial 7a+, but the project lip traverse into it looks quite good.

1. **Ganderhole Crack**   *4+*
   The crack.

2. **Fielder's Indirect**   *5*
   The wall on pockets after negotiating the rib.

3. **Fielder's Corner**   *6b*
   Classic cunningness up the groove. Or just yard on the mono.

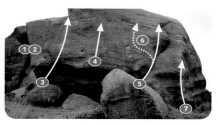

4. **Fielder's Wall**   *7a+*
   Use the large pocket (and the small pebble) to climb the wall.

5. **Elephant's Ear**   *4*
   The super-chunky flake. If you prefer to start from sitting it's 6c.

6. **Elephant's Eye**   *6b+*
   From the (super) flake reach left into the (nice) pockets.

7. **Clever Skin**   *7a*
   The classic arête is not very dermatologically friendly. Recent pebble snappage has made the starting pebble cluster much worse, much more painful and the problem is now much harder than it was and much less fun.
   (Martin Boysen but named by The Dawes)

It's unsure whether the wall to the right has been climbed. Rumour still points to an ascent by The Dawes.

The 'bun' shaped bit of rock on the right has a couple of problems on it, but they're all a bit pointless. There is also more bouldering on some roofs further right. They stay dry in the rain, but this is really their best feature. Problems from 4 – 6b can be contrived.

gib torr

Given its small size, this fine nugget of grit is home to a disproportionate number of great problems. Many of these problems climb strong independent lines on fantastic features and grades range from 4+ - 7c+. The crag is shady for most of the day and is rarely green.

John Cook on The Fin: *Alex Messenger* ▲

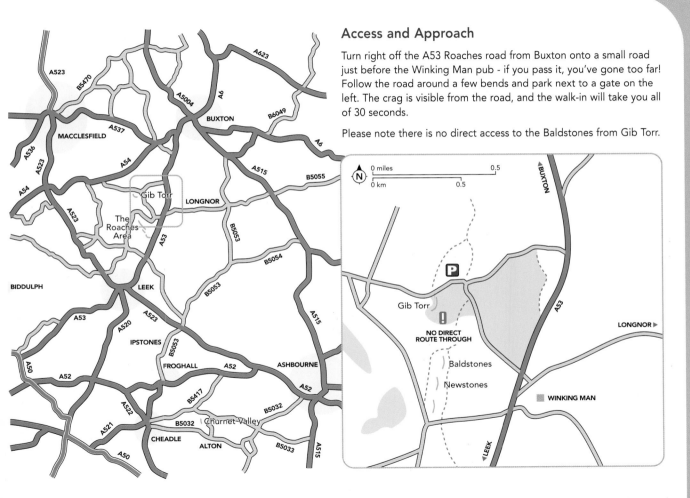

Access and Approach

Turn right off the A53 Roaches road from Buxton onto a small road just before the Winking Man pub - if you pass it, you've gone too far! Follow the road around a few bends and park next to a gate on the left. The crag is visible from the road, and the walk-in will take you all of 30 seconds.

Please note there is no direct access to the Baldstones from Gib Torr.

western crags

The Lower Tier

1. **Gibbering Wreck** *7b*
The massive roof on top of the tor is a highball classic. The big span out from a flake to a pocket over the lip gives the problem a passing resemblance to 'Big Boss' (but without Bruce Lee on a quest for justice and revenge). It was first soloed at E6, but it is now relatively safe with pads and spotters, so long as you miss the sign below. *(Andy Brown)*

   Left Fin *4+*
Climb the big holds in the sidewall left of the Fin.

2. **The Fin** *6c*
The undercut arête has a tricky move to gain the rounded, gritty top.

3. *7b*
The sit start to The Fin is superb. Start on a pair of low pockets and hug your way up the steep prow.

4. **The Fink** *7a+*
Climb the featured wall right of The Fin on big rounded slopers to the same gritty top-out. The sit start is a tough 7b.

5. *5*
The wall to the right of The Fink is lovely, but the landing isn't.

6. **Gibbering Left** *6b*
In a small scoop on the left side of the large overhanging prow is an ergonomic finger hold. Hang this and slap up and left to finish.

7. **Gibbering Right** *6c+*
A right-hand variation starting from the same finger hold. An extension continues rightwards along the lip at 7a+.

8. **Gibby Haines** *6b+*
Lunge upwards from an uncomfortable pocket and a sloper to gain the big rail and then top-out directly above.

9. **Stayin' Alive** *7b*
A fierce sitting start to Gibby Haines using a selection of sharp edges and painful pockets. Start on the large sidepull pocket under the overhang. *(John Welford)*

10. **Maurice Gibb** *7c+*
A massive (double) dyno finish to Gibby Haines. From the rail on Gibby Haines launch up and leftwards to land a jug just below the top. *(Pat Rainbird)*

11. **Porridge Wall** *5+*
From a low start on a finger jug head for a pocket above.

12. **Martin's Problem** *6b*
From a low start on a large hold, climb the wall above on pleasant ripples. *(Martin Boysen)*

13. **Stall** *7a*
The perfect sharp arête is climbed on the left-hand side. A technical classic. *(Martin Boysen)*

    Stall Sit Start *7c*
The sit start adds a series of dynamic and powerful slaps onto the original problem. Start matched on the finger jug left of the arête - the foot ramp is not to be used.

14. **Little Traverse** *5*
Traverse the lip of the little cave from left to right from sitting.

    Up and right from the main bulk of the lower tier is a small green wall with two rarely climbed problems.

    Gary's 5c *5+*
Climb the arête.

    Seams Green *6a+*
Climb up small holds on the wall to the right.

ramshaw

One of the fiercest looking crags in the Peak District; a series of battleship prows moored against the prevailing wind. Varied climbing on character-building rock rewards the visitor and the bouldering is significantly better than the crag's apparent lack of popularity would suggest. Much of the climbing can be described as 'real bouldering'- although the landings are generally grassy, there is no guarantee of a friendly camber. Ramshaw is not the home of the one-move wonder, several of the classic problems are seriously high, but a good mat will generally offer enough security. A hard circuit here is a good test of all round climbing ability and will feature slabs, offwidths, power pulls, even the odd E5 - all to be found scattered along the edge.

The crag dries quickly and catches the early morning sun, but it also gets a good amount of shade. The varied aspect of the many scattered problems usually guarantees something will be in condition. Don't be put off by the greenness, Don Whillans wouldn't have been.

◀ Sarah Harrison on Ossie's Bulge: *Ray Wood*

Access and Approach

From Buxton, drive under the obvious spikey crag overlooking the A53, turn right just after the crag, and park in a lay-by just over the brow. Paths lead up opposite the lay-by and along the top of the crag.

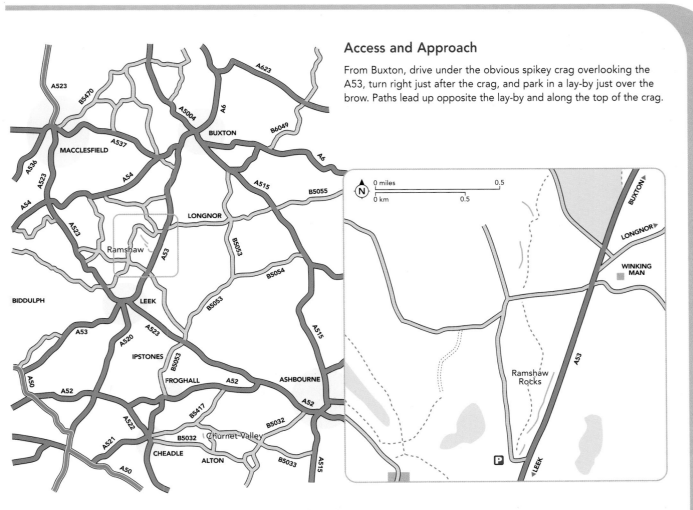

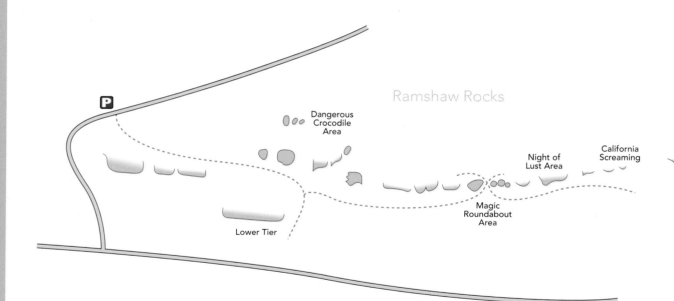

Ramshaw Rocks

Dangerous Crocodile Area

California Screaming

Night of Lust Area

Lower Tier

Magic Roundabout Area

Lucy Creamer on Cracked Arête: *Ray Wood* ▲

Dangerous Crocodile Area

Good quality bouldering, masquerading as a circuit. The problems lie to the right of the track. There are a few easy warm-ups scattered around the main challenges.

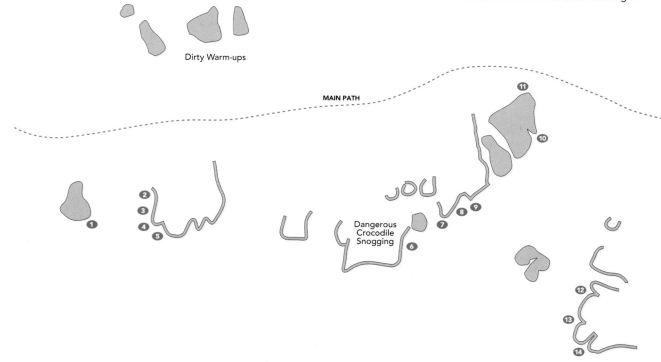

Dirty Warm-ups

MAIN PATH

Dangerous Crocodile Snogging

1. **Little Prow** *6c*
Situated on the isolated block in front of Ram Air. From the shelf make a tricky move onto the arête and then gain the top, easy when you know how. The arête to the left is a good warm-up.

2. **The Scoop** *4*
The easiest way up this superb block.

3. **The Lurch** *6b+*
From the flake swing left then up, via a hidden dish.

4. **Ossie's Bulge** *6b+*
Starting from the flake, climb straight up finishing left or, slightly harder, direct to a tricksome mantel.

5. **Ram Air** *7b+*
One of the classics of the crag. Climb up and left onto that rounded arête. The landing is definitely a 'two matter'. *(John Welford)*

6. **Elastic Wall** *6c*
Bounce up from the sidepull crimp to the top - hard for the short.

7. **The Arête** *6a*
Climb the arête on either side, the right-hand side being harder.

8. **5c Wall** *6a*
Climb the crimps. It's harder if you static it.

9. **Baby Groove** *Easy*
A pleasant groove.

10. **Hanging Crack** *5*
Why?

11. **Classic Mantel** *5*
Very short and very awkward.

12. **Johnny's Groove**
While we were able to repeat the first ascensionist's bizarre sequence, we were not able to grade it. Jump into a bridge position, top-out. Simple, although the starting hold has now broken.

13. **Crocodile Slot** *5*
It's an off width, and a bit high as well – nuff said!

14. **Right Slot** *5*
Another horror.

Magic Roundabout Boulders

The routes on the front of this buttress all have boulder problem starts for the confident. A very good bouldering area.

1. **Force Nine** *7a*
   Said to be E4 to the top, but a superb slab problem to the flake. *(Simon Nadin)*

2. **Be Calmed Right-Hand** *6c+*
   Gain the scoop from the right.

3. **Be Calmed** *6b+*
   From the arête swing right and mantel into the scoop. *(Richie Patterson)*

4. **Magic Arête** *4*
   A good problem.

5. **The Finger** *3*
   If you must.

6. **Jamless** *5*
   Much harder if you jam this perfect crack.

7. **Arête On Left** *7a*
   Quite high, the grade is for the gritty finale. Several mantelshelf problems exist to the left.

8. **Epilogue** *7a*
   Another hard and relatively high Ramshaw classic.

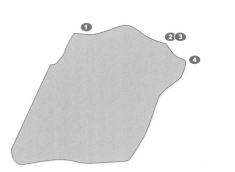

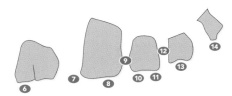

9. The Rammer 5
The best easy problem on grit? Don't get stuck, and let someone know where you are going.

10. Monologue 7c
Climb the very hard arête. *(Andi Turner)*

11. The Pinches 6a
Superb arête on great holds.

12. Practice Chimney 2+
Not one of grit's best problems.

13. Dialogue 7b+
Hug the rock to glory. Stunning.
(Andi Turner)

14. Cracked Arête 5
A warm-up, or a warm-down.

Across the grassy gully, under a large pinnacle lies a steep compact wall.

15. Press Direct 6b
Twin seams to a bounce to the base of the groove, finishing in the crack. 7a from sitting.

16. Lust Left-Hand 7b
Climb the crimpy handrail rightwards to the niche.

17. Night of Lust Start 6c
Start low and head up to the niche. Classic.

18. Runnel Entry 7a
From the same low start as previously mentioned, head up and right.

19. California Screaming 7b
The very compact arête just under the next buttress. Hard climbing, getting high for its finale. *(Tom Briggs)*

Shark's Fin 3
Steep fun 25m up and right of the last problem.

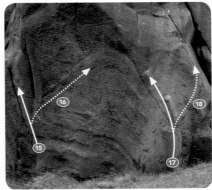

The Lower Tier

Classic rain-proof bouldering

Three problems exist on the undercut left-hand section.

Sensible Shoes 4
Cross the roof.

Crab Walk Direct 6a
The short hanging crack.

Roof Direct 6c
Climb the roof.

1. **Hemline** 7a
   A long traverse with some hard bits. Start on the left and head right under Colly Wobble, finishing just right of Tierdrop.

2. **Tit Grip** 7c+
   Dyno for the top off the, in some people's opinion, nipples, which keep breaking – ouch! *(Paul Higginson)*

3. **Tierdrop** 7a+
   Stunning. Climb up over the roof then lay one on for the good break. Sam's Left-Hand reaches left from the runnel to a slot then the top, 7b.
   (Nick Longland) (Sam's Left-Hand, Sam Whittaker)

S Harrison on Magic Arête: *R Wood* ▲

Ben Moon on Tierdrop: *Ray Wood* ▶

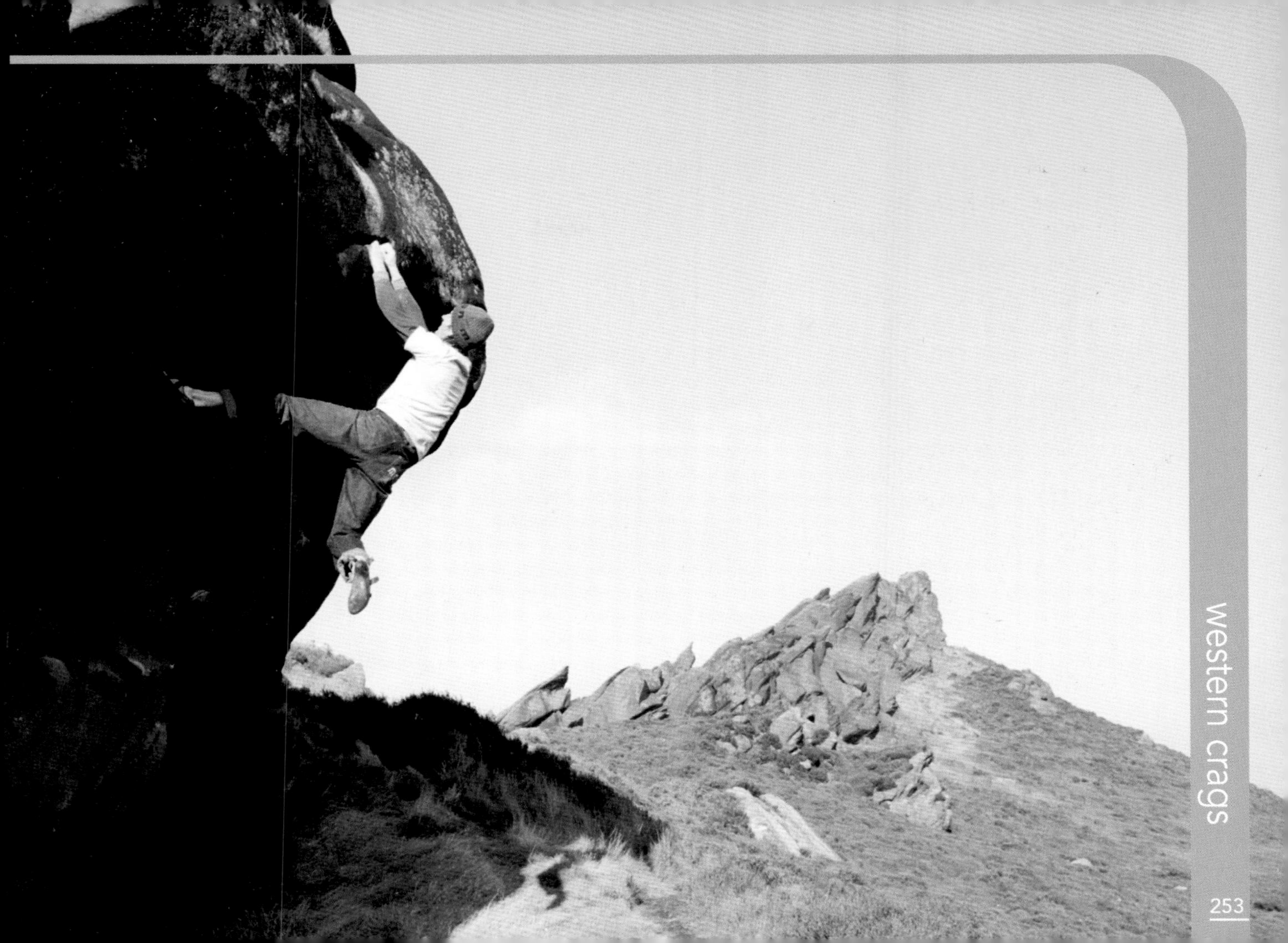

the roaches

The Roaches has some of the best routes and bouldering in the world. The climbing is spread out over a vast area and caters for all grades and all styles. With blank slabs on perfect grit, fine arêtes, proud flakes, beautiful fingertip ripple features, scallops, steep walls, roofs and the best traverse-line on grit, the Roaches has it all.

The moorland surrounding the Roaches is environmentally very important. Please keep to paths, and your dog under control, particularly on the Skyline and Clouds.

Katie Clough on a Roaches slab: *Stu Littlefair* ▲

Access and Approach

The Roaches lie behind Upper Hulme, just off the A53 between Leek and Buxton. Turn off the A53 towards Upper Hulme and drive through the village passing a ford and the factory. The road now winds uphill passing the Roaches Tea Rooms on the left and the imposing bulk of Hen Cloud on the right. There is a lot of designated parking beneath the crag, but this fills up fast, so please park considerately.

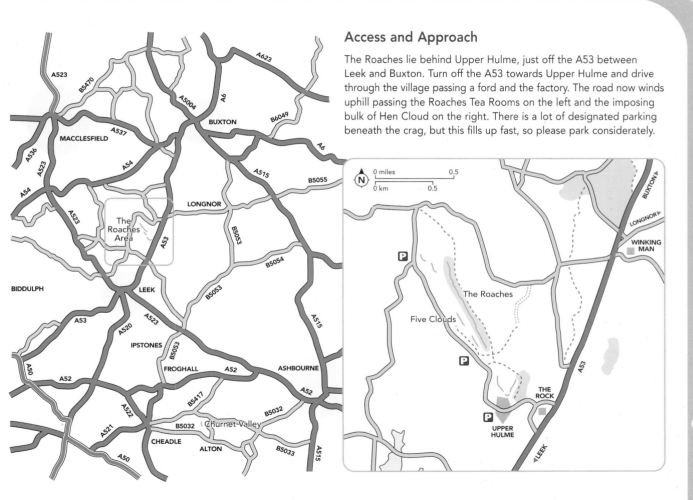

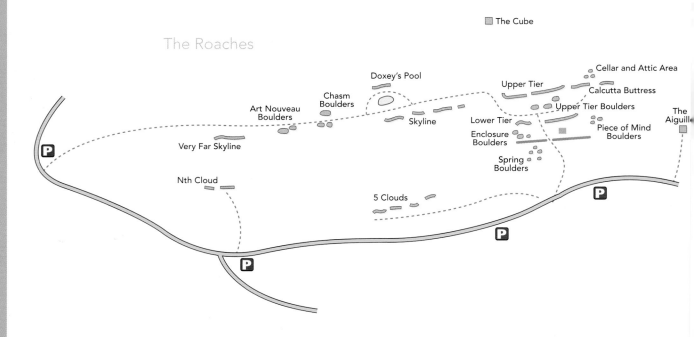

The Roaches

The Cube

Cellar and Attic Area

Doxey's Pool

Upper Tier

Calcutta Buttress

Chasm Boulders

Art Nouveau Boulders

Skyline

Upper Tier Boulders

The Aiguille

Lower Tier

Piece of Mind Boulders

Very Far Skyline

Enclosure Boulders

Spring Boulders

Nth Cloud

5 Clouds

P

P

P

P

P

Rupert Davies on The Inertia Reel Traverse: *Stu Littlefair* ▲

C3PO: *Sarah Davies* ▲

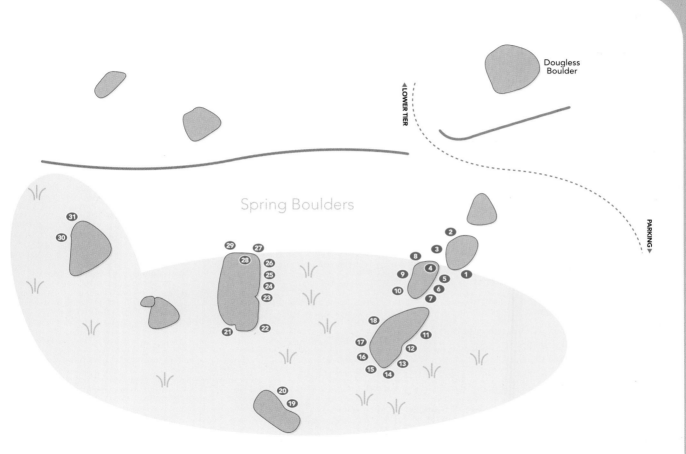

Dougless Boulder

Spring Boulders

Spring Boulders

The spring boulders offer a great selection of 'easy angled' problems that climb scoops, slabs and arêtes on rough, pebbly rock. They are open of aspect, quick to dry, close to the car and are surrounded by semi-permanent bog.

1. **Spring Roll** 4+
   The arête on the right-hand side.

2. **Slabby Seam** 3

3. *3*
   The blunt arête.

The next boulder is probably the best in this circuit. It not only has a fantastic array of smearing slab test-pieces that get gradually harder, but you can also walk up to it without sinking.

4. **Bobarête** 7a
   The big, bald arête is directly above an ankle-snapping hole that contains a spring. Which rather spoils it.

5. **Boba Fett** 7b+
   This is perhaps the hardest smearing problem in this guide. Ultra tenuous moves climb the slab left of the bald arête (without using it).

6. **C3PO** 7a
   The central line on the slab gives more faith-in-friction climbing, with only the odd pebble for assistance.

7. *6c*
   The left line on the slab is easier than the other two, but it is still delicate and requires clean technique.

8. **Easy Wall** 3

9. *5*
   From a sit start, climb the flake.

10. *4+*
    Climb the arête on the left-hand side.

11. **Scoops** 5+
    The scoops to the top. Graded for climbing using rock shoes and not wellies, but I know which I'd wear.

12. **Pebbles and Seam** 6a

13. **Pebbly Wall** 6c
    Hard pebble-pulling above the quagmire.

14. *6b*
    Climb the arête on the right.

15. *3+*
    The left side of the arête and the scoops.

16. *3+*
    The wall from undercuts.

17. *4*
    Big holds left of the arête.

18. *3+*
    Climb the scooped slab. Nice climbing above an often-dry landing. The slabs to the left are also 3+.

19. *5+*
    The appealing scoop.

20. *6a*
    Gain the hole and then the top.

21. **Violence** 6a
    The scoop is harder than it looks, but it is very good.

22. **Impotence** 6a
    Climb the blunt arête to the right.

23. **Seconds Out** 6a
    Climb the offwidth crack.

24. **The Grind** 7a
    Undercut the holes to reach the sloping top.

25. Skinned Rabbit *6b*
An almost identical problem to The Grind, situated a few holes to the right. 7a from a sitting (in your dinghy) start.

26. *6c+*
Climb the arête on the left-hand side.

27. *6c*
Climb the arête on the right-hand side.

28. Mr Nice *6b+*
The blank wall is climbed using the chipped foothold.

29. *6c*
From the right arête enter the scoop on the left and climb it to the top. Climbing the arête all the way on the left is 6b.

30. The Lurch *6b*
Jump to the scoop and top-out.

31. The Fly *7a+*
Climb the steep prow from a low start on the flake. The landing under this problem is so waterlogged that it actually flows. Quite fast.

Andy Higginson on problem 7: *Alex Messenger* ▲

The Inertia Reel Traverse: *Rupert Davies* ▲

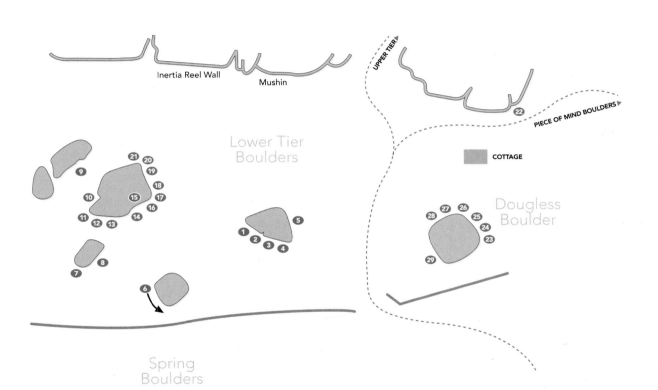

Inertia Reel Wall

Mushin

Lower Tier
Boulders

UPPER TIER

PIECE OF MIND BOULDERS

22

COTTAGE

Dougless
Boulder

9
21 20
19
18
10 15 17
16
11 14
12 13

5
1
2 3 4

28 27 26
25
24
23
29

7
8

6

Spring
Boulders

Lower Tier Boulders/
The Enclosure

The Lower Tier offers a classic circuit of easy slabs and arêtes on Velcro® rock, a few classic 7s and two stunning 'big numbers'. The trees can give shade in summer, but they also keep the boulders damp after rain. The Inertia Reel Wall and Mushin can both take seepage so finding them in condition can prove to be frustrating.

1. *4*
    Slab.

2. *3*
    Crack.

3. *4+*
    The slab right of the crack offers good smearing practice to help you get your gritstone head on.

4. *3+*
    The chips.

5. **The Flake** *4*
    'Nuff said.

6. **The Greener Traverse** *6b*
    Traverse down the ramp and slap back up to the rounded top. The crimpy sit start is 6b+ and the final slap up, on its own, is 6a.

7. *7a*
    Manteling onto the rounded top left of the left-hand arête is hard work.

Andy Higginson on The Big Dyno: *Rupert Davies/Alex Messenger* ▲

The Gutter: *Sarah Davies* ▲

8. *5 - 6b*
The obvious, independent problem up the front and using anything is 5. From a sit start on the jug left of centre it is 5+. Starting here but reaching left to the arête is 6a and, finally, starting here and going straight up eliminating the big undercut on the right is 6b.

9. *3 - 4+*
The slabby face is climbable everywhere, with all of the ways up being short and pleasant. The problems are all 3 or 3+ with the exception of the line just right of the centre, past a rounded feature, which is 4+.

10. *4*
The short slab.

11. *5*
Arête on the right-hand side.

12. Three Pocket Slab *6a*
The line of pockets up the otherwise blank slab is one of the best easy problems at the Roaches.

13. Parental Duties *7b*
The pebbly slab above the starting foot-pocket of the 6a. *(James Pearson)*

The ledge just right is more of a shrubbery than a boulder problem.

14. *3*
Climb the big flakes – the easiest way up.

15. *5*
The wall between the flakes and the diagonal crack is a bit worrying.

16. *4*
The diagonal crack and occasional plant.

17. Flake Crack *4*
The flaky crack perhaps?

18. Stretch and Mantel *6c*
Undercut up the wall. Congratulations, you've got your hands on the top, just the mantel to go then...

19. The Big Dyno *7a*
This cunningly named problem is a) a dyno, but more specifically, b) big. Also referred to as the Undercut Dyno because it starts on an undercut. Morpho. *(Richard Williams)*

20. Stretch Left *6a+*
Reach onto the finishing jug of the Big Dyno from the right arête and mantel. This problem is pretty much redundant since the Big Dyno was done.

21. Classic Arête *4+*
Big holds up the arête.

Right of the steps leading to the Upper Tier is the massive roof and prow of Valkyrie. At the bottom right of this prow is a small cave.

22. The Gutter *7a+*
From the back of the cave pull out to the lip and finish up the arête above. It would make a good sit start to the route Matinee.

The Dougless Boulder

The huge boulder in the grounds of the cottage is home to some big problems. They're all a bit green and a bit high, so it's unlikely that you'll be in a rush to do them.

23. Particle Exchange   *6c+*
Once an E6 getting on for E3, now, due to mats, it's a 6c+, getting on for E3. Climb the crack and tentatively step left to the arête. Highball.   *(Mark Katz)*

24. Dougless   *6b+*
Climb the crack and continue over the roundedness. Highball.

25. The Rumour...   *7b?*
...is that Simon Nadin climbed the rippled slab right of Dougless. He probably brushed it first.

26. Sketchy Rib   *6a*
The rib just right.

27. *3+*
Arête.

28. *6a*
Chips and flake up right.

29. Scratchy Scoop   *6a*
The scoop left of the big blunt arête, right of the carved steps, on the opposite side of the boulder (marked on the topo plan).

Mushin: *Sarah Davies* ▲

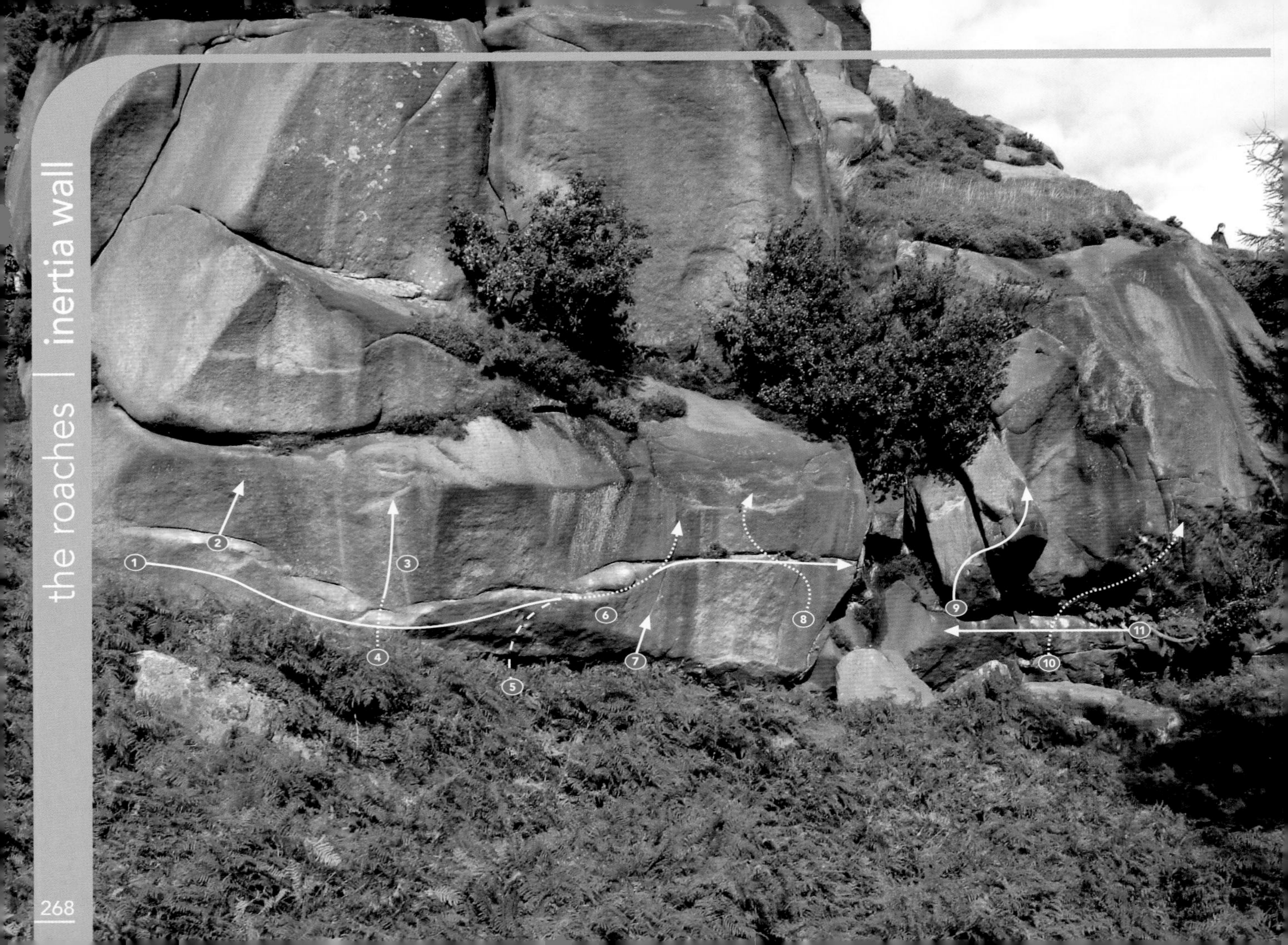
1
2
3
4
5
6
7
8
9
10
11

Inertia Wall

1. **The Inertia Reel Traverse**   *8a+*
A beautifully sculptured traverse, climbed from extreme left to extreme right. Some people have spent entire climbing careers trying to tick this.
(Jerry Moffatt)

2. **Ant Lives**   *7a*
A mantel of grimness onto the shelf.
(Nick Dixon)

3. **Inertia Reel**   *7a+*
Manteling, bridging, undercutting nonsense – brilliant. More than one finger pulley has been ruptured by that undercut.   *(Johnny Dawes)*

4. **Turbo**   *7c+*
The sit start to Inertia Reel. It's like a concentrated version of the stand-up, so if you didn't like Inertia Reel, you won't like this.   *(Rupert Davies)*

5. **Thud**   *7b*
Upside-down toe-hooking or a guns-out campus move. Start from the perfect scallop and the undercut under the roof, with your feet on the back wall and finish up Teck Crack Direct. It has also been done by starting matched on the undercuts, but they are quite fragile and often wet.   *(Paul Higginson)*

6. **Teck Crack Direct Start**   *6b+*
Traverse the slopey shelf up and right, then bounce for the top. Classic.

7. **Teck Crack Super Direct**   *7b+*
The thin seam to the finish of Teck Crack Direct. To start you will need to: 1) be tall 2) grow 3) stand on something.
(Paul Higginson)

8. **The Dignity of Labour**   *6c+*
Traverse the break left from the block, and lunge up to an intimidating finish.
(Nick Dixon)

To the right is a jutting prow with a steep undercut wall to the right, this is peppered with little dishes.

9. **A Modest Proposal**   *7a*
The jutting nose is approached from the left-most of the two prows, starting at the break. A variation - Skydivin' - jumps to the nose from the boulder. The offwidth roof crack also goes at 6b.
(Tom O'Rourke (AMP) Justin Critchlow/Paul Higginson (SD))

10. **Mushin**   *7c+*
The awesome bulge features climbing as God intended it to be – footless campussing on sloping dishes. It's worth brushing the top if you want to top-out, otherwise finish at the break and jump off like everyone else.   *(Ben Moon)*

11. **Boozy Traverse**   *6c+*
From the holly bush, shuffle leftwards beneath Mushin to take on the crux slopey section left of the crack. *(S Panton)*

Walking rightwards beneath the crag brings you to the boulders around the end slab – the Piece of Mind circuit. Although an extensive circuit has been documented (mostly with grades from 3 – 5+) on many of the problems the moves to pull on are also the top-outs i.e. many of them are a bit pointless. The rock can be a bit dirty too. There are a couple of decent problems in there, and if you have the excellent BMC Roaches guide and you're around that area anyway, check out Wildy's Arête (5+), which is o.k. and the scary Annie's Egg which is more of an E4 jump than a problem. You don't really need a guide to get you up most of the other problems.

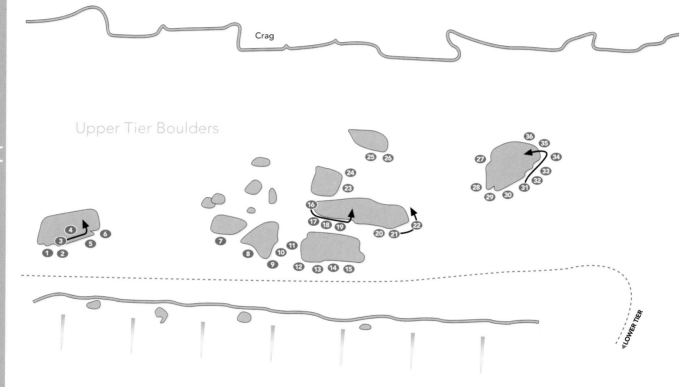

Crag

Upper Tier Boulders

▼LOWER TIER

Upper Tier Boulders

The Upper Tier boulders are very popular and have a spread of mostly easy problems on very good fine-grained rock. They dry much faster than the Lower Tier boulders making them a great place to warm up before trying your project downstairs. Approach up the steps from the Lower Tier.

1. *4*
The left arête.

2. *6a+*
Rock up leftwards from a round hold.

3. *6a*
A rising left to right traverse line on the high holds. A contorted sit start on undercuts and pinches is 6c+.

4. Grand Theft *7c*
A very hard and conditions dependant traverse along the slopey lip from the left arête to finish up problem 5.
(Justin Critchlow)

5. The Boss *6c*
Start low and inch awkwardly up to the ledge.

6. *5*
The arête. A variety of sitting starts are possible.

7. *3+*
A few very easy lines have been climbed on this boulder – take your pick.

8. *4*
The wall left of the arête.

9. *5+*
The slab and arête is an entertaining thrutch for those watching.

10. *6a*
Mantel onto the hanging slab from a low start.

11. *3+*
Big holes.

12. Joe's Arête *5+*
The classic arête is probably the most climbed problem in Staffordshire. It's polished, balancy and brilliant. The one-handed variation is also a must.
(Joe Brown)

13. *7a*
A frustrating eliminate right of the arête – pull up to the very slopey sidepull from a low start on the right-hand gaston and try to stay on long enough to reach the small high flakes.

14. *5+*
Another eliminate up the bigger flakes in the centre of the face.

15. Joe's Portholes *3+*
Climb more big holes or better still do one of these eliminates:

Mean Ol' Bastard *7b*
Sit start in the low holes and snatch up small gastons and crimps without using the big holes in the middle of the wall.
(Justin Critchlow)

Apocalypse Now *7a+*
A sitting start dyno from the low holes to the top. *(Mark Sharratt)*

16. **Nadin's Traverse**   *7a*
Start on big holds on the left arête, drop down to the big glued-up hold and traverse right on flatties and slopers to finish up the flake (problem 19).

Unsurprisingly there are several variations: finishing up the eliminate dyno finish to 19 is 7a+; continuing rightwards to finish up The Staircase is 7b; continuing further, staying below the top and finishing along Cooper's Traverse is 7b+.

17. *4*
The juggy arête from low.

18. **Glued Up**   *5+*
Start low on the glued jug and climb the wall. The Glued Up Dyno (from the glued jug to the top) is 7b.

19. *5*
Climb the flake. An eliminate dyno just left starts on the sloping finger rail at chest height and slaps for the top – 6c+.

20. **The Staircase**   *4+*
Climb the staircase-esque feature from a sit start.

21. **Cooper's Traverse**   *6b*
Start just right of The Staircase and traverse the lip rightwards until it gets easy.

22. *6b+*
Sit start under the bulge and snatch upwards to glory, or the top.

23. **Don's Crack**   *4+*
The crack. An eliminate just right (no crack, no arête) is 6b.

24. **Don's Arête**   *3+*
The arête.

25. *5*
Climb the wall past breaks.

26. *6a+*
The undercut nose from a hanging start. 'Broken Wing' starts up this and finishes up problem 25 – 7a.

27. *5*
The slippery and polished groove.

28. *5*
Climb the arête on the left-hand side.

29. *3+*
The easy groove.

30. **Flakes and Chips**   *4+*
Use polished chipped holds to gain the high flake. A contrived, but undeniably hard, eliminate project has been tried by many good climbers including Johnny Dawes, just right. 'One Inch Punch' attempts to slap to a pair of thin tile edges from a start undercutting the rib with feet on smears.

31. **Higginson's Arm**   *7b*
An eliminate traverse under the roof. Start on undercuts under Left Groove and traverse rightwards under the roof, along the lip of the boulder to finish up the Nose. *(Justin Critchlow)*

32. **Left Groove**   *6b*
A classic, climbing up the right-facing groove.

33. **Right Groove**   *6a*
The next groove-line right.

34. *5*
The arête, if you can call it that.

35. **The Nose**   *6b+*
Start hanging on the low break.

36. *5*
Climb jugs up another groove.

Calcutta Buttress

To the right of the Upper Tier Boulders as you approach up the steps from the lower tier is a steep buttress that is home to a range of problems that surmount its undercut base. The problems are fingery and powerful and well worth visiting if you can drag yourself away from the honey trap of the upper boulders.

1. **Bombay Overhang**   5
   The blunt left-most arête.

2. **Calcutta Crimp**   6b+
   From a jug under the roof, gain positive crimps over the lip and rock-over to the break.

3. **Sleeping with the Flowers**   7a
   A gem of a problem that takes the right arête on ripples from a sitting start under the roof. The big block on the right is out. *(Andi Turner/Justin Critchlow)*

4. **Dirtnap**   7b
   An extension to Sleeping with the Flowers. Once at the lip, continue leftwards to gain the break on the left side of the buttress and move up to join Bombay Overhang. *(Simon Willson)*

5. **Mistral Start**   6a
   Use either a long reach, or some small ripples, to reach better edges and then a flat hold on the left.

6. **Limbless Limbo Dancer**   6c
   From a low start under the roof, reach out to good holds and then make a big lunge to an incut hold at the top of the rib – finish at the break. *(Paul Higginson)*

7. **Dish Grab**   6b+
   From a low start, head for the good dish up and right.

8. **Calcutta Rib**   5+
   The crisp rib.

9. **Calcutta Traverse**   6a+
   Traverse the juggy shelf from right to left to finish at the crack. A low start begins in the mucky pit and adds a few harder moves on crimps onto the beginning of the traverse – The Black Hole Start, 7a.

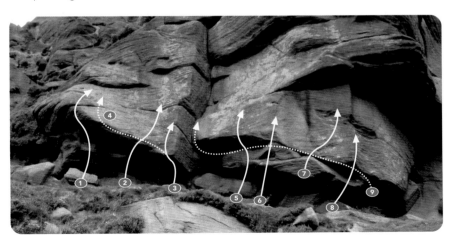

The Cellar and Attic Area

Above Calcutta Buttress there is a confusing maze of boulders containing a few hidden gems amongst some more mediocre problems. These are well worth seeking out if you have ticked the more mainstream circuits, or if you fancy a bit of esoterica. After a bit of wandering to orientate yourself, it should be easy enough to find the problems. The rock, especially on the back side of the boulders, is very soft and so many problems have been omitted to prevent further damage.

1. **Stretch Armstrong** 6c+
   Hard smearing up the right side of the slab. There are loads of other problems around here, but the rock quality is not great.

2. *5+*
   Reach slopey crimps on the lip from under the roof and then top-out more easily.

3. **The Squirm** 4+
   The crack and gap above.

4. **The Finger** 5+
   Move left to the 'finger' after climbing the arête.

5. **Little Wall** 4
   The easy wall.

6. *3+*
   The bulge above the crack.

7. *6a*
   Climb the arête on the left without using the sidewall on the boulder next to it.

8. **Sexy Steve** 6a+
   A squeezed-in problem up crimps left of the crack.

9. **Scrack** 3+
   The easy but nice crack.

10. *6a*
    A long move is needed to get up the wall right of the crack.

11. **Risky Runnel** 5+
    The runnel quickly gets scary and high.

12. *5+*
    The rippled wall is climbable all over at about the same grade.

13. *3+*
    The groove.

14. **Cellar Dwella** 7a+
    Slap to the top from sidepulls.
    (Justin Critchlow)

15. **Right Slab** 3
    The easy right-hand slab.

16. **Tiny Groove** 3+
    Climb the feature up the middle of the slab.

17. *3+*
    The left-hand line up the slab.

18. **The Gates** 6a+
    Climb the centre of the black slab.

19. **Crinkly Wall** 6a
    Delicate climbing up the wall.

20. *6b*
    Thrutch onto the arête.

21. **The Downpipe** 6c
    The hanging pipe is a fantastic feature that begs to be climbed.

22. **Pipe Entry** 7a+
    Not quite the hoped for sit start to The Downpipe: sit start right of the pipe, climb to the lip and reach left to the pipe to top-out. *(Andi Turner)*

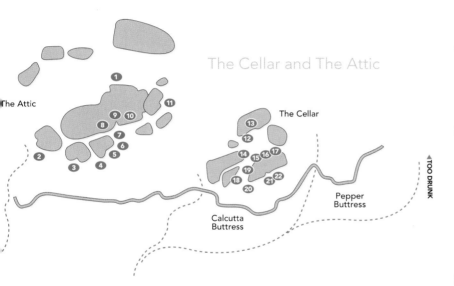

The Cellar and The Attic

The Attic

The Cellar

Calcutta Buttress

Pepper Buttress

TOO DRUNK ►

Too Drunk

The next buttress to the right of Calcutta Buttress is Pepper Buttress. Scout up the hill just after passing this buttress to find an obvious low overhanging boulder on the left. This is Too Drunk.

1. **Too Drunk** *7a*
   Climb the central line on the steep face from a sit start on the flake. Powerful moves using the rib and some slopey pockets above. *(Simon Panton)*

2. **Drunk Enough** *6c+*
   The steep right arête from a sitting start. *(Simon Panton)*

Simon Hudson on The Cube: *Alex Messenger* ▲

The Cube

An isolated monolith on the moorland behind the Upper Tier is home to a beautiful highball – The Cube – and a host of other problems. Access is sensitive. Approach from the right, not from the Skyline. At the right side of the Upper Tier take the track running back from the crag past old poles and 100 metres after a small stream, a vague path runs left off this to the Cube.

1. **Cube Traverse** *6a+*
Traverse the three faces of The Cube in a round-robin style.

2. **Flakes** *5*
Climb flakes up the wall.

3. **Cube Crack** *3+*
Climb the crack.

4. **Jump** *6c*
Dynamic slapping up the arête. 7a+ from a sit start.

5. **The Cube Direct** *7b+*
Climb direct up the face left of the start to The Cube to join that problem at the top.

6. **The Cube** *6b*
A brilliant highball, climbing the rippled face on small but always adequate holds. A hard start using a large pebble leads to easier climbing to the left side of the break. Move left and confidently pull up the upper wall. The Pube is an easier alternative finish up the arête.
(Nick Dixon)

7. **Right Pube** *6a+*
Climb the arête on the right.

8. **Back Crack** *5*
The crack on the far side of the block.

9. **Cave Exit** *6c+*
An awful problem climbing out of the dirty, low cave.

10. **K2** *3*
A cheval mountaineering up the ridge.

11. *4*
Climb the slab from the shallow crack.

12. **Summit Slab** *5*
Climb direct up to the highest point of the slab.

13. **Notch Slab** *4+*
The slab just right.

Doxey's Pool

Above the Skyline there is a mini-edge of boulders next to a small tarn, Doxey's Pool, named after the daughter of the occupant of Rock Hall, who was tragically raped and drowned here. To find it, walk along the path leading leftwards from the top of the Upper Tier. This small area is a fantastic bouldering spot with many good problems including an area classic: the Staffordshire Flyer. This problem used to have the added objective difficulty of being situated above a large boggy puddle, but recently the Bouldering Community Action Team has managed to drain much of the water away – thank you, whoever you are! The rock is nicely featured with many sloping ripples, but it has a thin skin with soft rock underneath. Please be careful and keep brushing to an absolute minimum. Paddling in the pool itself is not to be recommended, as the bottom is full of rotting peat which is easily stirred.

1. *6c*
   The left arête, behind the roof.

2. **Soggy Bottom Crack** *6a*
   The crack above the puddle.

3. *6a+*
   Jump to the ledge and mantel.

4. **The Staffordshire Flyer** *6b*
   The awesome overhang is overcome using a thin rail in the roof and jugs on the lip. It's totally classic and nowhere near as hard as it looks. Or is it?

5. The Arête *6c*
A sit start on undercuts bumps the grade to 7a+.

6. Another Nadin Traverse *7c*
Start as for The Arête (from sitting) and traverse the lip rightwards on poor slopers to gain the hanging flake on the next problem. Finish up this. Hard.
(Simon Nadin)

7. The Drowning Pool *7a+*
Start low on the jug, span left to a poor sloper and make a funky move to the hanging flake. Superb.

8. Groovy Crack *4*
Into the hanging crack.

9. *3+*
Climb the chipped wall.

10. *4+*
The flake line on the right.

11. *6a+*
Climb the arête on the left. Climbed on the right it's 5+.

12. *5+*
An eliminate up the flake only – no arête.

13. *6c+*
Start in a niche-like corner and climb up and right to gain a small pocket. Finish direct.

14. *6c*
The same pocket is gained from a start further right, below the arch feature.

15. *6a+*
Start as for 15, but follow the arch.

16. *6a+*
Direct into the flake at the end of the arch. A low start on the undercuts brings the grade up to 6b+ ish.

17. *6b+*
Climb the arête from low undercuts.

18. *3+*
The jamming crack.

19. *3+*
The arête.

20. Pancake *4*
Climb into, and out of, the big dish.

On the next block right are two further problems – the crack/groove and the arête right again. Both are 3+.

Problem 11: *Alex Messenger* ▲

Staffs Flyer: *Alex Messenger* ▲

Drowning Pool: *Alex Messenger* ▲

Roaches Skyline

Continuing along the path under Doxey's Pool, the Skyline area is reached. The next bouldering is located on two separate clumps of boulders by the path, both containing some fine, isolated problems – the Far Skyline Boulders. Finally, further still, is one last circuit beneath the path – The Very Far Skyline Boulders.

Far Skyline – Chasm Boulders

To be found some 200m or so further on from Doxey's Pool, between the paths, just after the path splits. Some of the problems are in the channels between the boulders and require attention to prevent unintentional bridging onto the opposite walls.

1. **Gritstone Pimple** *6b*
   A scary pull, using the pimple feature.

2. **Ramp** *4*
   Ascend the ramp, escaping rightwards at the top.

3. **Mantel** *4+*
   A mantel.

Matthew Coutts ▲

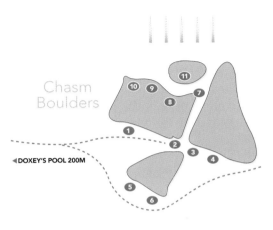

Chasm Boulders

◄ DOXEY'S POOL 200M

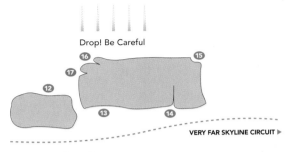

Drop! Be Careful

Art Nouveau Boulders

VERY FAR SKYLINE CIRCUIT ►

4. Harder Mantel *6a+*
Another mantel, this time harder.

5. *4*
Climb to the arête using a rounded feature.

6. Triptych Groove *7a+*
Climb the groove and arête from a sitting start. *(Andi Turner/Justin Critchlow)*

7. Acne Arête *7a*
The hanging arête - trying hard not to bridge. A sit start is a bit harder.
(Andi Turner)

8. Squeezer's Spots *6c*
The wall from sitting. *(Andi Turner)*

9. Spotter's Pop *6b*
The wall from a sit start on crimps.

10. Puss in Boots *6c*
Another sit start, with feet on the back.

11. Spotter's Slop *7a*
Sloper to top.

Art Nouveau Boulders

Some way on from the last boulders are some more - next to the path, above the route Art Nouveau. (Which would be the most beautiful highball 7b+, if the landing were not so awkward).

12. Mono Slab *3*
Easy slab.

13. Sidepull Wall *7a+*
The hard wall right of the arête.

14. *3*
The easy crack.

15. Flaky Romp *4*
Up flakes.

16. Juggy Flakeline *4*
Either get some spotters or don't fall off.

17. Crack and Arête *6a+*
As the name suggests …

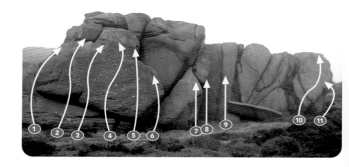

Very Far Skyline Boulders

Further still is the final bouldering up hereabouts. A good little circuit of easy problems on good rock. The boulders described are below the path, but there are more blocks above the path. The rock on these higher boulders is very soft, and climbing on them is very damaging, so you are requested not to.

1. **Rounded Arête** *3*
   Delicate and good.

2. **Open Groove** *5*
   Smear up the faint groove.

3. **Two Pocket Slab** *5*
   Past the twin pockets.

4. **Lazy Trout** *5*
   Climb the highest section of the slab, to a pocket.

5. *4+*
   Climb direct to the upper arête.

6. *5+*
   Tackle the steep arête. A sit start from a low slot is 7a.

7. *5+*
   The right side of the arête, 6c+ from sitting.

8. *5*
   The corner crack.

9. **Pinkies to Perkies** *3*
   The ace splitter crack.

10. *3*
   Walk up the slab.

11. **Inner Tube** *6a+*
   Sit start with hands in the hole and then go for the top.

12. *3*
   The wall.

13. *3*
The left crack.

14. *3*
The right crack.

15. *3*
Ramp features.

16. Flight Exam *4+*
Climb the slab, working the pocket for all it's worth.

17. *5*
Smear up and right from the pocket.

18. *6b+*
Climb the thin seams up the rib.

19. *6b*
The right arête.

The Aiguille

The small pinnacle between the Roaches and Hen Cloud has some highball problems that are too good to miss. It's easily seen from the road – simply park up and walk over to it.

1. Starlight Left *6b+*
Climb the left-hand face using both arêtes, to the break. Step right and climb the right arête to finish, or jump off.

2. Starlight and Storm *6c+*
The perfect highball arête is climbed on the right. Presumably named after the book by Gaston Rebuffat who gave his name to the gaston hold - none feature on this problem. *(John Allen/Martin Veale)*

3. Simon's Slab *7a+*
The centre of the slab. *(Simon Nadin)*

Pete Robbins on problem 4, Fourth Cloud: *Adam Long* ▲

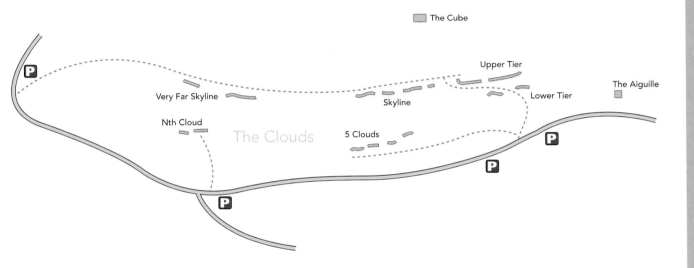

The Cube

Upper Tier

Very Far Skyline

Skyline

Lower Tier

The Aiguille

Nth Cloud

The Clouds

5 Clouds

The Five Clouds

This small line of outcrops below the Roaches Skyline is composed of some of the best gritstone to be found anywhere. The elements have conspired to produce wonderful, sculptural features on a much finer-grained rock than that which is to be found just a few hundred yards away at the Lower Tier.

There are virtually no pebbles to be found, yet the friction is unsurpassed.

Approach

Park on the road below the crag as you would for a visit to the main bulk of the Roaches. Walk through the gate towards the Lower Tier, but take a path immediately on the left that runs parallel with the road. The first outcrops become visible on the right after a few hundred metres.

Second Cloud

The Second Cloud has a small selection of perfect highballs.

1. **Communist Crack** *5*
    The sickle crack that slices the buttress in two is an awesome highball if you are confident at this grade. Climbed as a layback flake it is positive and satisfying all the way.

2. **Marxist Undertones** *6a*
    Lunge from the hole in the centre of the wall to the ledge and top-out much more easily up the arête above. There are two variations at the same grade – the undercuts on the right to the ledge, or using the hole for your right hand to gain the ledge using a flake on the left.

3. **Nadin's Secret Finger** *7b+*
    Climb the centre of the steepening wall, with slabby moves to start and small crimps higher up to reach into the big holds and a junction with Finger of Fate. *(Simon Nadin)*

4. **Finger of Fate** *6b*
    An elegant highball arête, climbed on the left. The awkward sloping landing means that you get gripped much sooner than it looks like you ought to. *(Simon Nadin)*

Third Cloud

The Third Cloud has two brilliant problems on the short wall to the left of the main face.

1. **Persistence**   *6b*
   The flakes at the end of the wall make a perfect problem.
   (Simon Nadin)

2. **Who Needs Ready Brek?**   *7c*
   The sinuous seam that winds its way across the blank face cries out to be climbed. Climb half-way up Persistence, paste your feet on smears, crimp down hard and follow it rightwards to its end, some better holds, and a final pull to jugs.   *(Simon Nadin)*

Rupert Davies on Who Needs Ready Brek?: *Alex Messenger* ▲

Fourth Cloud

The Fourth Cloud has a boulder beneath it that looks as though it was shaped with a giant spoon.

1. *6a*
The left arête.

2. Hard Arête *7a+*
The right arête is awkward to start.

3. Tetris *7c*
The sit-down start to the arête is a beautiful little beast. Technical and powerful moves up the steep rib lead to a final fight with the slopey upper arête.

4. *7a*
Rock onto the hanging slab above the scooped-out lower wall.

5. *7b*
Traverse the lip rightwards from the start of the last problem, to finish up the right arête.

On the hillside above and to the left (looking up) of the boulder is a friction slab with a few more pleasant problems. 'Holdless Slab' is the classic, up the right side of the slab, 6a, while the left arête is 6a+.

On the main buttress above the boluder is a lovely open scoop. This is Milky Buttons, 7b. (Justin Critchlow)

Nth Cloud

The Nth Cloud is somewhat separated from the other Clouds and it is best approached from the road via a track behind a gate, rather than from the Fourth Cloud. There are several buttresses with routes on them that can be bouldered out, but it is only the buttress included below that has any real bouldering - and it doesn't have much of that. The crag is included for the sake of the wonderful Swivel Finger – a real classic.

The climbing described is on the short wall to the left of the two higher buttresses.

1. **The Flakes** *6b*
   Easy moves on positive flakes lead to an unhelpful rounded scoop above an awful landing. I'm not selling this to you, am I?

2. **Swivel Finger** *6b*
   The arête, or massive flake, in the centre of the buttress is simply wonderful. A series of balancy barn-door moves are followed by a tricky top-out. A sit start adds fun, but nothing to the grade.

wimberry

Wimberry is practically ignored by many Peak climbers, which is good. The circuit is just as fine as any of the classic eastern venues, but it's only half as spoilt and it's twice as quiet. The boulders are strewn down the steep hillside below the crag and contain stacks of classic problems, many of which you probably won't have heard of. The rock is rough, but not painfully so, and of top-notch quality.

Access and Approach

The access and approach details are described for those approaching from the west. Wimberry is located just off the A635 Chew Valley road on the northeast side of Manchester, just east of Greenfield. After driving through Greenfield, take a road called Bank Lane on the right, then follow it down to the obvious pay and display car park next to the reservoir. Make sure that you do pay and display - you will get a parking ticket if you don't. To get to the boulders follow the track past the yachting club, turn right and follow the track with the stream on your left. The Sugarloaf is reached first, with the rest of the circuit scattered about the hillside above.

North-facing and exposed… actually the conditions are a lot better than this sounds. The boulders are quite sheltered and do not get as green as the crag itself. This exposure also means that the season lasts longer than at other venues, and with a stiff breeze good conditions can last almost into the summer.

Paul Worsdale on Fish Arête: *Rupert Davies* ▲

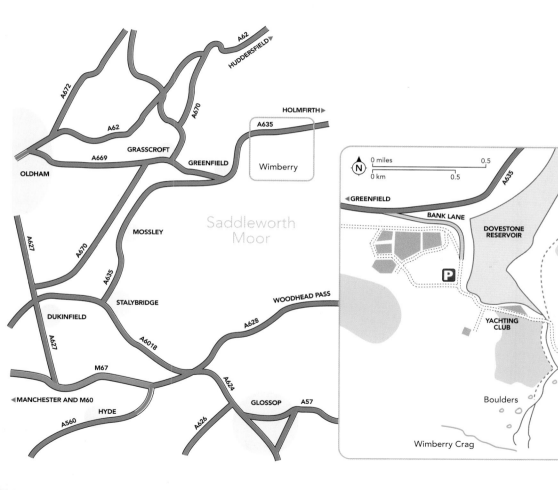

A672

A62 HUDDERSFIELD ▶

A670

HOLMFIRTH ▶

A635

A62

GRASSCROFT

GREENFIELD

Wimberry

A669

OLDHAM

Saddleworth
Moor

MOSSLEY

A627

A670

A635

STALYBRIDGE

WOODHEAD PASS

DUKINFIELD

A628

A627

A6018

M67

◀ MANCHESTER AND M60

A624

HYDE

GLOSSOP

A57

A560

A626

0 miles   0.5

0 km   0.5

N

A635

◀ GREENFIELD

BANK LANE

DOVESTONE
RESERVOIR

Dovestone Edge

P

YACHTING
CLUB

Boulders

Wimberry Crag

Dave Barrans on Stateside: *Mike Vincent* ▼

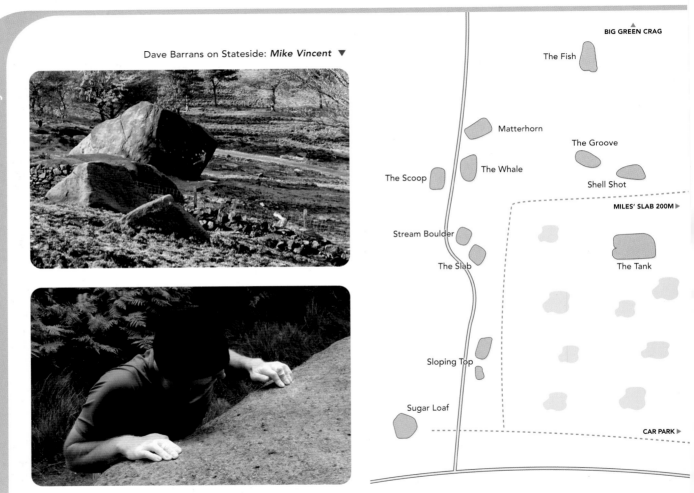

BIG GREEN CRAG ▲

The Fish

Matterhorn

The Groove

The Whale

The Scoop

Shell Shot

MILES' SLAB 200M ▶

Stream Boulder

The Tank

The Slab

Sloping Top

Sugar Loaf

CAR PARK ▶

Lee Anderson on Slap Happy: *Rupert Davies* ▲

Problem 52, Fish Boulder: *Davies Coll.* ▲

Sugar Loaf

Not the most appealing boulder on first sight, and covered with old chipped holds. Most of the stand-up starts, although good, tend to be climbing of the pulling-between-positive-chips sort. The sit starts, however, though they might not look like much on first acquaintance offer some fantastic and strange moves. The problems are described clockwise starting at the uphill face.

1. *6a+*
The blunt arête approached from the flake in the centre of the wall.

6b
Move right from the flake via a crimp.

7b
Sit start, with both hands on a low edge, match the rib above and layback to glory, finishing left or right as per the above problems. Unlikely, but great moves. *(Carl Kelsall)*

2. *3*
The way down and therefore it's debatable whether it should be advertised as a way up.

3. *4+*
Pockets, scoops & chips up the high wall.

4. Artificial Route *4+*
The short, hanging arête and wall above on chips.

Artificial Route Sit Start *7b*
Sit start hanging the low sloping boss, lock for flatties in the break using an unusual splits move, mantel and up. Harder than it looks. *(Lee Anderson)*

5. Baxter's Wall Direct *5+*
The next vague arête on the left is followed on more chips.

Brush Electric *7c*
A desperate sit start to Baxter's Wall, directly pulling into, and using, the lip of the little roof as an undercut to reach better holds above. *(Sam Whittaker)*

6. **Local Hero** *6b+*
The wall taken on crimps. Baxter's Wall starts up this and trends right to the arête – 6a+. There's also a fun eliminate dynoing from the large hold to the top at 7b ish.

7. *5+*
The rib just left on chipped holds.

7a
Sit start the rib on a chipped rounded dish, rock to crimp and use a mono and/or other features to finish up the 5+. *(Lee Anderson)*

8. *4*
The heavily chipped, slabby wall left again.

The next boulder up and right is Sloping Top. The block below this is home to two bits of fun.

9. *6b*
The undercut right arête, from a sit start, has a great move. If you are very strict and pull on to the front face using just the undercut and exit direct, it's much harder – in the region of 7a.

10. *4*
The unfortunately chipped slab is easy.

Katherine Sellars on Think Tank: **R Davies** ▲

Lee Anderson on Slap Happy: **R Davies** ▲

Adam Long on Project Dyno: **J Coefield** ▲

Sloping Top

11. *7c*

A sit start to the downhill face using a high right-hand crimpy sidepull to power up to the sloping top. Shorties may not be able to reach the starting hold from a sit start. 6c from a standing start.

12. Slap Happy *6c*

A sloping top classic. From the high right-hand hold, slap the sloping top, slap to match, but don't slap to mantel the top-out. A low (not sitting) start can be done from the flat undercut down and left – 7b+ but only the tall need apply.

13. Fat Slapper *6b+*

The featured, blunt arête.

Fat Slapper Sit Start *7a*

Sit start on a flatty (right) and undercut (left), slap up into the stand-up. Good moves. *(Paul Ingham)*

14. The Slot *5*

Undercut the slot.

15. *5*

The wall just left, with a left-hand sidepull. The arête left again is also 5.

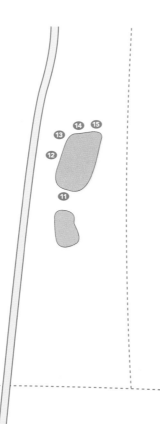

Adam Long on Slap Happy: *R Davies* ▲

The Slab

16. The Slab 4
The right arête of the slab.

17. *3+*
The centre of the chipped slab.

Stream Boulder

18. *4+*
The short arête on the downhill side.

19. *4*
The wall to the left.

20. *6a*
The groove above the stream. You have got to flash this if you want to stay dry – there's no padding out the landing of this one.

Further up the stream, on the right, is a block with a neglected gem on it. Sit start on the right, on slopes under the steepness, slap up to a final slopey exit above the worrying slope above the stream. 7a+.

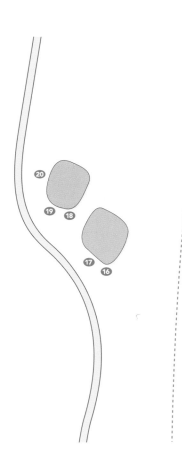

Sam Whittaker on Winsome: *Rupert Davies* ▶

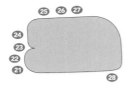

The Tank

21. Stateside *7c*
Steep laybacking up coarse but thin sidepulls, trending rightwards. The grade is earned by not using the chips - this is how it was first done.
(Miles Gibson)

22. *6c*
The wall between Stateside and Elephant's Bum using a nice fat pinch for your left hand.

23. Elephant's Bum *5*
Up to, then using the rounded crack feature.

24. *6c*
The slab left of the crack, right of the arête. There are two variations depending on whether you start with your left or with your right hand on the obvious pebble.

7b
A hard sit start to the slab off the chipped pocket, again with two variations on the pebble.

25. *4*
Chips just left of the arête.

26. *4*
Wall with flakes.

27. *4+*
Leftwards-slanting crack.

28. Think Tank *6b+*
The leftwards-rising line of flakes, from the right arête on the downhill face is a classic.

Left again is an old project dyno awaiting the world dyno champion. Some of the best efforts so far have been hitting the rock only inches below the jug (and landing about 10ft away).

Shell Shot

29. Shell Shot *4*
The downhill arête.

30. Shell Shock *4*
The slab just right.

31. The Cannon *6a*
A bit eliminate – up to flakes right again.

The wall on the downhill face is 7a

The Groove

The next small boulder up and left of Shell Shot.

32. *6b*
The lovely short groove from a sit start.

33. *7a*
Right to left traverse along the top of the boulder from the right (not quite on the arête) to finish up the 6b groove.
(Lee Anderson)

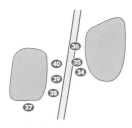

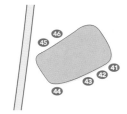

The Whale

34. *4+*
The stream-facing crack line.

35. *6b+*
The bulging wall just left is very good –
for full local approval make sure that
you don't use the crack for your feet.

36. *5+*
Pockets and wall. The problem is quite
good, but much better is the eliminate –
no pockets, just the right-facing big
rounded flake/blob. Now try and pull
on. Starting at 6b, you get an extra
grade for every two seconds you stay
off the floor up to a theoretical limit of
7a+ if you top it out up the scoop.

7b
Traverse leftwards from the crack to
finish up the pockets, staying low on
slopers. Good conditions essential.
(Sam Whittaker)

The Scoop

37. Steve's Wall *7a+*
The downhill-facing wall starting just left
of the arête and trending left across the
slab on pebbles. *(Steve Fisher)*

38. *5+*
The left side of the scoop.

39. *5+*
Direct up the wall above the scoop.

40. The Scoop *4*
Into the scoop and out of it on
the right. Nice.

Matterhorn

41. *6a*
The arête on the left-hand side.
Good climbing.

42. Winsome *7a*
A Chew Valley classic up the worryingly
high slab on pebbles. Keep on that
line – the problem goes straight up,
not leftwards onto the good foot and
handholds. *(John Allen)*

43. West's Route *5+*
Climb the features and overlap just left
of centre.

44. The Nipple *6a*
The arête on the right-hand side.

45. *6a*
An eliminate up the black slab.

46. *4*
Chips up the wall to the left.

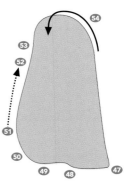

Lee Anderson on Ego: *Adam Long* ▲

There is more bouldering on the blocks below the crag, way up the hillside.

The Fish

47. Fish Arête *6c+*

The stunning arête and rib are perfect grit features. Climb them with a flowing sequence to a final slap for the top.

Fish Arête Sit Start *7b+*

The sit start adds more moves slapping up the arête and rib, which can only be a good thing. Totally classic. Bottom end of the grade.

48. The Groove *6c*

A standing start (right hand in the groove, left on crimp) to climb the short hanging groove. A great problem. Starting a move lower on the slopey crimps in the vague break and slapping into the groove above is 7b.

49. You're Joking! *7b*

From the slopey crimps in the vague break slap to the top. Very similar to a similarly named problem on the Eastern edges, but not as hard. *(Adam Long)*

50. *6b*

Mantel out the overhanging lip.

51. *6a+*

From a low start on a sloping shelf, move right onto better shelves and then the top. Satisfying.

7a

Traverse leftwards on features below the top from the same low hanging start as the previous problem to finish up the next problem. *(Sam Whittaker)*

52. *6b+*

A good little sitting start on the short rib leads to slopey dishes and the top. Really nice moves.

6c+

A traverse into the previous problem from the low handrail to the left.

53. Ego *7b+*

A fantastic hard problem. Starting on the low handrail, slap out to a pair of terrible slopers, do a tricky move to bring your other hand out, and then go for the top. The problem is independent but the slopers are very close to those on the similar problem just right, so make sure that you keep on the line. *(Carl Kelsall)*

54. The Coarse Traverse *7a*

Sit start on the left-hand side of the large overhang and traverse the lip rightwards, footless or with heels, to finish up the vague nose.

Miles' Slab

Walk parallel with the main crag back towards the parking on a level with the Shell Shot boulder for about 150m and you will happen upon this well-hidden slab.

Miles' Slab *7b+*

A cunning slab test piece that's more involved than the usual grit padding and pebbles lark. Jump into the high foot-scoop and contrive a sequence upwards using the dish and mono. *(Miles Gibson)*

6c

The left-hand side of the right arête.

Paul Worsdale on Miles' Slab: *R Davies* ▲

Limestone
area

Rubicon Wall
Raven Tor
Stoney Middleton

Matthew Coutts ▲

rubicon wall

Rubicon wall is the first of the steep, hardcore limestone bouldering venues in the Peak. Like its soul brothers Raven Tor and Stoney Middleton, the climbing is steep, polished, powerful and fingery.

Rubicon is riddled with eliminates. However, unlike 'The Tor' and Stoney, the best problems here are mostly independent, and so it is only these problems that are described – if you want eliminates then bag a local or make some up for yourself.

Andy Harris on Kudos Wall: *Rich Heap* ▲

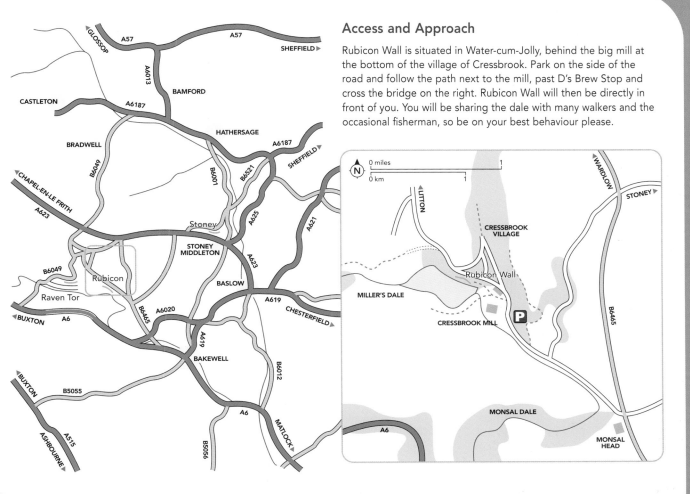

Access and Approach

Rubicon Wall is situated in Water-cum-Jolly, behind the big mill at the bottom of the village of Cressbrook. Park on the side of the road and follow the path next to the mill, past D's Brew Stop and cross the bridge on the right. Rubicon Wall will then be directly in front of you. You will be sharing the dale with many walkers and the occasional fisherman, so be on your best behaviour please.

limestone area

Traverses Area

The first area to be reached is the most popular. It has some pumpy training traverses and a few good up problems. The potential for eliminates is unlimited.

1. *5*
   The standard warm-up traverse. Start at the extreme left of the bay and join the conga shuffling right on big holds. Or do it the other way, it doesn't matter, there's no rules, that's the joy of climbing.

2. *6b+*
   Traverse the lowest line of slots through the alcove. It can be done either way, but right to left is nicest. A classic.

3. *6a*
   The middle traverse line.

4. *5+*
   The top traverse line.

5. *6b*
   From the jugs in the middle of the traverse lines, trend up and left to the break on edges.

6. *6b*
   As above but trend right.

7. *5+*
   Flakes and pockets up to the ledge.

8. *6a+*
   Climb diagonally through the bulge.

9. **Toenail Pie** *5*
   Haul up jugs past the sign to the break.

10. **Debris Groove** *6a*
    The right side of the prow.

11. *6b+*
    Climb small crimps and pockets up the right side of the groove.

Davies Coll. ▶

Kudos Wall

This small, steep wall has a concentration of hard, fingery and powerful problems.

1. **A Bigger Splash** *7a+*
    From the jugs on the right-hand side of the wall, climb up to more jugs using painful flakes and crimps.

2. **The Press** *7b+*
    Press off the opposing gastons to a sharp crimp, and then up for the jug.

a) **Kneeling Start** *7c+*
    Start on the finger rail and reach into The Press.

b) **Low Right Sitting Start** *8a*
    Sit start The Press under the start of A Bigger Splash.

c) **Low Left Sitting Start** *8a+*
    Start sitting with hands in the low slots down and left.

3. **A Bigger Splash Direct** *7b*
    Use The Press' gaston as a lay away for your right-hand and a small undercut for your left – then slap into the jug.

a) **Kneeling Start** *7b+*
    Start on the finger rail and pull into A Bigger Splash Direct.

b) **Low Right Sitting Start** *7c*
    Start under A Bigger Splash and traverse left into the stand-up.

c) **Tsunami** *8a*
    The low left sitting start with hands in the low slots down and left.

4. **The Pinch** *7b+*
    An eliminate. Start with both hands matched on the poor slopers and pinches just below the undercut on A Bigger Splash Direct. Pull on, and then slap into the big sidepull jug up and left. That's it.

5. **A Bigger Tail** *7a*
    Jump to good edges then pull up more edges to gain the high jugs.

6. **Kudos** *7a+*
    Start on the jugs on the left of the wall, pull up to sidepulls using a pocket and pull left into the flakes to finish. The easiest way takes the lowest sidepull with the left hand and the higher on the right with your right before slapping up, while 'Kudos Hard Way' takes the lower sidepull with the right hand and rocks out to the flake, 7b. A sit start is 7b+.

7. **A Miller's Tale** *6b+*
    Climb into the big hole from a sit start.

To the left are various routes, the starts of which can be bouldered out, but to prevent excessive polish they are not described. Further left still, the wall slabs out and an awkward traverse can be made.

The Dragon Flight Traverse *6a+*
Traverse the slabby face from right to left on extremely polished holds.

raven tor

Raven Tor is where finger strength was invented, the original laboratory of power. The problems are steep and brutally powerful, very polished and often painful, but ultimately rewarding. The bouldering at Raven Tor was historically used as training for the routes, so many of the problems are eliminates that have been devised to maximise power and even those that follow natural lines have accepted 'rules'. If this seems like an unnecessary throwback to a period of bouldering when difficulty was sought rather than avoided, then feel free to climb the problems however you like; but if you wish to climb the problems as they were historically done then read on - every problem is described in pedantic detail.

Raven Tor stays dry in the rain (once seepage has dried up) and is shady in the morning and late evening. Although the grades start at about 5+, you will not get much out of a visit unless you climb at least 7a.

◀ Andy Harris on Out of My Tree: *Rich Heap*

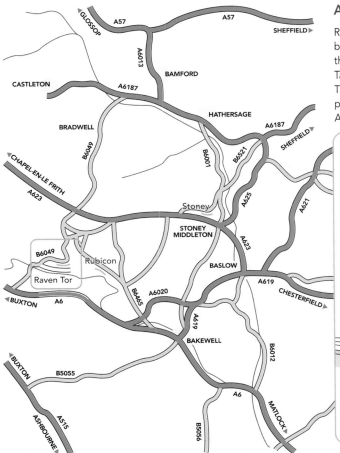

Access and Approach

Raven Tor is situated in Miller's Dale just off the B6049 road between Tideswell and the A6. From the A6, drive down the hill on the B6049, around a few bends and under the big railway bridge. Take the next turn on the right to the Angler's Rest pub. From Tideswell the turning is on the left, at the bottom of the hill, after passing the Youth Hostel on the left. In Miller's Dale, drive past the Angler's Rest and continue for half a mile – the crag is on the left.

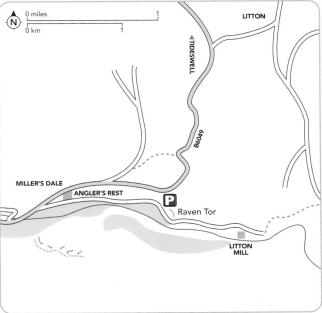

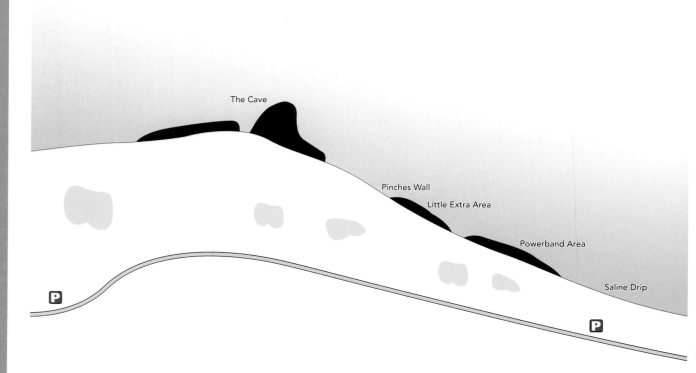

The Cave

Pinches Wall

Little Extra Area

Powerband Area

Saline Drip

The Cave

1. **Ben's Roof**   *7c+*
   An endurance problem that is both powerful and painful in equal measure. Sit start on often damp sidepulls in the back right-hand side of the cave, cross the cave leftwards to the side wall on scoops and crimps and then exit on undercuts, slopers and yet more crimps to finish below the top roof. The exit by itself is unlikely to have been, 'Too Hard for Mark Leach,' 6c. An extension start has been climbed starting way back in the cave - the crux is climbing the original when your feet and hands are covered in mud. *(Ben Moon)*

2. *7c*
   Start on a slot in the middle of the cave on the right, pull out to a crimp and an undercut on the lip and then pull rightwards to the finishing jug on the Weedkiller Traverse.

3. **The Weedkiller Traverse**   *7a+*
   Start on large holds just right of the pillar and traverse the lip of the cave leftwards on the lowest line of slots and edges. Pull up to the large jug. Footless it is 7c+.

4. **Basher's Problem**   *6c+*
   Cross the roof from the back wall on undercuts to slots on the traverse, gain pockets above, a small crimp and finally the flat jug up and left. A harder, right-hand variation is 7a+, and traversing into the problem along the high line of pockets above the Weedkiller Traverse from the start of that problem is 7b.
   (Martin Atkinson)

The holds

1. Big rippled sidepull
2. Slopey undercut
3. Very poor sloper/pinch
4. Bobbly pinch/crimp
5. 'Concept' edge
6. Poor sloper/crimp and good thumb sprag
7. Pinch
8. 'Matchbox' edge
9. Poor slopey crimp
10. Sidepull/pinch
11. Good, big, flat hold
12. Sloping 3 finger drag
13. Sharp flatty
14. Jugs
15. Jugs
16. 'Bear claw' pinch
17. Poor pinch
18. Poor rounded pinch
19. Poor edge/slot
20. Slopey sidepull
21. Very small edge
22. Jugs
23. Highest small slot

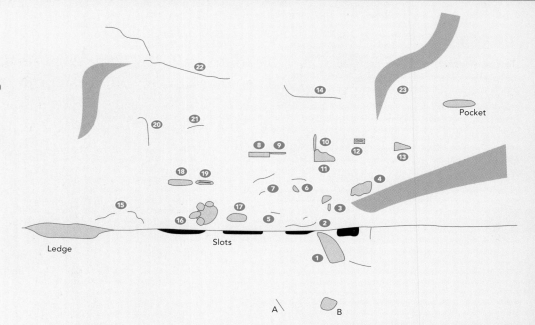

Pocket

Ledge

Slots

A

B

The Pinches Wall

Tens of eliminates have been contrived on this tiny but incredibly versatile section of rock. Grades are meaningless on this wall because many problems don't even involve moving your feet and once wired they are more about body position than pulling. The problems are listed from easiest to hardest, the easiest being about 6a, and the hardest about 8a, but take these grades with a pinch of salt.

For each problem the handholds are described in sequence with the starting holds in brackets, but you can use any footholds unless otherwise stated.

1. (L1, R1) R11, L8, L14, R14.
2. (L1, R1) R11, L14, R14.
3. (L1, R1) R13, L13.
4. (L1, R1) L8, R14, L14.
5. (L1, R1) L7, R11, L14, R14.
6. (L1, R1) L7, R12, L14, R14.
7. (L1, R1) L9, R14, L14.
8. (L15, R15) L20, R22, L22.
9. (L1, R1) R6, L8, R14, L14.
10. (L1, R1) R10, L14, R14.
11. (L1, R1) R8, L22, R22.
12. (L1, R1) L14, R14 dyno.
13. (L1, R1) R4, L8, R14, L14.
14. (L15, R15) R slots, L11, R23, L14, R14.
15. (L1, R1) L11, R foot A, R14, L14.
16. (L15, R15) R7, L8, R14, L14.
17. (L1, R1) R4, L9, R14, L14.
18. (L1, R1) R2, feet A and B, R14, L14.
19. (L1, R1) L3, R12, L12.
20. (L15, R15) R7, L9, R14, L14.
21. (L1, R1) R7, L21, R22, L22.
22. The Bear Claw (L15, R15) R16, L18, R19, L20, R22, L22.
23. (L15, R15) R16, L19, R7, L8, R11, L13, pocket, continue right to finish up Little Extra Start.
24. (L15, R15) R16, L19, R7, R14, L14.
25. (L1, R1) L5, R7, L9, R14, L14.
26. (L1, R1) L17, R7, L9, R14, L14.
27. Malc's One Armer (L9) - do a one arm pull up.

Little Extra Area

1. **Little Extra Direct Start** *7a*
   From slots under the bulge span out to the greasy flat hold (mono optional) and lock or pop to the jug out right. Share to finish.

2. *7c*
   A powerful eliminate. Start once again on slots under the bulge, match a pair of undercuts and make a big move to the high sloper and slap left to the jug from here. Climbing the same problem but using the diagonal crimp underneath the sloper is 7b+.

3. *7c*
   Another eliminate. From the same slots reach out and use the fingery edge/pocket hold to get the crozzly sidepull above and finish on the jug.

4. **Hooligan Start** *8a+*
   An extremely hard problem slapping for a small crimp from a tiny left-hand undercut and a totally inadequate pinch. Once at the crimp another hard move up and right gains a further crimp allowing the flakes above to be reached. The grade is for pulling on before going for the edge. *(Steve Dunning)*

5. **Ben's Traverse** *7c+*
   Traverse left from the start of Out of My Tree to the Pinches Wall. Contorted, tenuous, powerful and in need of weeding. *(Ben Moon)*

Powerband Area

1. **Boot Boys Start** *6c*
Big undercuts and sidepulls left of
the pillar are used to gain the big
glue-covered jug.

2. **Out of My Tree Start** *7b*
The steep wall above the pillar is
climbed by twisting your fingers into
the painful and greasy slots. Finish on
the jug. *(Andy Pollitt)*

3. **Pump Up the Power** *7c+*
The vague hanging grooveline on small
but positive crimps. The hard section is
only finished when you move out left
onto the good flatty at 15ft, so you're
virtually soloing. 8a+ (route grade) if you
take a rope. *(Ben Moon)*

4. **Rattle and Hump Start** *7a+*
Any which way up to the big jug two
metres up. All methods are powerful
and fingery.

5. **Power Humps** *7b*

An extension to the Rattle and Hump Start, starting on the first two slots of the Powerband. The harder (and better) method is to go straight up from the two higher slots to the pair of crimps rather than traverse left to the start of the stand-up – 7b+.

6. **Powerband** *7c*

Start on the right-most pair of twin slots and traverse all the way left to the pillar. It is generally accepted that you should stay high on pinches through the middle section rather than dropping down low into a mono (Powerless), and the original finishing sequence drops down to the undercuts on the pillar from the painful two-finger pocket. Totally classic.

For hunters of Raven Tor esoterica, there is Under the Powerband – climb the last section of the Powerband by keeping low and palming off the roof. (Jerry Moffatt)

Strict Blueband *7c+*

Reverse Powerband, keeping high over the middle section (no use of undercut vertical slot or the big square pocket) and finish without the final pocket on the higher line on slots.

7. **Staminaband** *8a*

An extension start to Powerband from under Super High Intensity Body Building. Start on pockets and traverse left, with a hard sequence using the low slot and the sloper, into undercuts and then into Powerband. The big high pocket just after the start is out.
(Ben Moon)

Staminahumps *7c+*

Sit start of Staminaband into Powerhumps – the hard way.

**Staminaband/
Pump Up the Power Link** *8b+*

Ben Moon's old training project finally realised. 9a route grade. *(John Gaskins)*

8a+

Link Staminaband and Ben's Traverse. Although you can get a full rest (not to mention a cup of tea, sandwich, etc.) on the pedestal at the end of Staminaband, you have got to do the whole thing again if you fall off Ben's Traverse. *(Andy Harris)*

8. **Saline Drip** *7a*

Climb the fingery wall on the other side of the tree to the right of the start of Staminaband to jugs. Reverse or jump.

stoney middleton

Stoney is not included because it's a great place to climb, but because of its important history. When you first encounter the vertical slickness and finger strength building gloss of Minus Ten, the stench of Carl's Wark and the impossible number of problems revolving around one hold in Tom's roof, you may wonder why you're here. But stick with it - there's probably no other crag in the UK with so many hard problems packed into such a small space.

Almost every problem at Stoney is an eliminate, which means that despite all the listed problems being hard, there's good sport to be had at all grades by doing your own thing. Please bear in mind that eliminate grades are much more approximate than normal because there are no alternative sequences to suit different people. So if you're told not to use that hold, and do the next bit like this, just remember that this is where training (and modern climbing) was born. Bouldering on limestone isn't about lines, soaring features and the easy sequence; it's about tiny holds, desperate moves and making it as hard as possible.

Whilst some problems have been lost in the mists of the 80s, we've done our best to straighten things out and interpret them for the new millenium. The training diaries and memory banks of Sheffield's finest (and oldest?) have been scoured, so enjoy the new (well 10-20 years old) stuff while it's still fresh!

Nowhere are the conditions as reliable as they are at Stoney. If the grit is dripping and Raven Tor and Rubicon are sopping wet, chances are that Stoney will still be dry. If you're lucky you might even get to experience the elusive 'sticky damp', the most hallowed of all conditions when grades drop and gravity seems to loosen its grip.

◀ Andy Harris on Nasty Traverse: *Rich Heap*

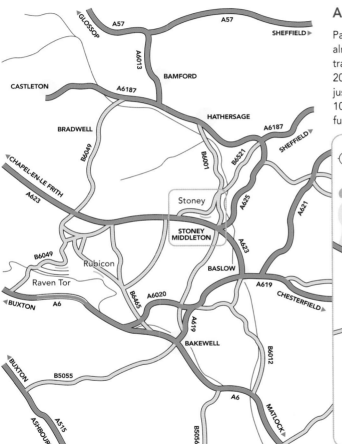

Access and Approach

Parking is in the large lay-by on the edge of Stoney Middleton, almost opposite the Café/Bistro. 150m up from the car park is a track on the right directly below Garage Buttress. Follow this for 200m and you'll find Tom's Roof after a 10m scramble up the gully, just before Bitter Fingers wall. For Minus 10, continue for another 100m and turn right. Carl's Wark is on the lower tier another 30m further off the main path, just drop down left on either side.

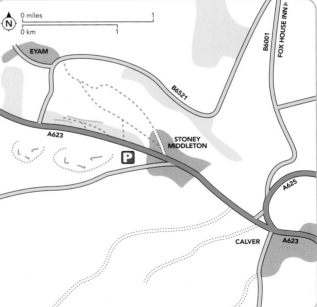

Love it or loath it, Stoney is the home of hard Peak bouldering and it played a key role in pushing climbing standards in the 80's. Thanks to the forefathers of UK bouldering: Proctor, Allen, Moffatt, Stokes and Kirton, we're left with a crag as rich in history as it is in polish. Back in the late 70s/early 80s there were no such things as climbing walls and training merely consisted of doing some weights and a few pull ups. Then along came a few climbers who thought that bouldering around on the limestone of Stoney would be good conditioning for the routes they aspired to. Tom's roof was, therefore, perhaps the world's first climbing 'cellar' and spawned the latter in-house venues of Pollitt, Moon and Moffatt. It might be surprising to learn that this grotty cave is where Jerry trained for those hard 'sends' in America. Tom's Roof may also lay claim to the world's first glued-on hold. Around 1975, the late Tom Proctor stuck on that classic edge in the centre of the roof. A builder by trade, Tom covered the hold in Araldite and then held it in place with a scaffolding pole - thus creating the most solid hold at Stoney.

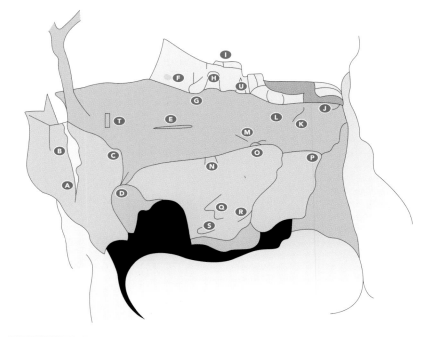

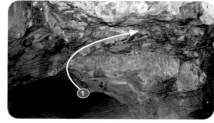

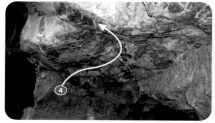

The holds

A. Lower side pull

B. Upper side pull

C. Big fat undercut/jams

D. Pocket at base of rib

E. Classic, slick glued-on edge

F. Poor pinch on lip of roof

G. Square pinch

H. Big slick jug

I. Crumbling slot and jug

J. Undercut pinches

K. Edge in roof

L. Flat hold in roof

M. Small edge

N. Pinch

O. Small slot

P. Large flake

Q. Low edge

R. Foot jam

S. Low foothold/toelock

T. Pinch in roof near lip

U. Triangular pinch

Tom's Roof

Rules is rules, so follow your left hand (LH) and right hand (RH), and go footless when told to do so. On first acquaintance with the place you may become confused, as there appears to be only one hold.

1. **Tom's Original** *7a*
   (RH-C, LH-C), RH-E, LH-E, RH-H, LH-H, RH-J, LH-J. Feet anywhere.

2. **The Womb** *6c*
   Jam out from the back of the hole to D, and then add a finish of your choice.

3. **Power Allowance** *7b*
   (RH-C, LH-C) RH-E, LH-E, RH-G, right foot toe jam H, RH-E, LH-C, RH-C. Feet anywhere but side wall.

4. **Swing Thing** *7b+*
   (LH-B, RH-A) RH-E, LH-E, footless, RH-H, LH-H Feet on back wall only. There and back is 7c+.

5. **Quintesscence** *8a*
   (LH-B, RH-A) LH-T, RH-F, footless, LH-H, RH-H. Feet on back wall only. Jerry was so desperate to repeat this Kirton nasty that he stripped down to his underpants and took off his rock boots in an effort to lose weight.

6. **Pete's Power Pull** *7c+*
   (LH-C, RH-C) LH-E, footless, RH-H, LH-H.

7. **Rack and Ruin** *7c*
   (LH-small pocket right of D, RH-pinch rib right of D) RH-E, LH-Q, LH-L, LH-I, RH-H, LH-H. Feet back wall for 1st move, then side wall.

8. **Jerryatricks** *7c+*
   Link the following problems without getting off; Womb, Swing Thing, Tom's Original in reverse, and Power Allowance. Pumped?

9. **Jerry's Problem** *7c+*
   Often done incorrectly, so read carefully. (LH-C, RH-C) RH-E, LH-E, footless, RH-little crimp directly below left-hand slot I, LH-left-hand slot I, RH-large jug I.

10. *7c*
    (LH-B, RH-A) RH-E, LH-E, footless, RH-U, LH-L, LH-H, RH-H Feet on back wall only.

11. *7c*
    (LH-Q) RH-O, LH-E, RH-E, footless LH-B, LH-A Feet on S and back wall.

12. **Figure of 8** *7b+*
    (LH-C, RH-C) RH-E, LH-Q, RH-U, LH-E, RH-C, LH-C Feet back wall & S.

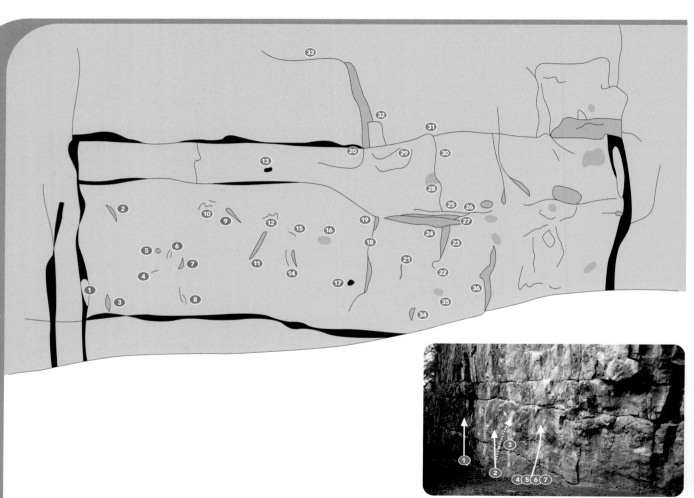

The holds

1. Chockstone/jug
2. Sidepull
3. Sidepull
4. Edge
5. Small, shallow pocket
6. Vague fin
7. Crimp
8. Slopey sidepull
9. Small ramp
10. Spikey edge
11. Sidepull
12. Edges
13. Sharp pocket
14. Sidepull/pinch
15. Edge
16. Smear
17. Perfect three finger pocket
18. Sidepull
19. Polished foothold in break
20. Quartzy edges
21. Vague sidepull
22. Undercut dish
23. Large, slopey sidepull
24. Thin seam
25. Good edge
26. Quartzy crimp
27. Slopey edge
28. Crimpy sloper
29. Quartzy edges
30. Good, smooth sidepull
31. Juggy ledge
32. Good edge in groove
33. Juggy ledge

Minus 10

Don't worry about the polish, just think how well you'll be climbing when you learn to use it. This is technical stuff indeed and the grit will feel twice as grippy after a few sessions here.

1. **Quent's Dyno** *7b*
   From the jug (1) and crack launch for the big jugs at the start of the Upper Break. Very morpho.

2. **The JABP** *7c*
   Done and named by Moffatt after a rumour that John Allen had done it. He hadn't. Use the small shallow pocket (5) with the left and pinch the vague fin (6). Pull on, feet anywhere and reach the next break with your right. As fingery as it gets.

3. *7b+*
   Starting on sidepulls (3 & 8) with feet low, pull on, right foot in break and balance over to ramp (9) with left. Match this and reach to sharp pocket (13) with right and leap for the top break 33.

4. *7a+*
   Use pocket (17) with left and gaston (21) with right. Egyptian feet up onto small edges above the low break. Reach edge 28 and crank through for the edge in the groove 32, using poor edges for your feet. Feet on smears below 2nd break and lurch over for (33) with right.

5. **Easy Dynos**
   Using pocket (17) with left and undercut (22), dyno to break off small edges above low break with left, right or both. A great introduction to dynoing.

6. **One Arm Bandit** *7b*
   With your left in 17 and your right behind your back, dyno for the jug 31 with your left! Can be done with the other hand at the same grade.

7. **Kirton Dyno** *7a+*
   Start with your right on (19), left in the break and toe in (17), leap for (33).

The holds

17. Perfect three finger pocket
18. Sidepull
19. Polished foothold in break
20. Quartzy edges
21. Vague sidepull
22. Undercut dish
23. Large, slopey sidepull
24. Thin seam
25. Good edge
26. Quartzy crimp
27. Slopey edge
28. Crimpy sloper
29. Quartzy edges
30. Good, smooth sidepull
31. Juggy ledge
32. Good edge in groove
33. Juggy ledge
34. Sidepull
35. Polished dish
36. Sidepull
37. Poor smear (no more resin, please)
38. Poor crimp
39. Crozzly crimp
40. Sharp undercut
41. (Right-hand) thin horizontal edge
42. Pinch
43. Big, fat sloper
44. Poor, three finger sloper
45. Jugs behind block
46. Round, smooth sidepull
47. Sloping dish
48. Big sidepull
49. Undercut in roof
50. Pinch on lip of roof
51. Sloper
52. Juggy Block
53. Flatty above sidepull
54. Slopey gaston
55. 3 downward sloping edges - always use lowest, poorest edge as per foothold eliminator!

8. Sean's Problem *7b+*
Left on (34), right on (36) and feet in the low break, reach the shallow dish (38) and crimp (24) (thumb around side edge). Feet up on tiny edges (no break for this move) and reach over to edge (28) with right, and incut (32) with left. Feet on smears below 2nd break and lurch over for (33) with right. Superb.

Using sidepull (23) instead of edge (24) is 7c. Even better.

9. Zippy's Sidepull *7b+*
Left on (34), right on (36) and feet in the low break. Get top of sidepull (23) with your right and put toe in shallow pocket (35). Lurch for jug (31).

10. Lucian's Undercut *7a*
Easier version of the previous problem. Using undercut (22) instead of (23). Peculiarly, Lucian knows nothing about this problem.

11. *6c+*
Left on (34) and right on (36) reach up to scoop (22) with your right. Reach up to (19) then (30) and (33).

For the following 3 problems please refer to our handy foothold eliminator to ensure the full tick. I hope that you've not been using the wrong footholds all this time?

12. Zippy's Problem *7b+*
Start with left on edge 36, right on pinch 42 and outside edge of left foot on 41. Up to sloper 44 with left, swap feet on 41. Reach the sloper (47) with your right (no holding the good bit at the back). Now place left foot on foothold 55, slap up for sidepull (48) and reach the top (52) with right foot on pinch (42). Sorry.

13. *7c*
As for problem 12 but instead of reaching sidepull (48), reach pinch (50) then right hand to (53) with toe on smear (43). Missing out ledge (53) by dynoing for jug 52 is 7c+.

14. *7c*
As for problem 12 to sloper (47). Swap feet on edge 41, reach ripple 54 with left. Right foot on smear (43), grunt to pinch (50) with right and flick to edge (51) then footless to jug (52).

Megatron – problem 19, page 329

The holds

17. Perfect three finger pocket
18. Sidepull
19. Polished foothold in break
20. Quartzy edges
21. Vague sidepull
22. Undercut dish
23. Large, slopey sidepull
24. Thin seam
25. Good edge
26. Quartzy crimp
27. Slopey edge
28. Crimpy sloper
29. Quartzy edges
30. Good, smooth sidepull
31. Juggy ledge
32. Good edge in groove
33. Juggy ledge
34. Sidepull
35. Polished dish
36. Sidepull
37. Poor smear (no more resin, please)
38. Poor crimp
39. Crozzly crimp
40. Sharp undercut
41. (Right-hand) thin horizontal edge
42. Pinch
43. Big, fat sloper
44. Poor, three finger sloper
45. Jugs behind block
46. Round, smooth sidepull
47. Sloping dish
48. Big sidepull
49. Undercut in roof
50. Pinch on lip of roof
51. Sloper
52. Juggy Block
53. Flatty above sidepull
54. Slopey gaston
55. 3 downward sloping edges - always use lowest, poorest edge as per foothold eliminator!

15. Pinch 2 *7c+ (8a+)*

Ben Moon growling in slow mo. Stuart Cameron not doing it. You got it! Once the hardest eliminate around and highlight of One Summer. There is a massive variation in grade depending on who you ask and exactly how they did it.

Start with left on edge (36), right on pinch (42) and outside edge of left foot on (41). Up to sloper (44) with left, swap feet on (41). Left toe onto smear (37) and dyno with right for pinch on lip (50). Right foot up to smear (43) and dyno again for edge (51) with left. Then the top (52).

16. Nasty Traverse *7c+*

Start with left on edge (36), right on pinch (42) and outside edge of left foot on (4). Up to crozzly crimp (39) with left, swap feet and left foot to small edge above low break. Right hand to poor crimp (38) and fall into crimp (24 -thumb around side edge). Finish as for Sean's Problem. Nasty.

17. The Double Double *6c*

Classic 70s double dynoing. From the good flakes (45) and edge (46), dyno to opposing sides of the block (48) and the side below (53). Then the jug (52).

18. Young American *7a+ (Originally B2)*

Done by visiting American Christian Griffith (he of thong fame), hence the name. Dyno straight from (45) and (46) to (52) with feet on (43) and edges to the left. Classic!

19. Megatron *7a+*

Dyno from edge A to jug B. Megatron Turbo double dynos to jug B, no change in grade.

There are three left to right traverses; two along the obvious upper and middle breaks, while a tricky traverse takes a line of holds below the middle break. You can use whatever footholds you like.

20. The Upper Break *5*

21. The Middle Break *6b*

It starts off fine, but you may struggle with the final moves. Pumpy.

22. The Wall Traverse *6c+*

Quite awkward passing the JA.

George's Wall

In between Tom's Roof and Minus 10 is this clean little wall.

1. *7a+*
    Big dyno from the jug in the low break to the obvious sloper.

2. *6a+*
    The vague groove.

Carl's Wark

A bit smelly and lonely, but it has some good routes, some ok problems and a classic limestone traverse.

1. **Carl's Wark Traverse**   *7b*
A low-level traverse, starting from the crack and heading right on a variety of pockets and edges, to finish up the flakes to the break, that being the start to Bubbles Wall E3 6a.

   More Air than Chocolate   *6a*
Climb pockets on the left-hand side of the wall, trending right to a groove.

2. **Au Revoir Mono Doigt**   *7b*
Old school bouldering and quite hard. Climb the highball centre of the wall.

3. **Soapsuds Traverse**   *6b+*
Situated to the right of the main wall is the Soapsuds wall - ironically it's a bit dirty. Start on the left and make an awkward move into the crack, climb it, traverse the second break back left and climb down to the start.

The old skool: *Al Williams* ▶

Gritstone
SCIENCE : 1
ARÊTE-NOLOGY
10 cutting edge angles

01. **Crescent Arête** *5+ Stanage*
Popular but still one of the best.

02. **Heart Arête** *6b Eagle Tor*
Cute, bulbous and tricky.

03. **Brain Dead** *6c Cratcliffe*
Worryingly high and off the
beaten track.

04. **Fish Arête** *6c+ Wimberry*
A perfect feature, easy for the grade
and climbs well – the essential tick.

05. **Clever Skin** *7a Baldstones*
Harder after pebbles have broken,
but still balancy, tippy-offy climbing
up lava-lamp-wax curves.

06. **Sean's Arête** *7b Curbar*
Balance and grit poise needed only,
there's no strength required.
Bring your grit Karma.

07. **Big Al Qaeda** *7b Robin Hood's Stride*
Some find it fairly easy, some fairly hard.
It's all in the footwork.

08. **Desparête** *7b+ Burbage South*
Two arêtes for the price of one.
Monkey-up-a-stick-ing.

09. **Flatworld** *7c Baslow*
Hard pulls up a sharp arête,
but with no arête moves on it at all.

10. **Careless Torque** *8a Stanage*
The daddy.

Gritstone
SCIENCE : 2
SLAB-OSOPHY

10 steps along the path of gritstone zen

01. Pock Man *5+ Burbage South*
Delicate and popular, but no walk over.

02. Three Pocket Slab *6a Roaches*
Straight-forward pulling until the last
cautious moves.

03. Beauty *6c Stanage*
Tentative steps onto barely
there footholds.

04. C3PO *7a Roaches*
Padding and pebbles to test the faith.

05. Slab right of Crescent Arête
7a Stanage
Tricky pebble and pocket pulling up a
beautiful curving face.

06. Satin *7a Stanage*
A steep hanging slab featuring a hard
rockover on crimps.

07. Miles' Slab *7b+ Wimberry*
Big foot and handholds –
now try using them.

08. Boba Fett *7b+ Roaches*
Release yourself to the friction.
There are no holds.

09. Pressure Drop *7c Stanage*
Manteling onto coin edges.

10. Walk on By *7c+ Curbar*
Almost a wall, but the key is in
trusting and standing on your feet.
The tiny crimps will torture your tips.

Leo Houlding on Satin: *Adam Long* ▶

Gritstone
SCIENCE :3
DYNO-CIDE
10 killer jumps

01. Sly Stallone *6b+ Newstones*
About as easy as proper dynos get.

02. Crash and Gurn *7a Burbage South*
Sitting start dyno to a big, often water-filled, jug. More timing than anything.

03. The Big Dyno *7a Roaches*
The real thing - full flight between big holds.

04. Green Room Slap *7a+ Stanage*
More of a lunge as two points of contact are kept throughout, but the top hold is frustrating to latch despite being good. Probably possible static.

05. Buckstone Dyno *7b Stanage*
Big holds, but a long flight.

06. JetPack *7b Froggatt*
Well hidden with a strange trajectory.

07. Rocket Man *7b+ Burbage Bridge*
One of the best moves in the valley.

08. Hurricane *7c Curbar*
Getting the distance is hard, sticking the top is harder.

09. Maurice Gibb *7c+ Gibb Tor*
The biggest naturally two-handed dyno on grit? (The biggest in the country?)

10. Tank Dyno *Wimberry*
Still a project, but it will go - and it won't be silly hard. At least 5 - 6 ft between big holds up a steep wall. This project NEEDS to be done.

Mark Sharratt on The Big Dyno: *Alex Messenger* ▶

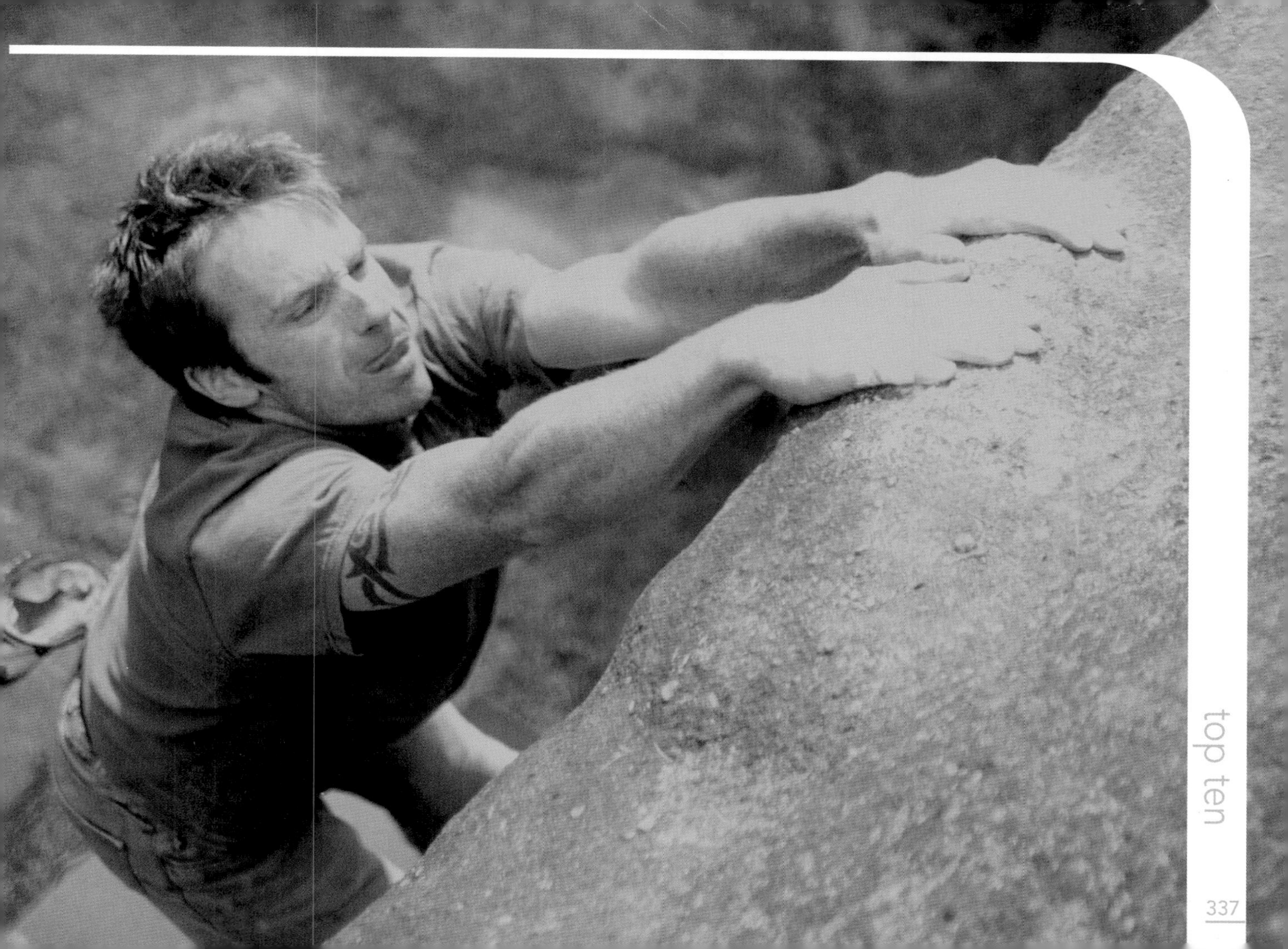

Gritstone
SCIENCE : 4
ROOF-ISM

10 trips to the lab of steepness

01. Staffordshire Flyer *6b Roaches*
Big footholds make this surprisingly easy given the size of the holds in the roof.

02. Left-Hand Stepped Roof Problem
6c Secret Garden
Lovely moves matching the sloping block in the roof.

03. Razor Roof *6c Cratcliffe*
A satisfying pull on skin destroying holds.

04. Diamond White Left-Hand
7a White Edge
Obscure esoterica, but good climbing through a big roof.

05. Short Sean's Reachy Roof *7a Rowtor*
Undercutting rounded nothings in a horizontal roof. Not that reachy either.

06. Cinzano Roof *7b Burbage North*
Hidden roof at one of the most popular venues in the Peak. A good find.

07. Mark's Roof *7b Gardom's North*
It's big and it hurts. Gritstone wrestling on some of the biggest holds around.

08. P Crack *7b Cratcliffe*
Pockets, slopers, double toe-hooks and proper roof work lead to a finish up the hanging crack.

09. Shit *7b+ Higgar Tor*
Reasonable moves on small holds through the roof are followed by the crux of Piss.

10. Brass Monkeys *7c Stanage*
Burly slapping while totally inverted.

Staffs Flyer: *Alex Messenger* ▶

Gritstone
SCIENCE : 5
TRAV-CENDENTALISM

10 STAGES ON THE ROAD TO SIDEWAYS NIRVANA

01. The Cobra *4+ Burbage*
Nice flowing traverse:
a good introduction.

02. The Walnut *6c Baslow*
Long, pumpy and steep,
but no hard moves.

03. The Green Traverse *7a Stanage*
Short, with positive holds and
burly moves.

04. Hamper's Hang *7a Stanage*
Done in its entirety this is a
long workout.

05. Jerry's Traverse *7b Cratcliffe*
Footless fun along the slots.

06. Long Wall Traverse *7b Churnet*
Massive traverse of three halves,
with a puzzle-solving pebble finish.

07. Wright's Traverse *7b Churnet*
Another long trip, this time with
gymnastic moves on big positive
holds through the steepness.

08. 7b lip traverse *7b Stanage Right*
One of the best examples of
grit shuffling.

09. Ben's Extension *8a Stanage*
Eliminate but great moves –
the dropdown is a great example
of gritstone 'knack'.

10. Inertia Reel Traverse *8a+ Roaches*
Powerful and technical crux on marginal
slopers and blind toe-hooks. Stunning.

Jerry's Traverse: *Pete O'Donovan* ▶

Grading SCIENCE

A graded list of the best of the named problems from Font 3+ - 8b+, in absolute order of difficulty.

8b+

Staminaband/PUTP Link

8b

The Ace
Close of Business
8 Ball

8a+

Low Left Start, The Press
Hooligan Start
Inertia Reel Traverse
Sweet Thing
Ben's Extension into Danny's Prob
Stamina Band into Ben's Traverse
Work Hard

8a

Careless Torque
Ben's Extension
Superbloc
Staminaband
Nik's Wall
Solomon's Seal
Blazing 48's
Westworld
Slingshot
La Terrace
Blind Drunk (original way)
Intense (jump start)
Full Power
Bohemian Grove
Tsunami
Jason's Traverse
The Joker

7c+

Help the Young Sit Start
Striker
Walk on By
Hats for Weasels
Chequer's Groove
Stump Hole Cavern (dyno finish)
Mushin
Low Rider
Feel Good
Domes Sit Start
Raw Deal
The Choker
Darkstar
Ben's Roof
Pump up the Power
Western Eyes
Master Kush
Tit Grip
Ben's Traverse
Turbo
Left Hand Man Direct
The Terrace
Zorev Sit Start
No Mercy
Maurice Gibb
Brad Pit

7c

Barry Sheene
Danny's Problem
Silk Sit Start
Brad's Wall
Submergence (original way)
Little Pig
Hurricane
Mark's Roof Direct
Pressure Drop
Mona
Soul Power
Grand Theft
Tetris

Blind Fig
Rollerwall
Spartacus
Bizarre
Sweet Release
Pea Crab Shuffle
Heartland
Stall Sit Start
Monologue
Powerband
Who Needs Ready Brek?
Quine
Spring Voyage
Brass Monkeys
Higher Ground
Middle Man
Jerry's Traverse (Stanage)
Ben's Wall (RHS)
White Rose
Them!
Flatworld
Great White
Ben's Wall (Curbar)
Play Hard
The Growler
Zaff Skoczylas
Giza
Zorev
Famous Grouse Sit Start

7b+

Ego
Jason's Roof
West Side Story
Eastwood Traverse
Shit
Boba Fett
Green Room Slap Sit Start
Autumn
Ram Air
Dick Williams
Fireball

Nadin's Secret Finger
Guplets on Toast Sit Start
Blind Ali
Blind Date
Once Upon a Time
Mike Tyson
The Rib
Face Arête
Mint 400
Stump Hole Cavern (first bit)
Dialogue
No Regrets
Press
Zippattrocity
The Green Man
Desparête
Talk to Me Martin
Bentley's Gonna Sort You Out
Miles' Slab
Fact Hunt
China in your Hands
Mother's Pride
Zaff's Problem
The Storm
The Hit Man
All Sit Down
Suavito
Left Hand Man
No Class
Deliverance
Fish Arête Sit Start
Rocket Man

7b

Jetpack
The Beast
T Crack
Dreaming the Eagle
Fist Full Left
The Bear Pit
For a Few Beagles More
I'm Tense

P Crack
Out of My Tree Start
Parental Duties
Big Al Qaeda
Dissolution
Zippy's Traverse
Brutal Arête
Cream
Little Gem
The Sheep Assis
Pogle's Wood Sit Start
Gibbering Wreck
California Screaming
The Yoghurt Hypnotist
Stayin Alive
Bigger Splash Direct
Cinzano Roof
Faze Action
Fuji Heavy Industries
True Git
Full Virgin Wall Traverse
Jerry's Traverse (Cratcliffe)
Pig Heart Boy
Direct Start to Perfect Day
Master Chef
Pets Win Prizes
Simple Simon
Leather Joy Boys
Buckstone Dyno
Leroy Slips a Disk
Captain Hook
Happy Campus
Mark's Roof
David
Blood Falls
Rambeau
Back in the YMCA
Mammoth Book of UFO's
Sean's Arête
Whitebait
Beneath the Breadline
Hats for Clowns

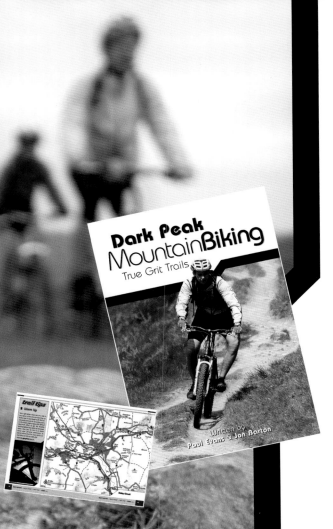

7b

Green Death Super Direct Start
The Nostril
Chip Shop Brawl
Twister
Wrights Rock Traverse
72 Direct
Piss
Pooh
Lust Left

7a+

Weedkiller Traverse
Rattle and Hump Start
Purple Haze
Inertia Reel
The Gutter
Kudos
Brad's Rib
The Hard Arête
Velvet Crab
A Fist Full of Beagles
The Beagle Has Landed
Where Beagles Dare
Electrical Storm
Pebble Mill Traverse
Trellis
Green Room Slap
Little Rascal
Tierdrop
The Arête (Higgar Tor)
The Drowning Pool
Help the Young
Baldstones Traverse
Fielder's Wall
Hurry on Sundown
The Alliance
Curvaceous
Brad's Block Traverse
The Fink
Brad's Arête
Pet Cemetery
S & M
Dry Wit in a Wet Country

A Bigger Splash
Rose and the Self-Employed...
The Parson's Finch
Wish
Simon's Slab
Grizzly Arête
Full Green Traverse
Nightsalt
Dragon Slayer
Soft on the G
Skinless Wonder
Blunted
Tombstone
Early Doors
Silk
All Quiet Direct
Chapel of Rest
Direct Start to Downhill Racer
Bin Laden's Cave
Hemline
To Be Or Not To Be
Big Brother

7a

Little Extra Direct Start
Stall
Clever Skin
The Good the Bad and the Beagle
The Undercut
The Jackalope
Too Drunk
Bus Stop Mantel
Sloper Traverse
Above and Beyond...
Ten Inch Zombies
Sleeping with the Flowers
Winsome
Elmer Fudd
Little Richard
David Traverse
Home Cooking
Ousal Low Traverse
Mark's Roof Left-Hand
Epilogue

Rollin Pat
Force Nine
Nadin's Traverse (Upper Tier)
The Big Dyno
Jerry's Arête
Pat's Roof
Beach Ball
Help The Aged
Honorary Caley
The Nose (Burbage West)
Fishboy
Attitude Inspector
Jellyeyes
Kim Span
Dirty Bitch
Crash and Gurn
The Crack
Boing Boy
C3P0
Ant Lives
Trackside
Hampers Hang
Domes
A Bigger Tail
Satin
Mermaid
Gorilla Warfare
Short Sean's Reachy Roof
Fat Slapper Sit Start
Green Flag
Breakfast
The Green Traverse
Diamond White Left Hand

6c+

Basher's Problem
Ape Drape
Starlight and Storm
Proper Grit
Stallone Arête
The Dignity of Labour
The Sheep
72
Gibbering Right

Captain Quark
Elastic Wall
Fish Arête
The Deep End

6c

Triangular Wall
The Fin
Limbless Limbo Dancer
Jump
Slap Happy
Serpico
Banana Finger Direct
Brain Dead
Stretch and Mantel
The Groove
Home Cooking Slab
Night of Lust
Sickle Crack
Angel Falls
Abyss
Barrel Slap Problem
Safe Bet
7 Ball
Bulb Sit Start
The Arête (Doxey's Pool)
Hideous Hidare
Not to be Taken Away
Adults Only
Right Spur
Tourette's Arête
Beauty
The Walnut
Razor Roof
Walnut Whip (Secret Garden)
J-Warkin' Sit Start

6b+

Local Hero
Conan The Librarian
Teck Crack Direct
Think Tank
Like a Beagle Over Troubled Water
Elephant's Eye

Crash Test
Cool Running
Sly Stallone
Original Sloper Traverse
Little Brother
G -Thang
Ogilvie's Direct
Gibby Haines
Finger of Fate

6b

Nicotine Stain
Arête Problem (Remergence)
Fielder's Corner
Alternative Three
Strawberries
The Greener Traverse
Boeing
Leggit
The Flakes
Swivel Finger
Remergence
Charlies Overhang
Oedipus Traverse
The Arête (Joe's Slab)
Ripple
Persistence
Technical Master
Heart Arête
Cool Running Left Hand
Staffordshire Flyer
The Cube
Headspin
Wobble Block
New York New York
Bullworker
My Left Foot
Nobody Knows

6a+

Elf Cap
Original (Clifftop Boulders)
Oyster Cap
Varicose
Pine Wall
Seams Green
Calcutta Traverse
The Gates
Crack and Arête (Newstones)
Invisible Touch
Go West

6a

Debris Groove
Go West
Marxist Undertones
5c.Wall (Ramshaw)
Lurcher Direct
Lost In France
The Pinches
All Quiet on the Eastern Front
Three Pocket Slab
Tiger
Pebble Wall, Curbar
Banana Finger
Right Arête (Burbage West)
Joe's Original
Parachute
Fat World

5+

Crescent Arête
Pebble Arête
Joe's Arête (Roaches)
Pock Man
Puck
Chips
Cleo's Edge
The Wafer
Sick
The Lone Slab
The Tufa
The Hourglass

5

Communist Crack
Pudding
Mini Prow
Brush
Corpse Crack
Beagles About
Elephant's Bum
Nunn's Eliminate
The Curse
Pock
Pocket Wall
Dork Child
Blue Cap
Chieftain

4+

Pullover
The Chant
Classic Arête (Roaches)
Flight Exam
The Cobra

4

Elephant's Ear
20 ft Crack
Magic Arête

3+

Beyond the End
Pebble Face

3

Men Only

Index of problems

Still keen?

You've ticked the guide and you still haven't found anything better to do with your life? Here's a load of stuff that's not in the guide.

Birchen Edge, southern edges – several good boulder problems disguised as routes on the main edge and a couple of boulders on the top with good, easy problems graded from 3 – 5.

Bosley Cloud – just south of Macclesfield. **Summit Arete** is a highball 7a depending on where you start, with the start being the crux. Just left is **Codfinger Workout**, 7a+.

Carhead Rocks - situated over the moor in front of the popular end at Stanage, it is small, insignificant with few problems of merit. A good recent addition is **Just Like Honey**, 7c+ on the detached block away from the main edge *(John Welford)*.

Derwent Edge, eastern edges – a previously partially documented area with outcrops stretching into the distance. Lots to do. Approach from Cutthroat Bridge on the A57.

Dogs Dinner Buttress, Cheedale - hidden behind the giant rhubarb and old sport climbers on the opposite side of the river to The Cornice, it's got a few good up problems and an incomplete 50+ foot French 9a traverse.

Gradbach Hill, Staffordshire - **The Green Streak** on the Yawning Stone is a good, high 7a+.

Grinah Stones, Bleaklow – more incredible boulders in the middle of nowhere, and a good few hours walk from the road.

Hen Cloud, Staffordshire - Nadin's old route **Touch** is a highball 7a+. If you contour the crag rightwards there are some boulders in a wood at the end. Called The Magic Wood it's not to be confused with the other Magic Wood in Switzerland because it's nowhere near as good.

Hobson Moor Quarry, nr. Stalybridge – lots of eliminates and a great big traverse.

Rheinstor, Youlgreave – lots of problems on limestone pockets that are mainly the starts of routes - bail out at the break. Two low traverses also exist - grades up to 7a.

Running Hill Pits, Chew Valley – **Scoop de Grace**, 7c/E5 7a, in the second quarry on the right, is an awesome highball. The steep groove on the right side of the first quarry on the left is called **The Groove** and goes at 7a+, with some easier stuff on either side.

Woolpacks, Kinder – An awesome boulder field above Kinder's southern edges, with some unfortunately soft rock in places.

Yorkshire – Lots of pleasing bouldering. Good for an afternoon at least.

Finally, a quick selection of routes that can all be climbed as highballs using mats and spotters:

Down to Earth *(E4 6a)* – Bamford Edge

Golden Days *(E3 6b)*, **The Runnel** *(E2 6b)* - Black Rocks

Art of Japan *(E1 6b)*, **Rise of the Robots** *(HVS 5b)* – Curbar

Master of Thought *(E2 5c)* – Gardoms

Wild Thing *(E1 5c)* - Roaches Skyline

DIY *(E3 6a)*, **Sithee** *(E1 6a)*, **Pigs Ear** *(E1 6a)*, **Shock Horror Slab** *(E1 6a)*, **Germ** *(E2 6a)*, **Microbe** *(HVS 5c)* – Stanage

Tensile Test *(E1 5c)* – Wharncliffe *(popular end)*